S0-CFS-921

Livonia Public Library
ALFRED NOBLE BRANCH
32901 PLYMOUTH ROAD
Livonia, Michigan 48150-1793
421-6600
LIVN # 19

623.88
S

Practical and Ornamental Knots

George Russell Shaw

Livonia Public Library
ALFRED NOBLE BRANCH
32901 PLYMOUTH ROAD
Livonia, Michigan 48150-1793
421-6600
LIVN # 19

DOVER PUBLICATIONS, INC.
Mineola, New York

MAR 3 1 2009

Copyright

Copyright © 1924, 1933 by George Russell Shaw.
All rights reserved.

Bibliographical Note

This Dover edition is a republication of the second edition of *Knots: Useful & Ornamental*, published by Houghton Mifflin Company, Boston, in 1933.

Library of Congress Cataloging-in-Publication Data

Shaw, George Russell, b. 1848.
Practical and ornamental knots / George Russell Shaw.
p. cm.
Reprint. Originally published: 2nd ed. Boston : Houghton, Mifflin, 1933.
ISBN-13: 978-0-486-46020-8
ISBN-10: 0-486-46020-7
1. Knots and splices. I. Title.

VM533.B53 2008
623.88'82—dc22

2007041873

Manufactured in the United States of America
Dover Publications, Inc., 31 East 2nd Street, Mineola, N.Y. 11501

3 9082 11317 6211

INSCRIBED
TO
ROBERT GOULD SHAW
BY HIS
BROTHER

IN the United States, the study of knots has moved westward and may be found in the curriculum of western State Colleges. There the AB seaman, the familiar tar of the deep seas, finds a worthy coadjutor in the Mexican Vaquerro, the mounted Cowboy, skilful in the training of horses, in the embellishment of saddlery, very skilful with the rope, bringing with him names of Spanish origin — lasso, cinch, lariat, latigo hondo — now permanently grafted on the English tongue as it is spoken in all the ranches beyond the Mississippi.

In many details incidental to the care and breeding of stock, to the cultivation of land, to the harvest, its storage and transportation, there are occasions for the use of cordage where the knowledge of reliable knots, appropriate for whatso ever emergency, is an important part of the ranchman's education.

In the first edition, #64 braid of the New Bedford Textile Co. was recommended for practice in tying knots. If the ends when cut, are dipped in paste or rubber cement and are rolled between the fingers, the strands will not unravel and a rigid end will result, very convenient for reeving through eyelets or loops.

CONTENTS

CONTENTS

DEFINITIONS

The End of a Line
is the part that ties the Knot
shown thus
on the drawings

The Standing Part
is the rest of the Line
shown unfinished
on the drawings
as at A

A
Standing Part
End

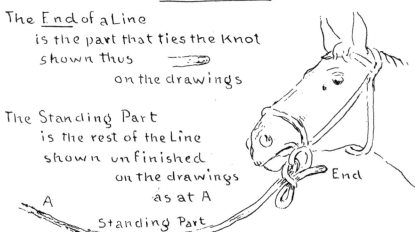

The Bight is the part of the line between its ends

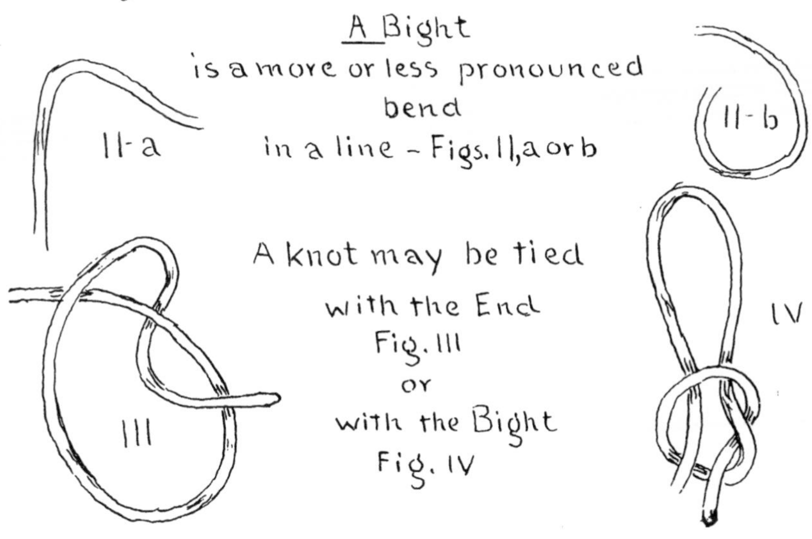
II-a
II-b
III
IV

A Bight
is a more or less pronounced
bend
in a line – Figs. II, a or b

A knot may be tied
with the End
Fig. III
or
with the Bight
Fig. IV

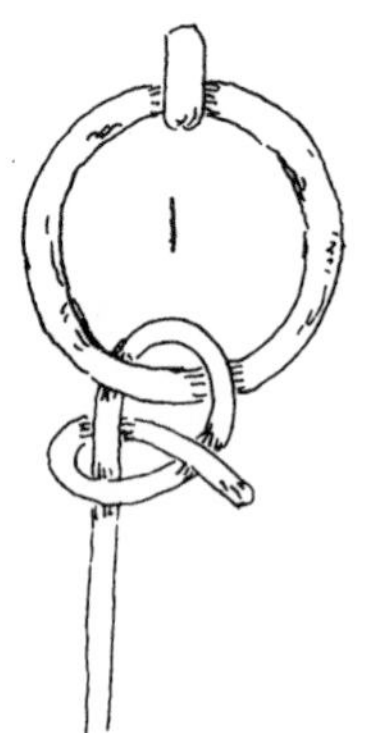

A HITCH

as here understood
is a Knot
tied to a
ring, spar, post, cable
or
other anchorage
not a part of the knot itself

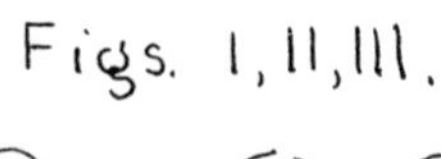

Figs. I, II, III.

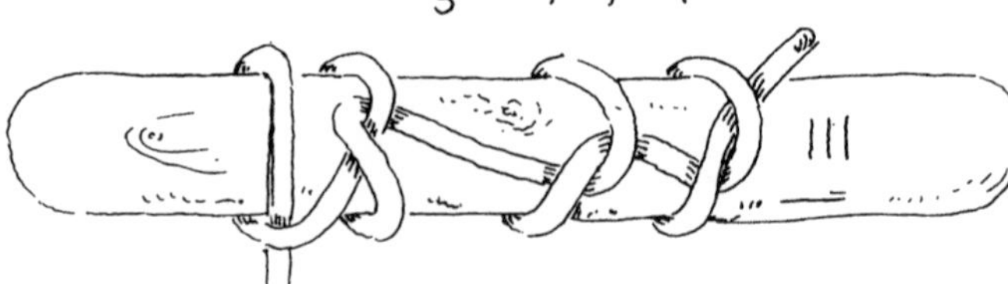
III

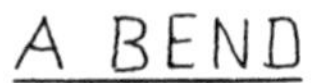

A BEND

is a Knot uniting
two lines
or two parts of the same line
where
each line or each part
is an integral part of the Knot

Figs IV, V, VI.

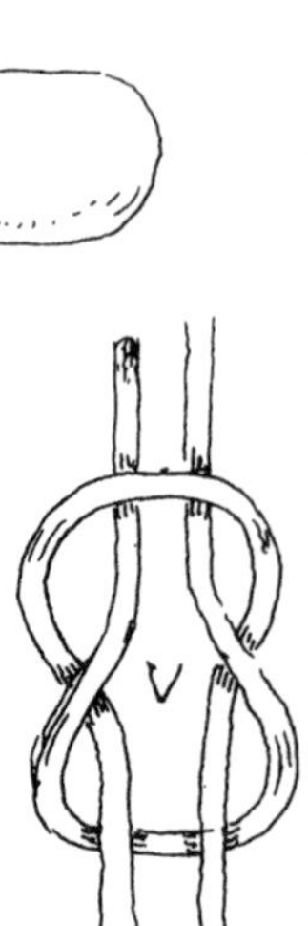
V

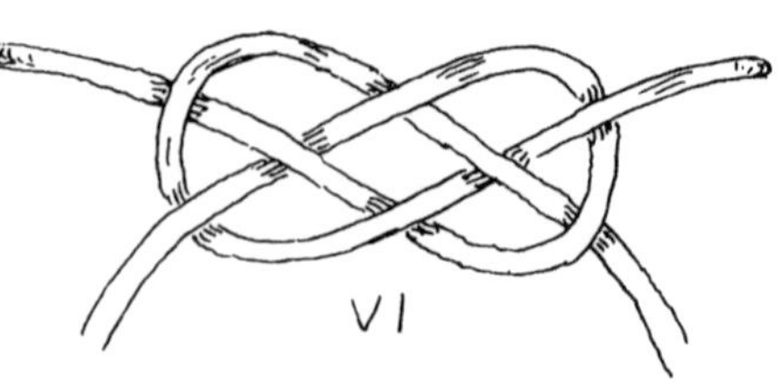

NOOSE and LOOP

A Noose
is tied with
a Hitch
of one of its parts A-A
around the other B-B,
which remains straight. Fig. I

A Loop
is tied with
a Bend
where both parts C & D combine
to form the Knot
Fig II

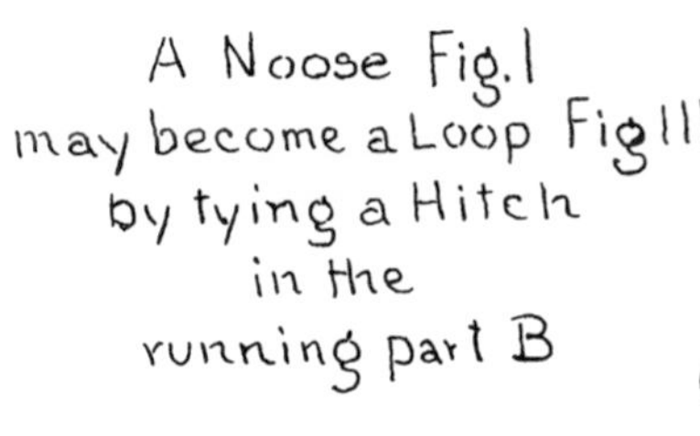

A Noose Fig. I
may become a Loop Fig III
by tying a Hitch
in the
running part B

A Loop Fig II
may become a Noose Fig. IV
when one
of its parts C-C-C
can be straightened

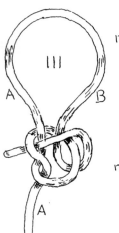

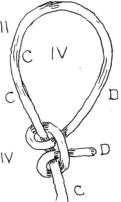

4

HALF HITCH

A round turn of a line about a post or a spar
One part
of the line
bears or Jams upon the other
Figs. I & II

I

II

or

A Turn
of the end of a line
around the
standing part
Figs III, IV

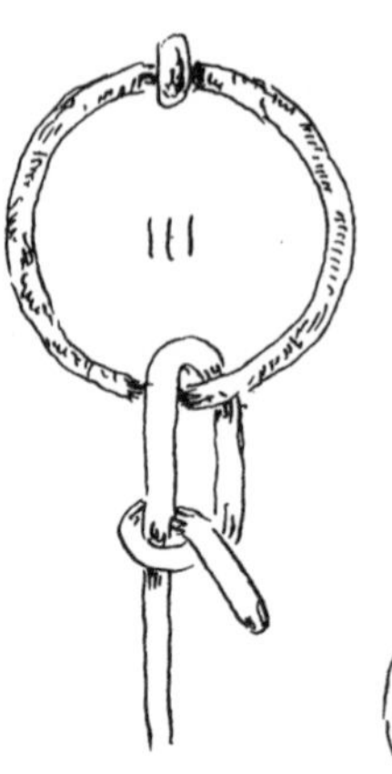
III

IV

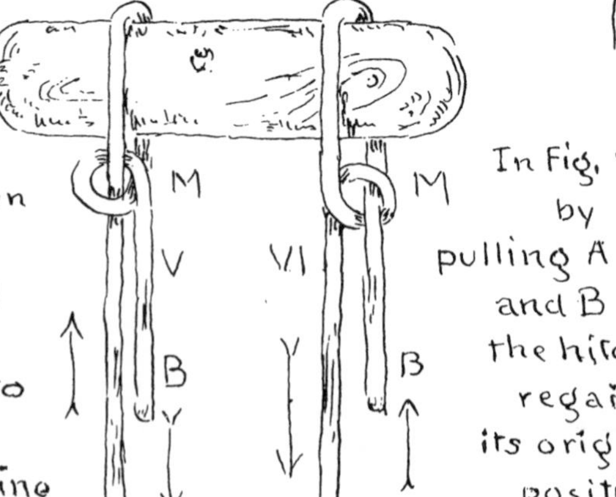
M
V
VI
M
B
B
A
A

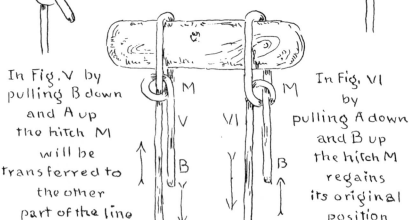

In Fig. V by pulling B down and A up the hitch M will be transferred to the other part of the line Fig. VI

In Fig. VI by pulling A down and B up the hitch M regains its original position

TWO HALF HITCHES

I
Lark

II
Clove

It will be seen later that the knot of Fig. I - Lark is a form of the Reef Knot page 19

Fig II - Clove is a form of the Granny

Page 32

III
Crossed
Lark

Fig. III - Crossed Lark is a form of the Oblique Square Knot page 20

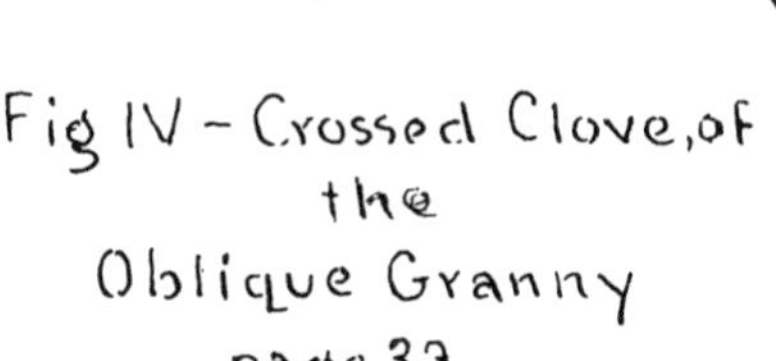

Fig IV - Crossed Clove, of the Oblique Granny page 33

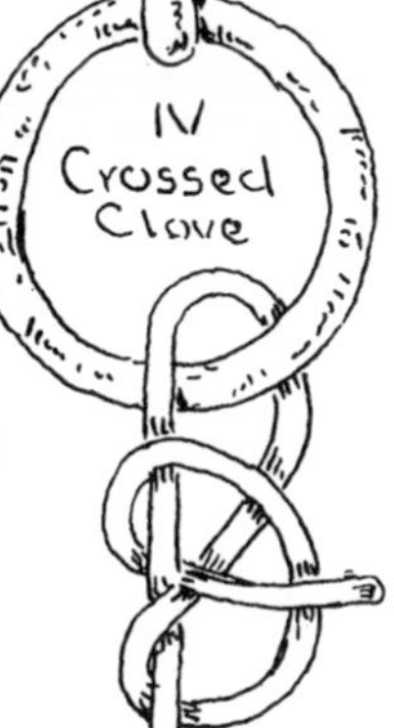
IV
Crossed
Clove

LARK'S HEAD

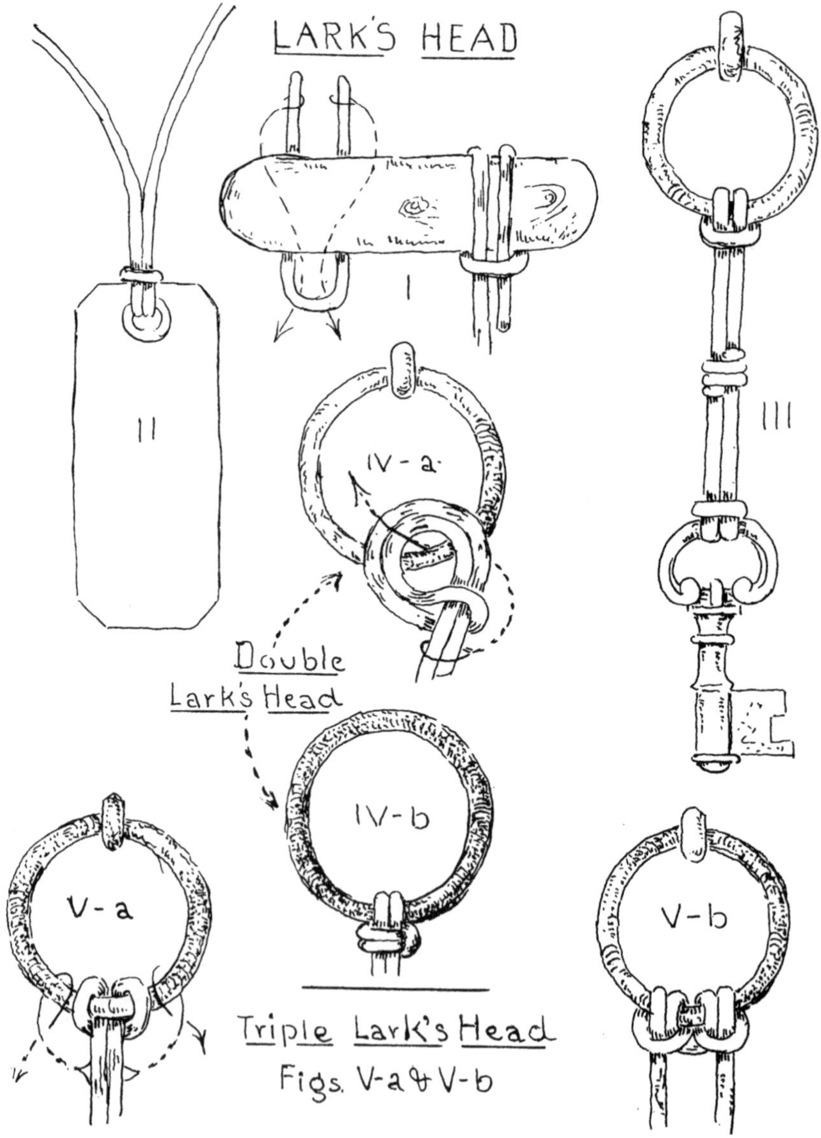

I
II
III
IV-a
Double Lark's Head
IV-b
V-a
V-b

Triple Lark's Head

Figs. V-a & V-b

7

CLOVE HITCH

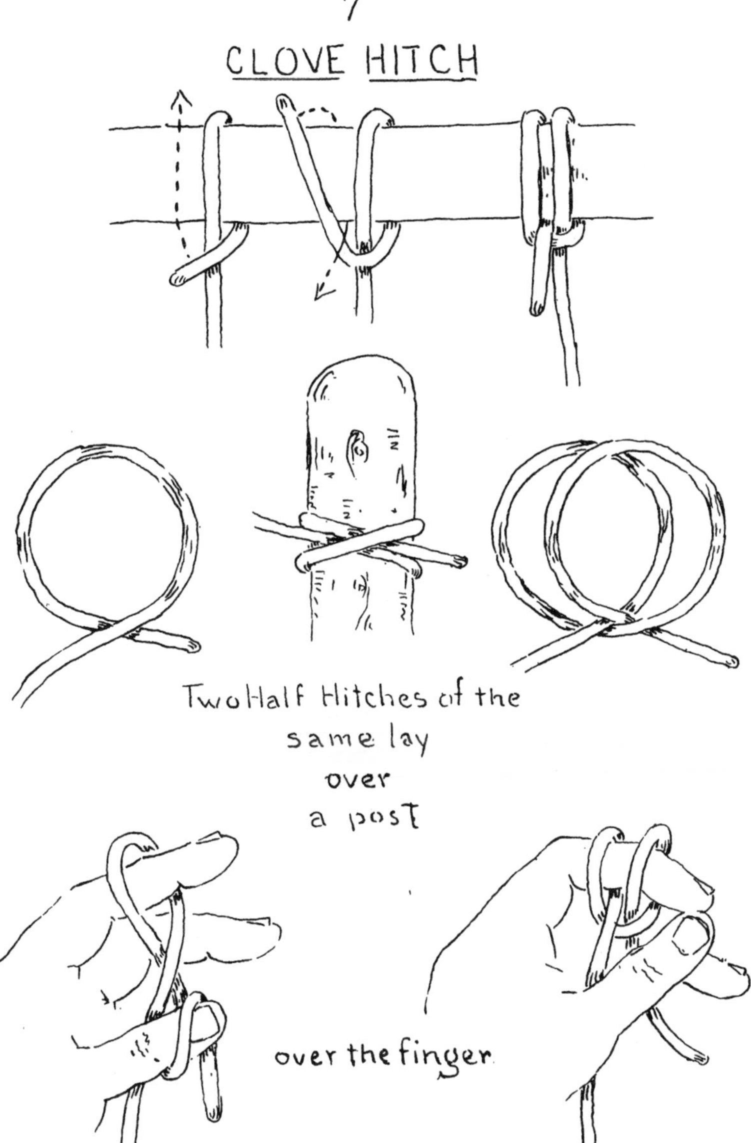
Two Half Hitches of the
same lay
over
a post
over the finger

8

CLOVE HITCH

with Double Loop Figs. I—III

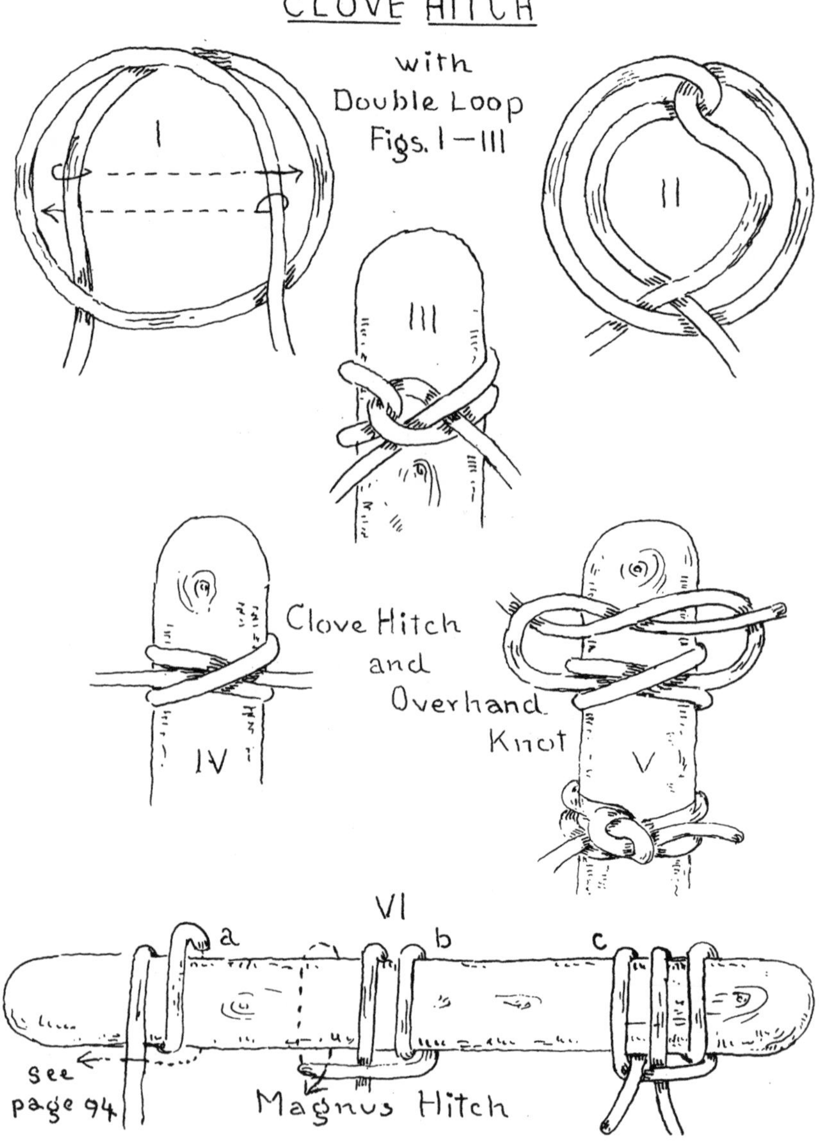

I
II
III
Clove Hitch
and
Overhand
Knot
IV
V
VI
a
b
c
see
page 94
Magnus Hitch

OVERHAND KNOT

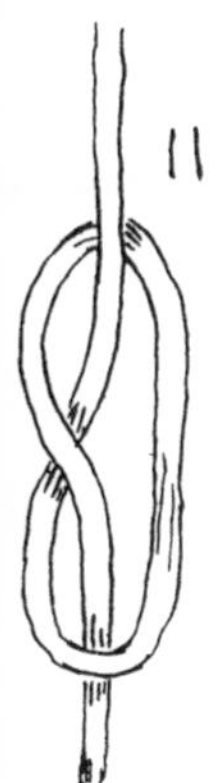
II

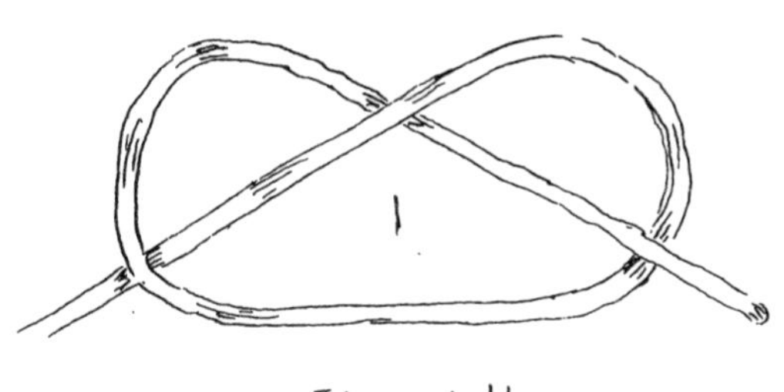
I

III

Figs. I, II
Overhand Knot

Fig. III
Overhand Noose
The Knot tied with the bight of the line

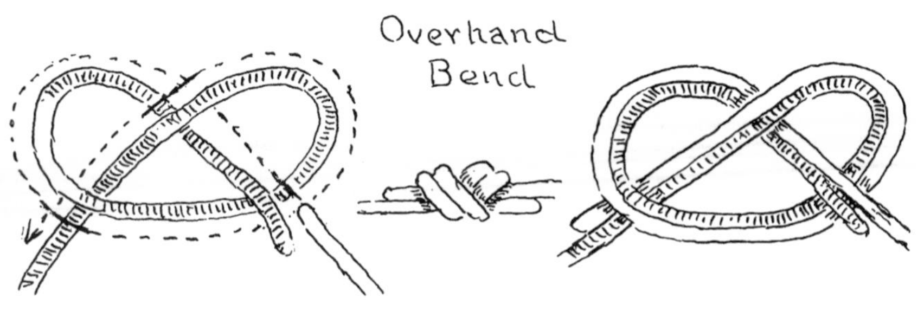

Overhand
Bend

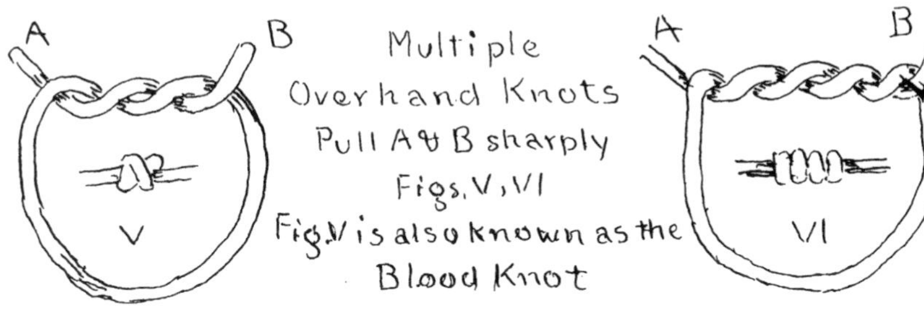
A
B
V
A
B
VI

Multiple
Overhand Knots
Pull A & B sharply
Figs. V, VI
Fig. VI is also known as the
Blood Knot

10

TWIN OVERHAND KNOTS

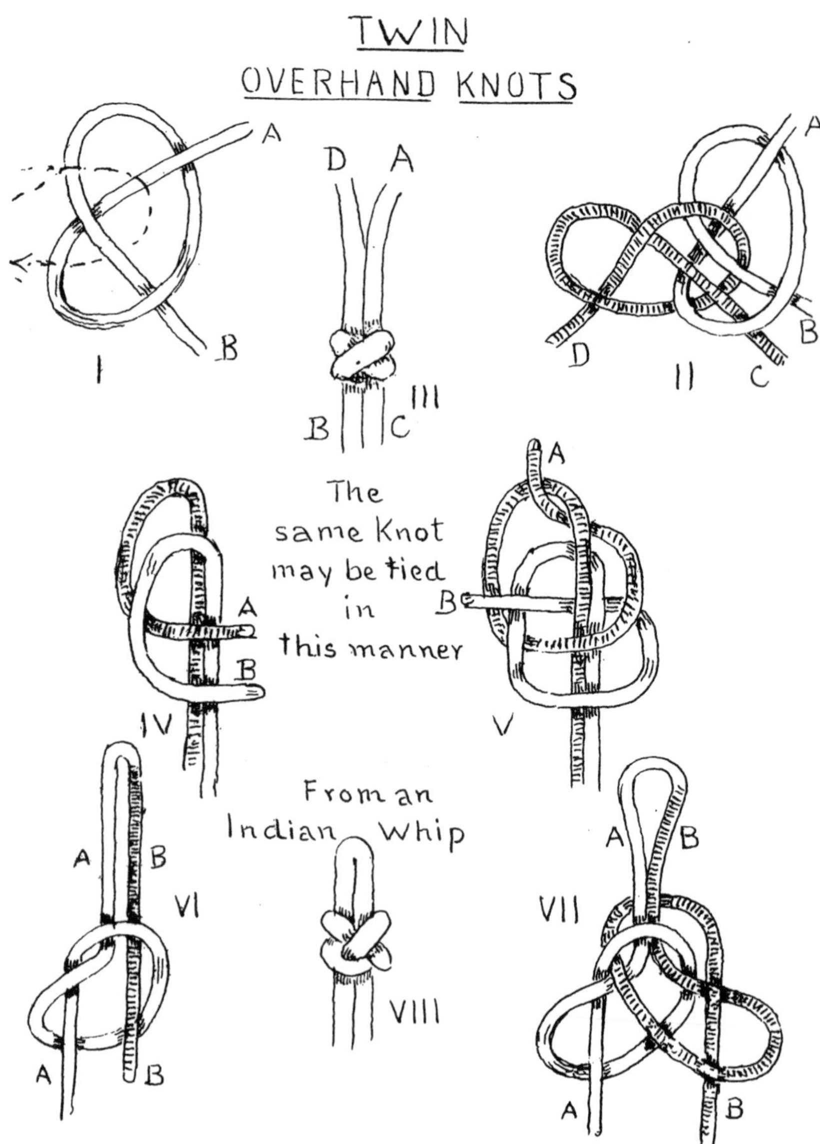

A
B
I
D
A
B
C
III
A
D
B
C
II
A
B
IV
The same Knot may be tied in this manner
A
B
V
From an Indian Whip
A
B
VI
A
B
VIII
A
B
VII
A
B

THE OVERHAND KNOT

when tied with a paper band takes the form of a pentagon

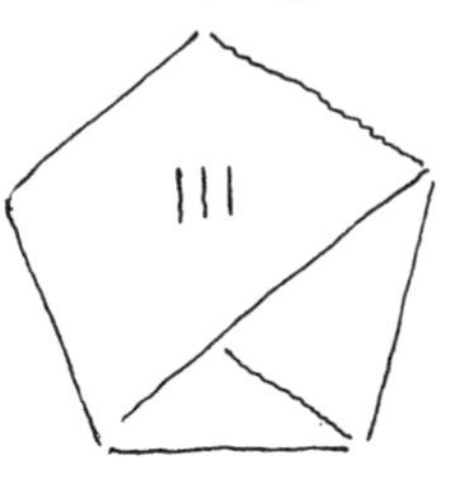
III

II

Let one end of a length of tape be turned over three times and then be pasted onto the other end, Fig. IV

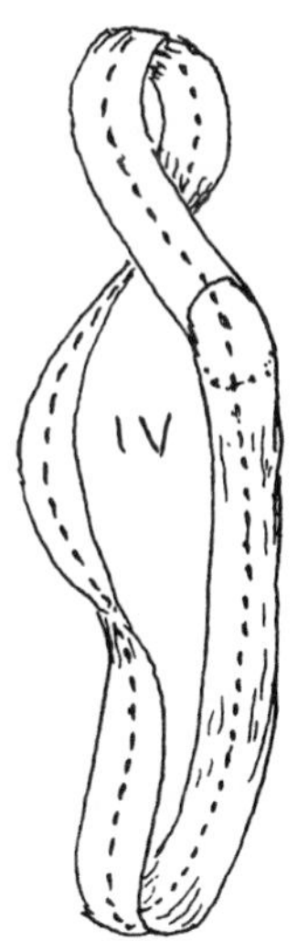
IV

If the tape is cut through along the dotted line it becomes an endless Overhand Knot Fig. V.

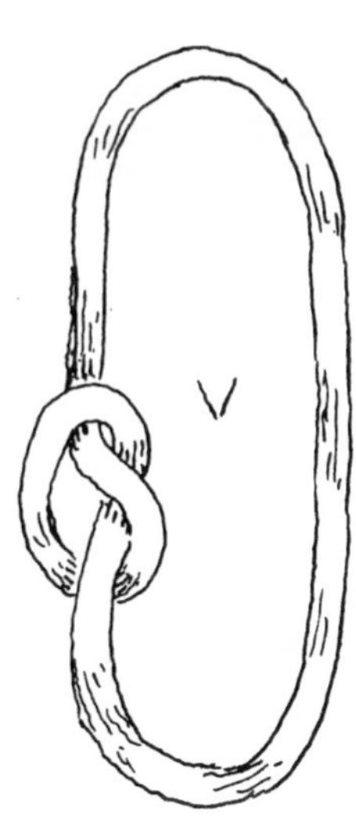
V

FIGURE OF EIGHT

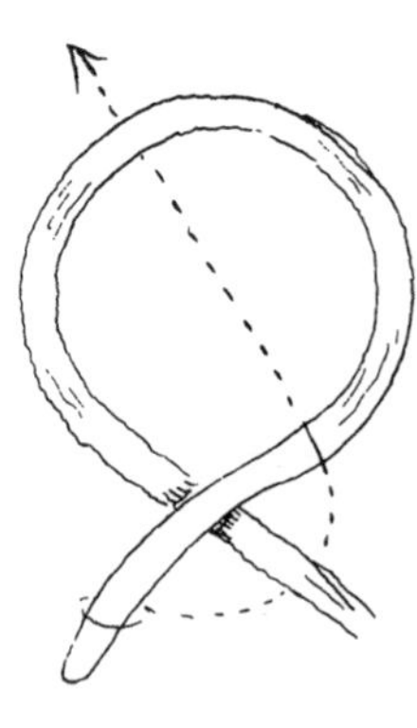

FIGURE OF EIGHT BEND

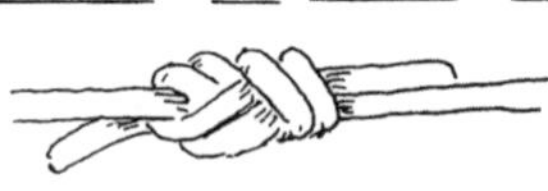

Figure of Eight and the Miller's Knot

See page 106

Fig. of 8

B
I
A

Lay A over onto B Figs. I, II

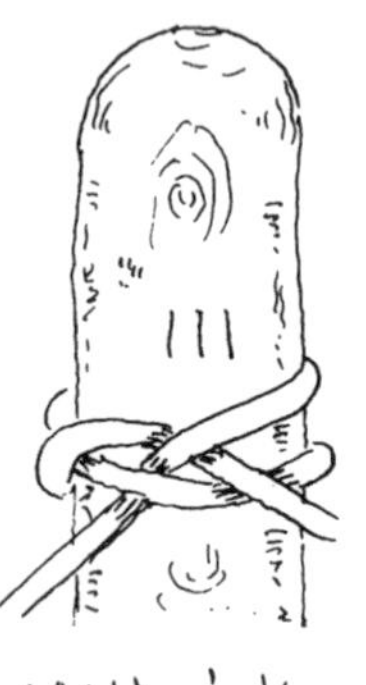
III

Miller's Knot

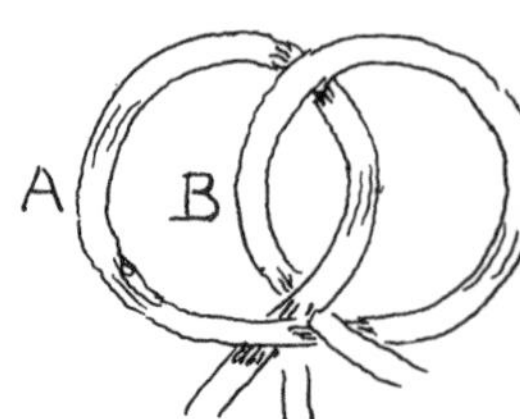
A
B
II

Throw the two loops over a post Fig III

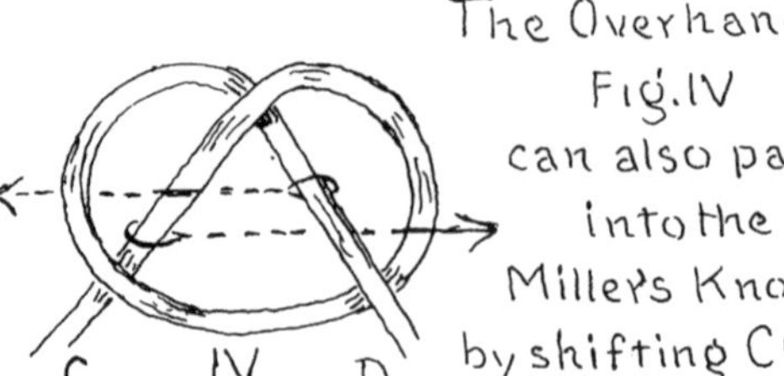
C
IV
D

The Overhand Knot Fig. IV can also pass into the Miller's Knot by shifting C & D

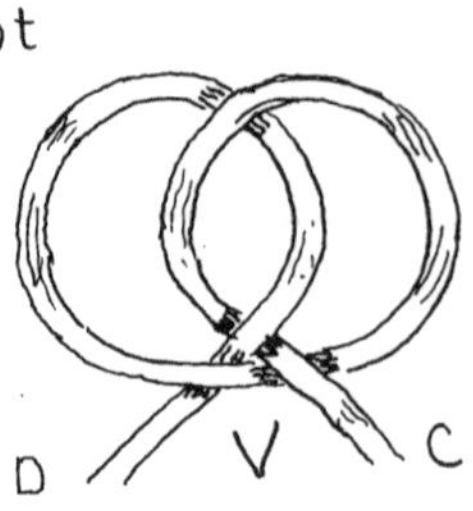
D
V
C

FIGURE OF EIGHT

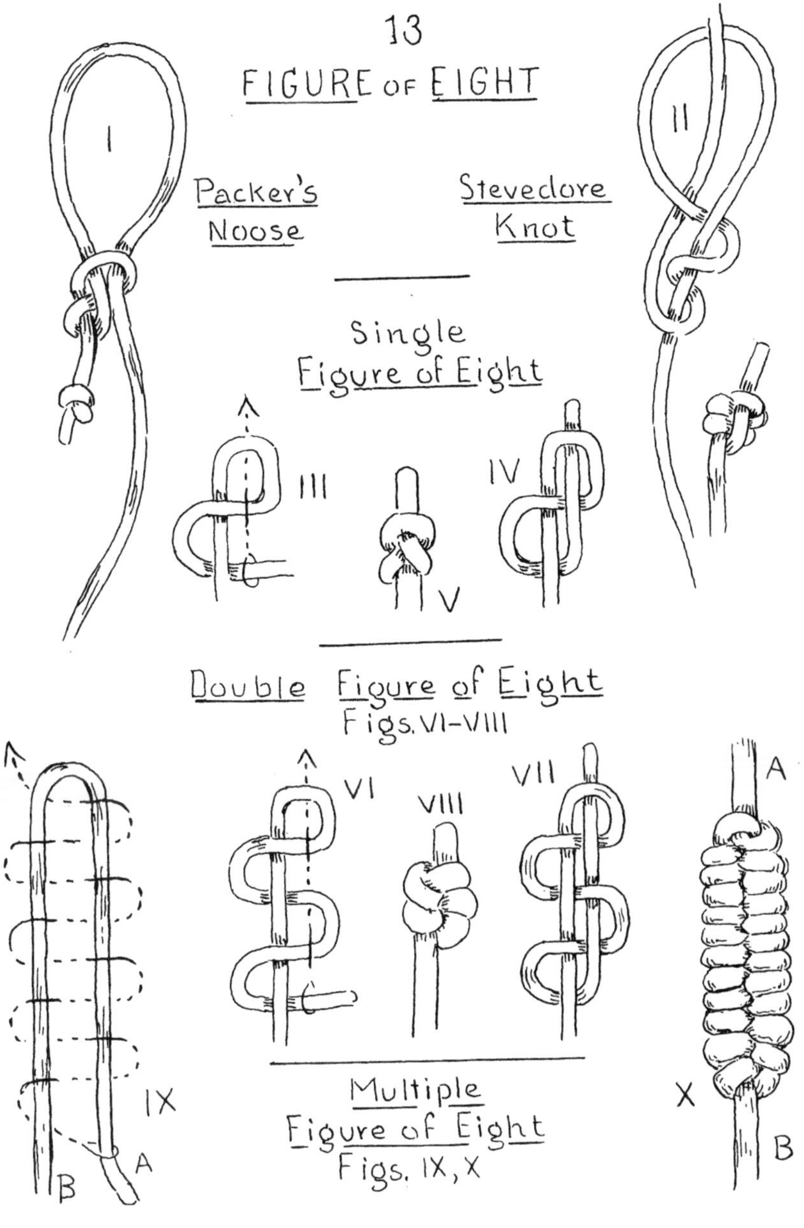

Packer's Noose

Stevedore Knot

Single Figure of Eight

Double Figure of Eight

Figs. VI–VIII

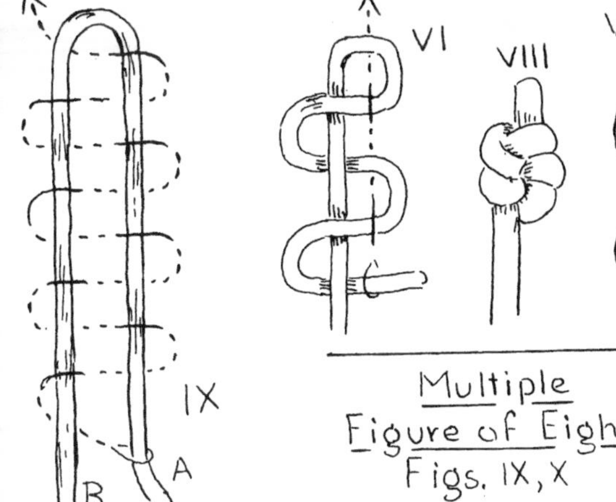
VI
IX
A
B

Multiple Figure of Eight

Figs. IX, X

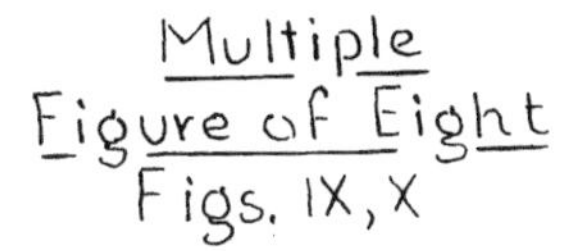

M

ANALYSIS

of the Bends of the forms M & N

N

CENTER

A

A One line lies on the other

B The two lines interlace

B

ENDS

Ends not crossed in the Bight

1 – Ends on same side of the Bight

2 – Ends on different sides of Bight

Ends are crossed in the Bight

3 – The Braiding is not regular

4 – The Braiding is regular

There are 20 possible combinations

1-A-1 1-A-2 1-A-3 1-A-4 2-A-2 2-A-3 2-A-4 3-A-3 3-A-4 4-A-4

1-B-1 1-B-2 1-B-3 1-B-4 2-B-2 2-B-3 2-B-4 3-B-3 3-B-4 4-B-4

15
Among the twenty combinations there are eight knots
1
A
1
REEF KNOT
1
A
3
WEAVER'S KNOT
3
A
3
HALF GRANNY
2
B
2
GRANNY
3
B
2
SINGLE CARRICK
2
B
4
HALF CARRICK
3
B
4
DOUBLE CARRICK (1)
4
B
4
DOUBLE CARRICK (2)

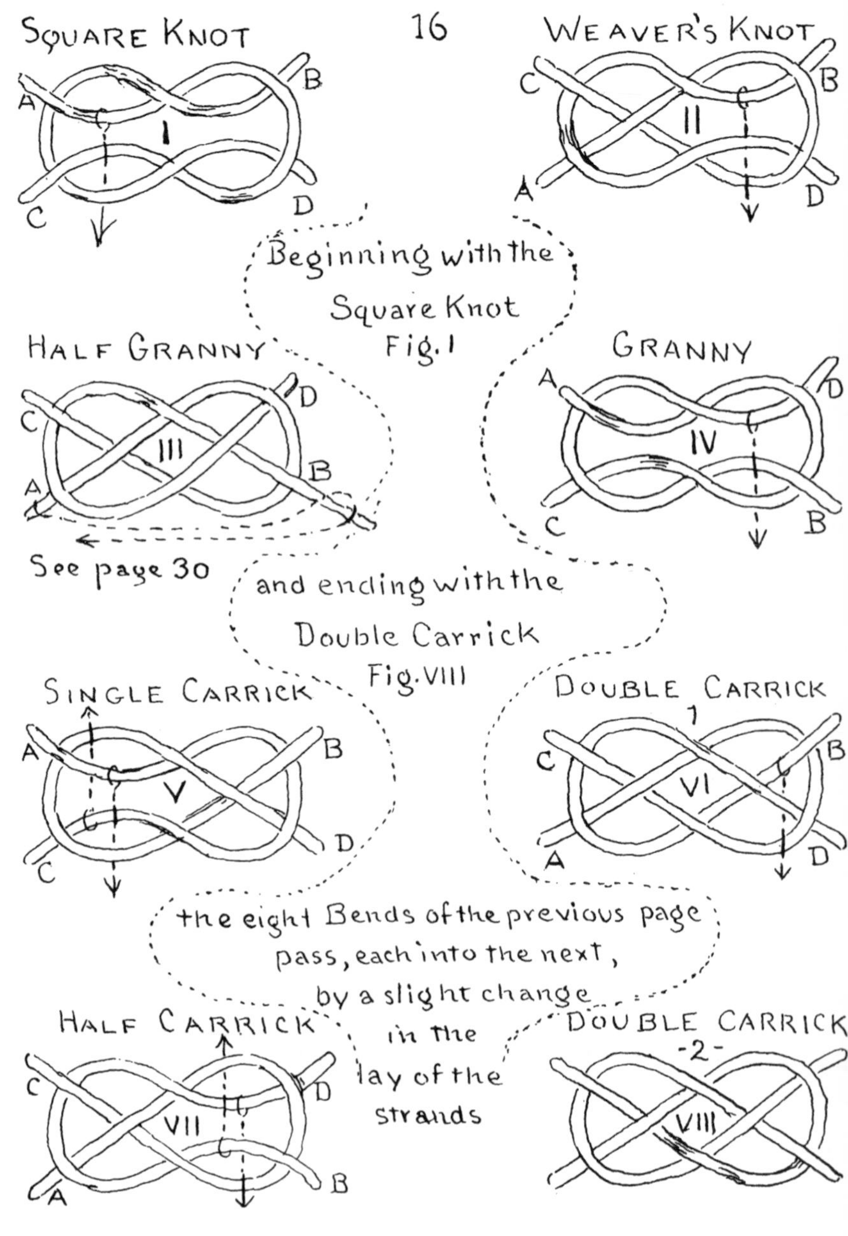
SQUARE KNOT
A
B
I
C
D
WEAVER'S KNOT
C
B
II
A
D
Beginning with the
Square Knot
Fig. I
HALF GRANNY
C
D
III
A
B
See page 30
GRANNY
A
D
IV
C
B
and ending with the
Double Carrick
Fig. VIII
SINGLE CARRICK
A
B
V
C
D
DOUBLE CARRICK
1
C
B
VI
A
D
the eight Bends of the previous page
pass, each into the next,
by a slight change
in the
lay of the
strands
HALF CARRICK
C
D
VII
A
B
DOUBLE CARRICK
-2-
VIII

OBLIQUE BENDS

The strands of the eight bends are drawn together by pulling the ends A and D or B and C

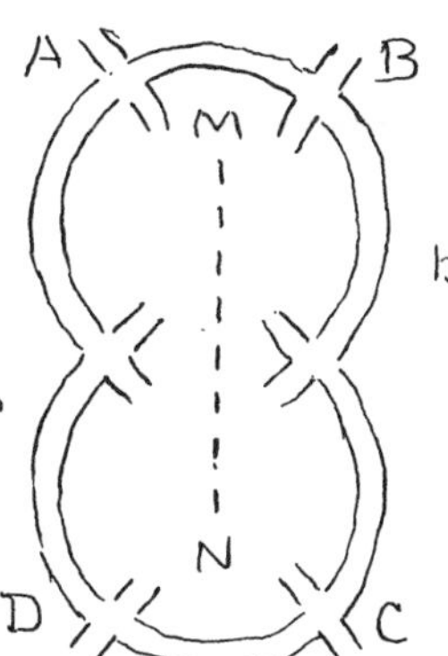
A
B
M
N
D
C

the strain being directly parallel with the axis M-N

But the strain can be applied to A and C or to B and D in a direction oblique to the axis.

The Oblique Bends will be explained in later pages where each is an intermediate stage in the tying of a Loop peculiar to that Bend alone

---

The distinction between Direct and Oblique is better presented when the Bends are tied with the ends of a single line

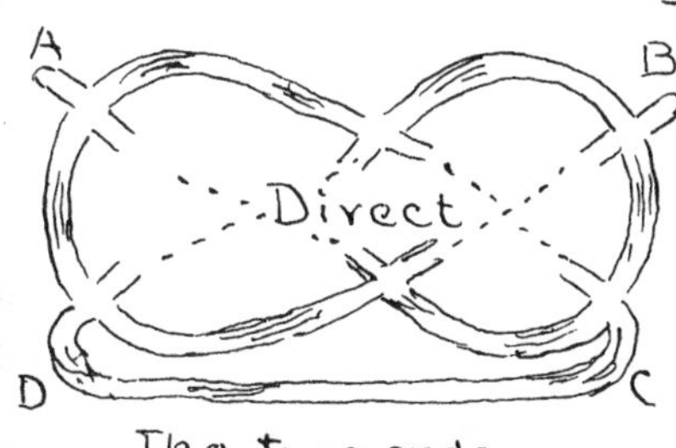
A
B
Direct
D
C

The two ends A & B are on the same side of the knot

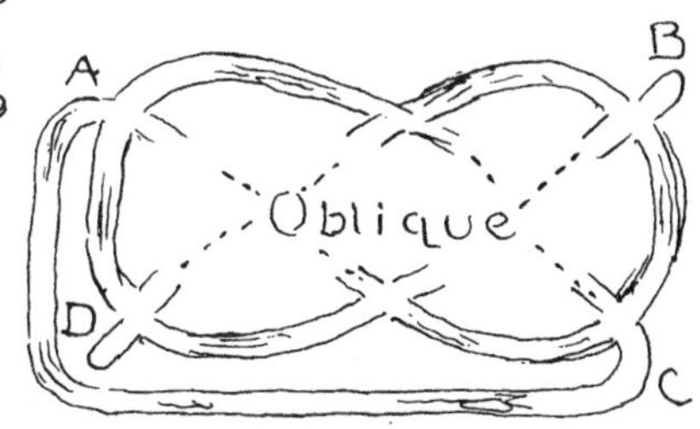
A
B
Oblique
D
C

The two ends B & D are on opposite sides of the Knot

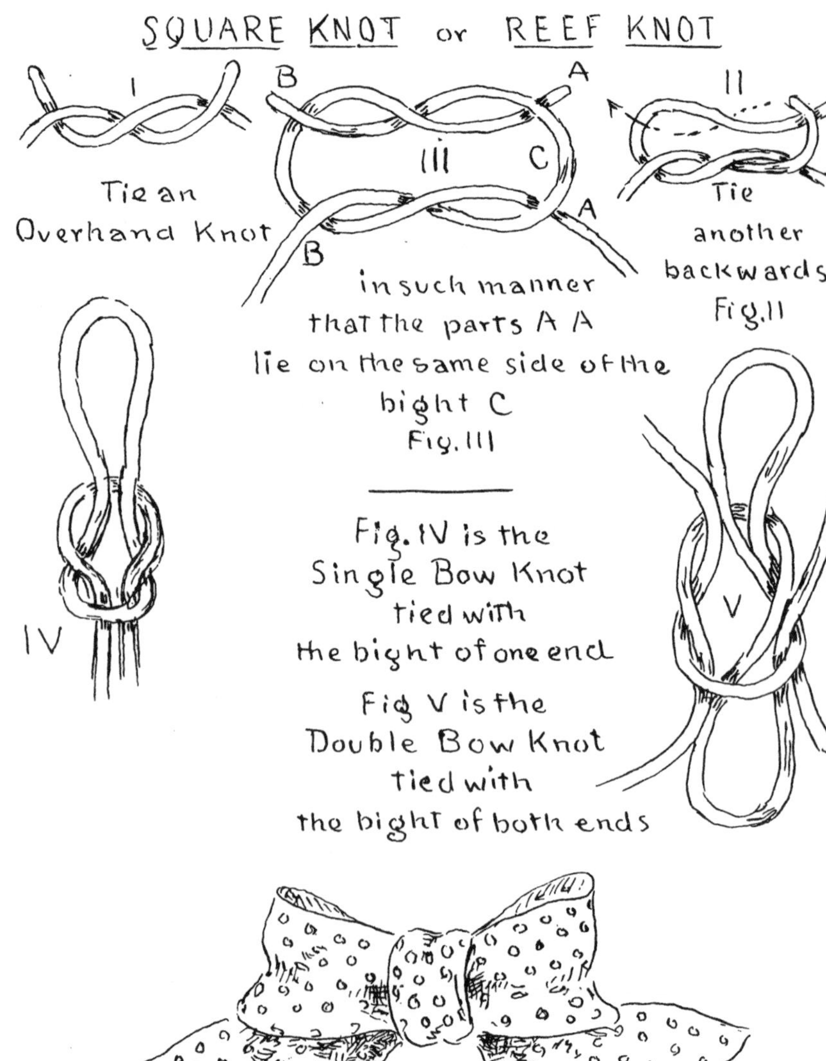
SQUARE KNOT or REEF KNOT
I
Tie an
Overhand Knot
B
A
III
C
A
B
in such manner
that the parts A A
lie on the same side of the
bight C
Fig. III
II
Tie
another
backwards
Fig. II
IV
Fig. IV is the
Single Bow Knot
tied with
the bight of one end
Fig V is the
Double Bow Knot
tied with
the bight of both ends
V

SQUARE KNOT AND LARK'S HEAD

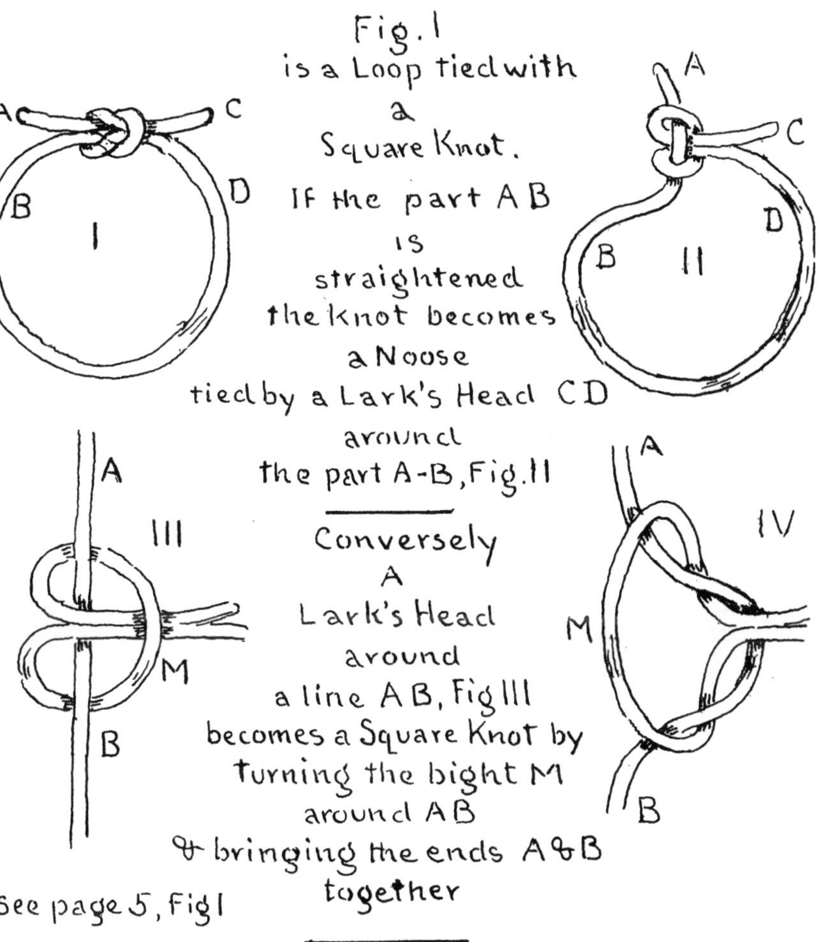
Fig. I
is a Loop tied with
a
Square Knot.
If the part A B
is
straightened
the knot becomes
a Noose
tied by a Lark's Head CD
around
the part A-B, Fig. II
Conversely
A
Lark's Head
around
a line A B, Fig III
becomes a Square Knot by
turning the bight M
around A B
& bringing the ends A & B
together
A
C
B
D
I
II
III
IV
M
See page 5, Fig I

To untie a Square Knot, straighten one of the 2 strands
Grasp the resulting Lark's Head
and strip it quickly from the straight strand

20

OBLIQUE SQUARE KNOT

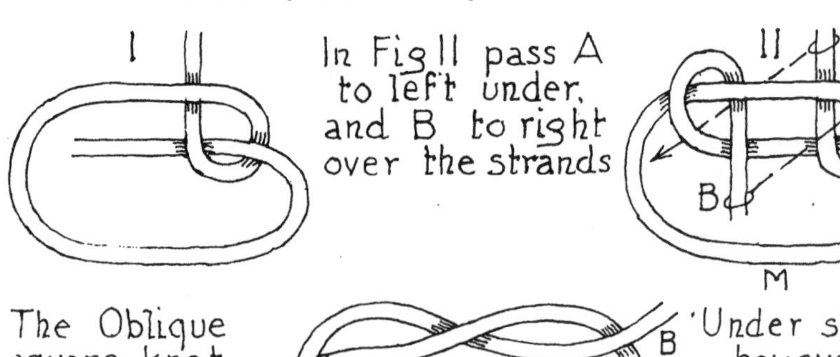
I
II
A
B
M

In Fig II pass A to left under, and B to right over the strands

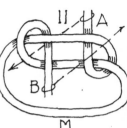

The Oblique square knot also known as the Thief Knot

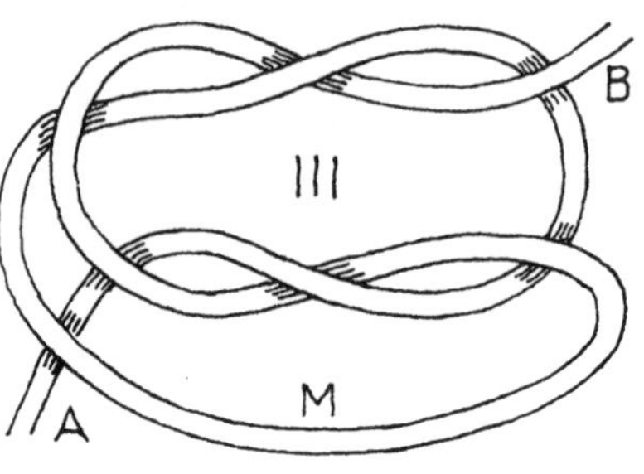
III
B
A
M

Under strain however slight, it slips apart.

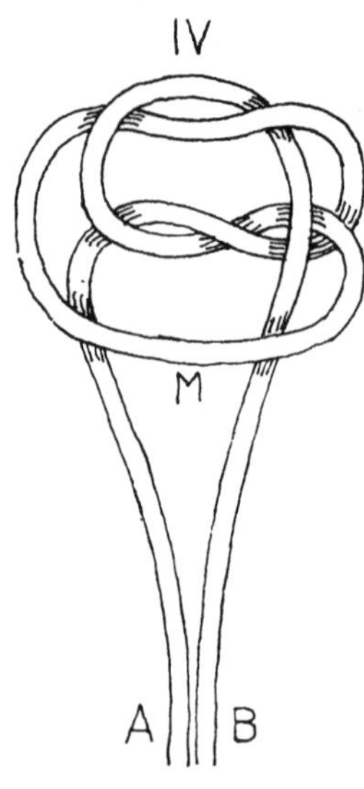
IV
M
A
B

See page 5

But in Fig. III bring the ends A & B together, Fig IV. then with A & B in one hand and the part M in the other hand the knot becomes a reliable Japanese Loop.

V
M
See
page
148

MARLINE - OR ROPE YARN KNOT

Marline is laid with two strands

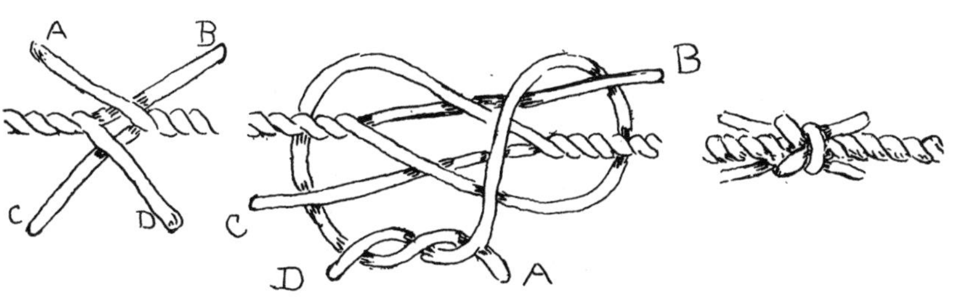
A
B
C
D
B
C
D
A

The Surgeons' Knot is a Square Knot of which th first part, Fig. V-a, is a double Overhand Knot

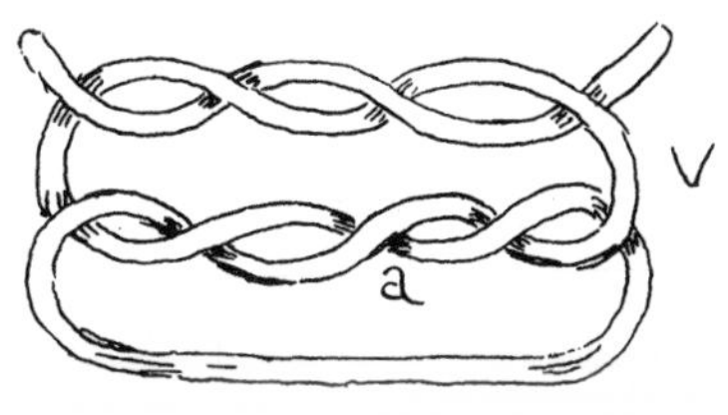
V
a

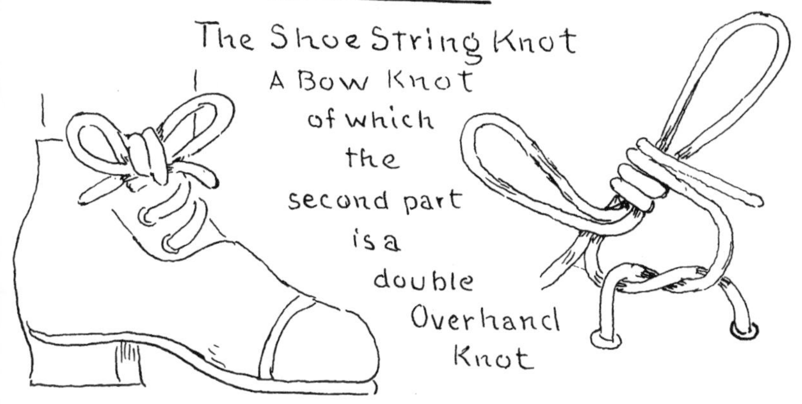

The Shoe String Knot

A Bow Knot of which the second part is a double Overhand Knot

Under several names as
Weaver's Knot - Sheet Bend-Bowline & others, is
a combination of a Loop AB with
a Half Hitch CD

Fig. I
is the Direct form of the knot,
the two ends (both And C)
being on the same side of the knot

Fig. II
is the Oblique form of the knot.
the two ends A&C being
on opposite sides

Fig. III
is the Oblique form
tied with one line.

Fig. IV
A&C are brought
together.

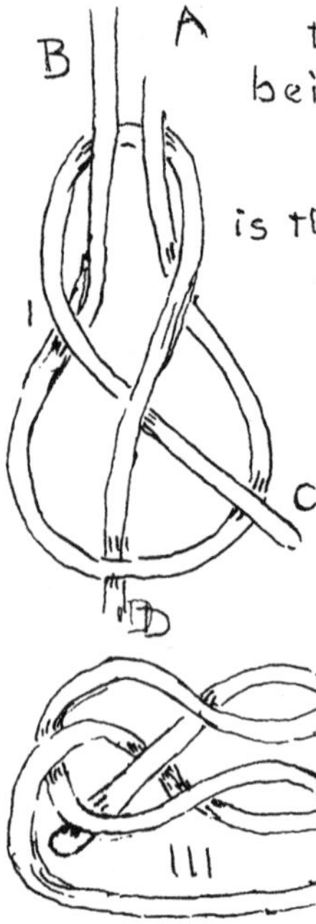

B A I C D

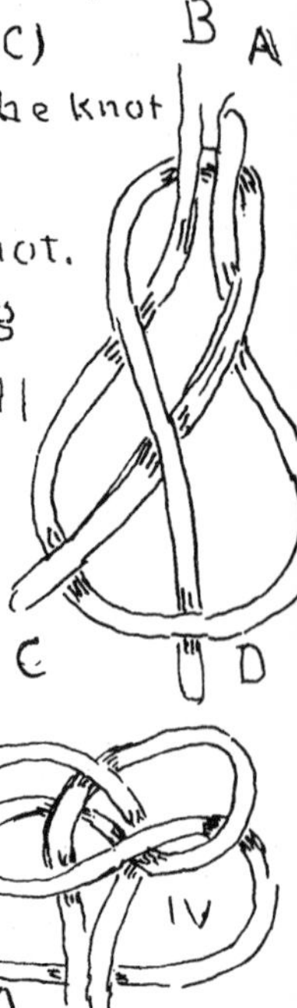

B A II C D

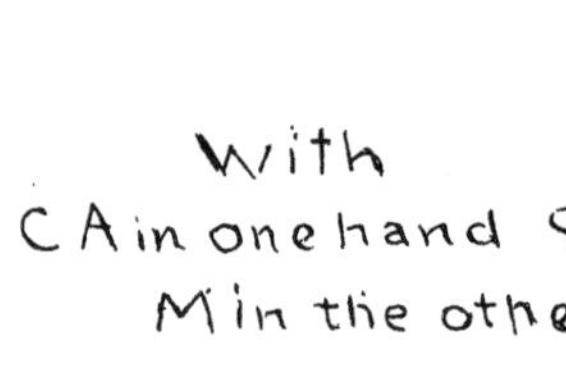

III

V

M C A IV

With
C A in one hand &
M in the other

The Knot
becomes a loop

WEAVER'S KNOT

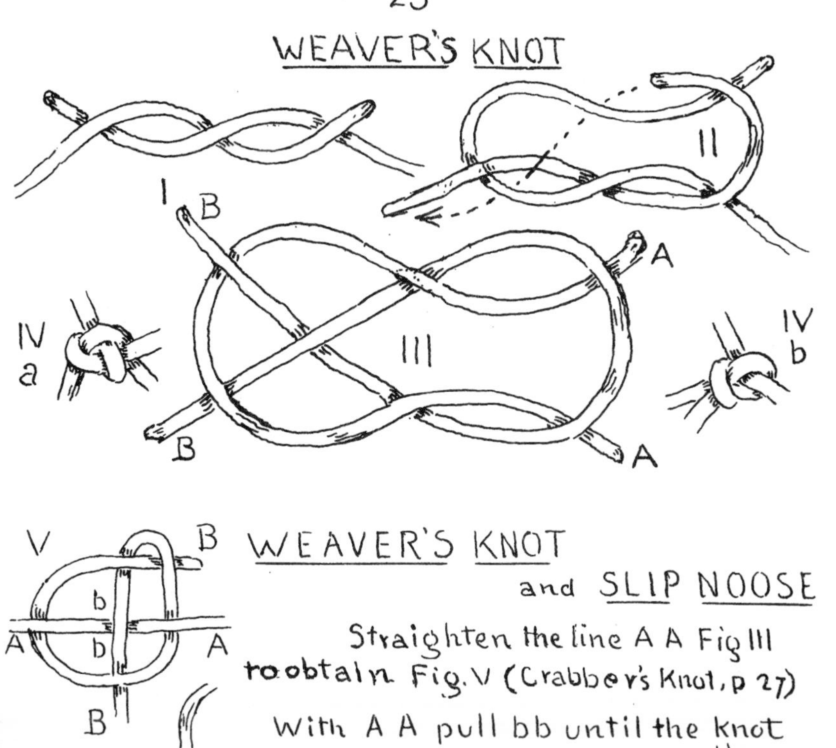
I
II
III
IV a
IV b
A
B
V
b

WEAVER'S KNOT and SLIP NOOSE

Straighten the line A A Fig III to obtain Fig. V (Crabber's Knot, p 27)

With A A pull bb until the knot becomes a Noose Fig. VI

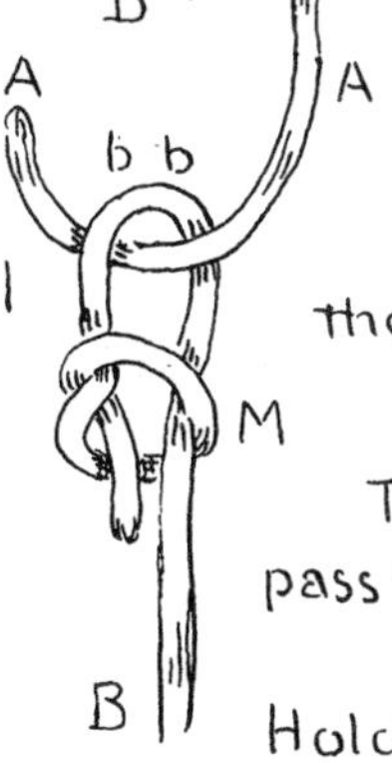

Therefore the Weaver's Knot may be tied as follows

Tie a Noose with one line, pass the other line through its eye Fig. VI

Hold A A together, pull B and slip the collar, M, up onto the loop formed by A A, Fig. VII

24

WEAVER'S KNOT

I

II

III

Another Method

Figs. IV, V, VI

IV

V

VI

The combination of a Loop with a Half Hitch
Is a reliable Knot
for joining two lines of
unequal size

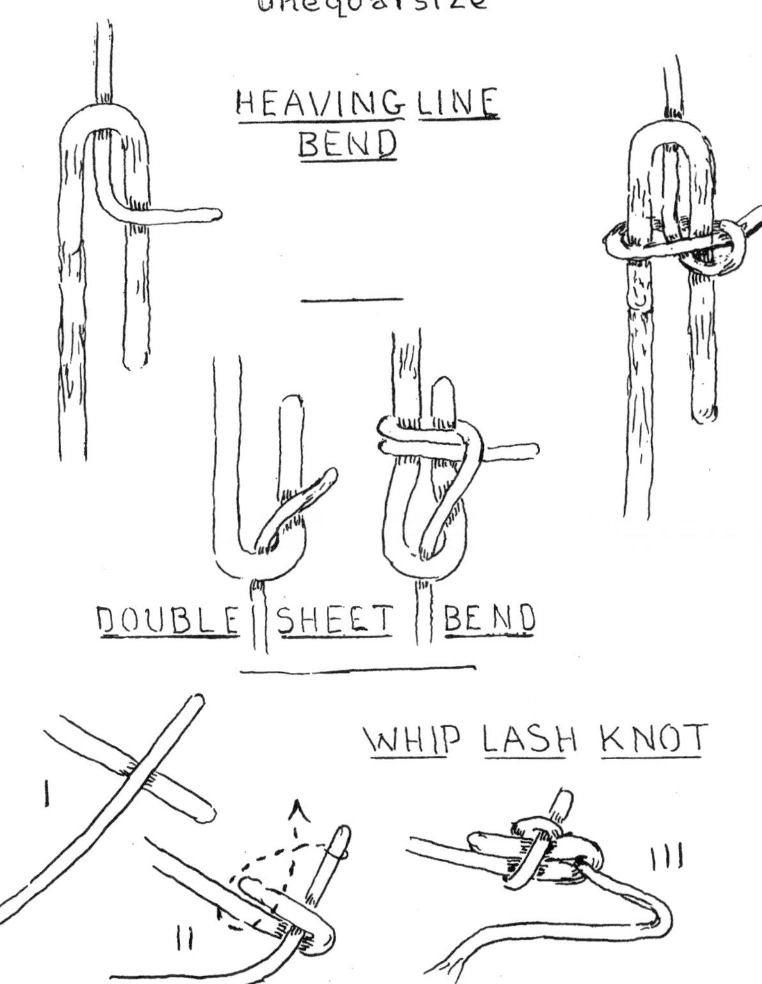
HEAVING LINE
BEND
DOUBLE SHEET BEND
WHIP LASH KNOT
I
II
III

BOWLINE

Lay the end A on the standing part B

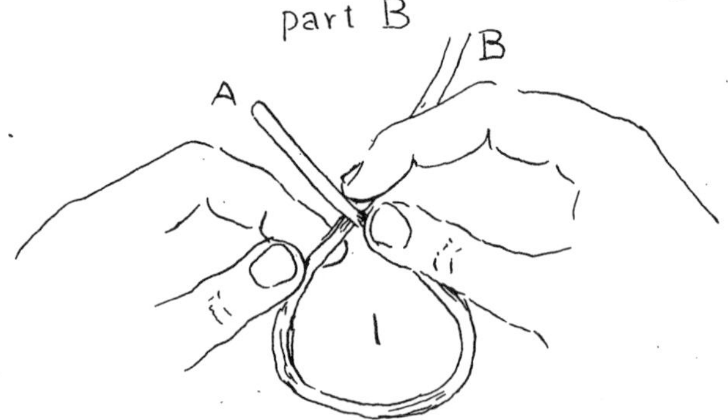
B
A
I

Turn the palm of the right hand up, Forming a loop with the end A through the loop

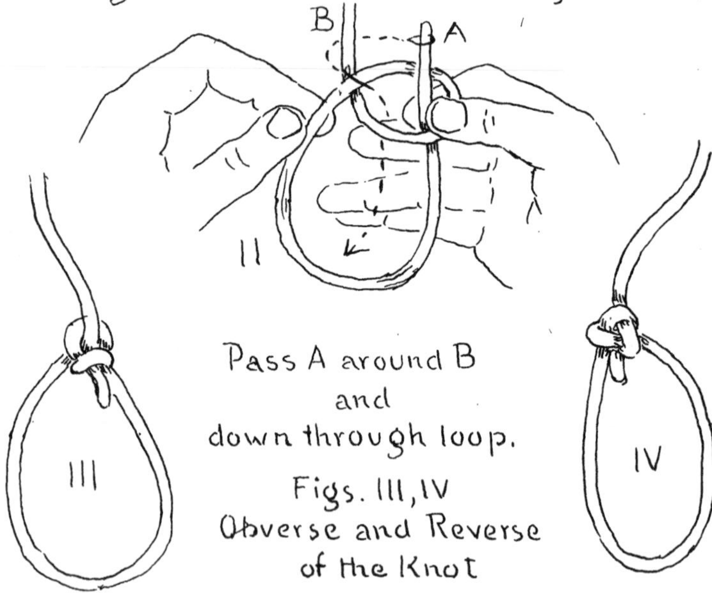
B
A
II
III
IV

Pass A around B and down through loop.

Figs. III, IV Obverse and Reverse of the Knot

RUNNING BOWLINE

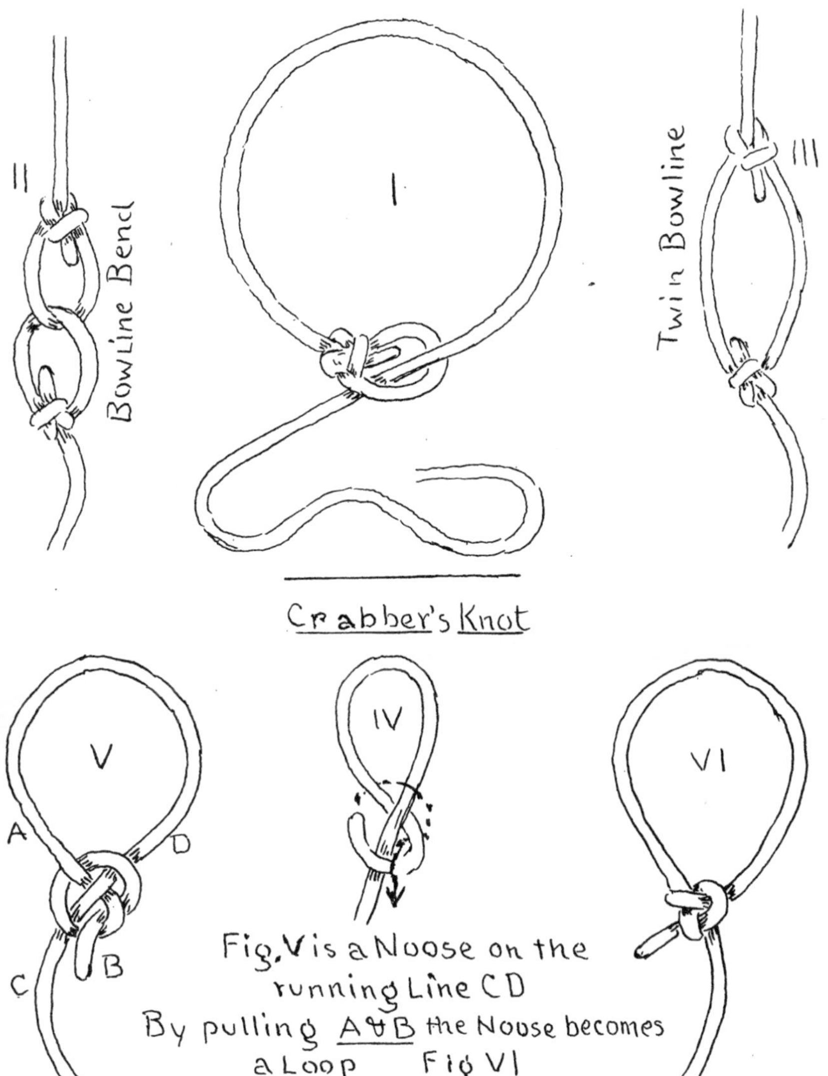
II
Bowline Bend
I
Twin Bowline
III
IV
V
A
D
C
B
VI

Crabber's Knot

Fig. V is a Noose on the running Line CD
By pulling A & B the Noose becomes a Loop Fig VI

PORTUGUESE BOWLINE

Chaise de Calfat Caulker's Chair

Fig. I - is a double Loop

Fig. II - Where end A crosses the part B tie a Bowline (III-IV) around the two lines

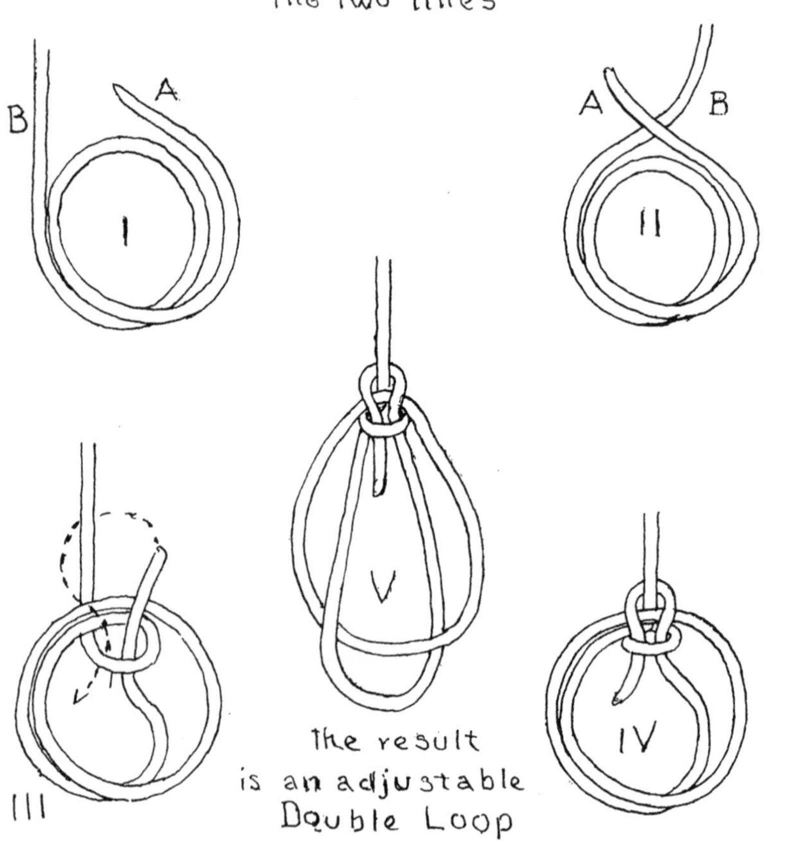

B
A
I
A
B
II
V
III
IV

the result is an adjustable Double Loop

BOWLINE - ON - BIGHT

This Knot
may be tied with the bight
on any part of the line
A short length of a long rope
may be used without
cutting it

With the Loop A
tie an Overhand Knot
Fig. I

Pass the Loop A
back under the Knot
Fig. II

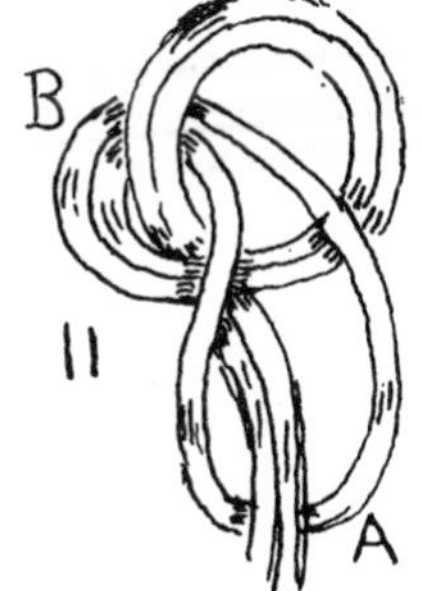
B
II
A

With the strands at B
Fig. II
pull the loop A into the position
shown in Figs. III-(a & b).

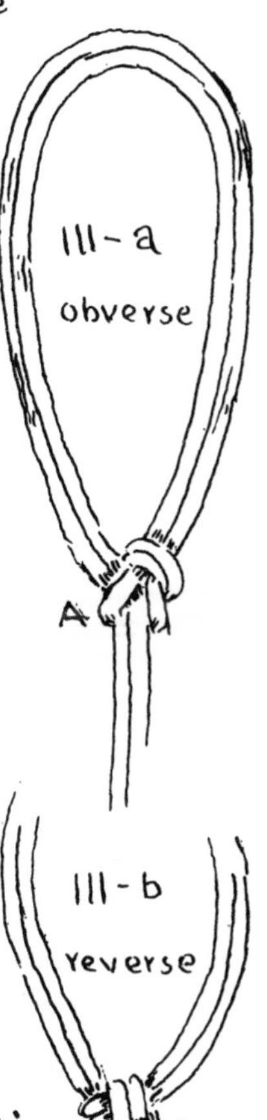
III - a
obverse
A
III - b
reverse
A

HALF GRANNY

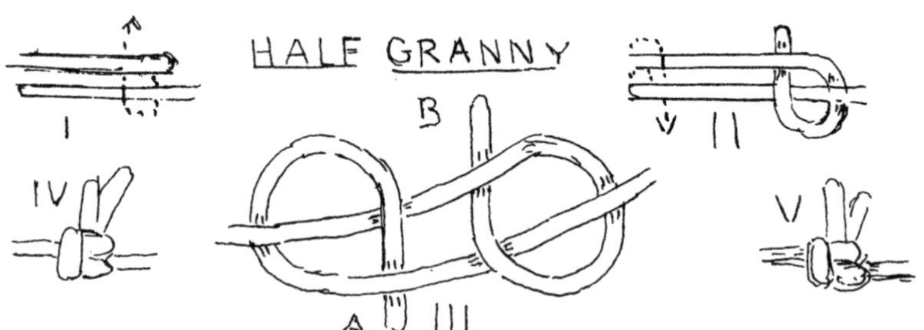
I
B
II
IV
V
A
III

This knot, when pulled taut, is peculiar
Figs. IV, V
The two ends lie side by side
The two faces; both obverse and reverse, are alike.

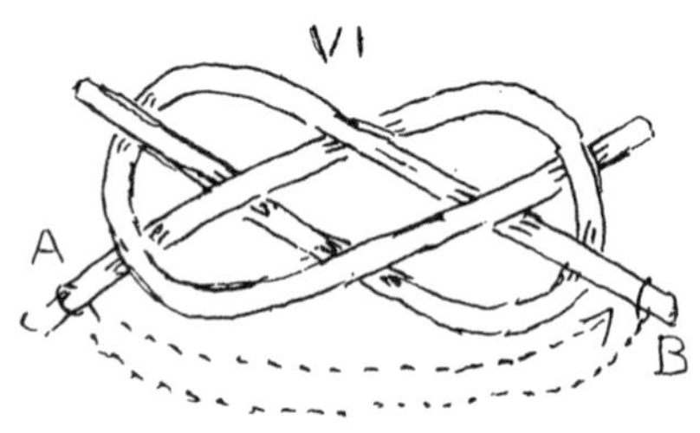
VI
A
B

Fig. VI
is the form of the knot shown on pages 15-16. When pulled taut, it takes the form shown in Fig. IV (or V)

In Fig. VI interchange A & B to form VII
In Fig. VII turn the right hand half of the knot over to form Fig. VIII (or Fig. III above)
III, VI & VII, when taut are alike and are forms of the HALF GRANNY

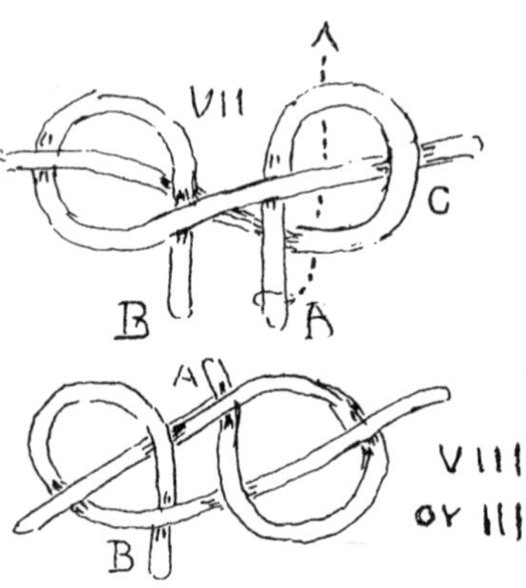
VII
C
B
A
A
B
VIII
or III

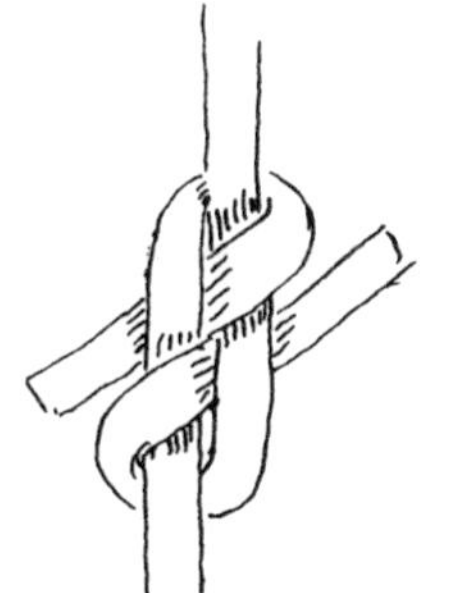

THE GRASS KNOT

is the Half Granny as a bend for straps, straw, grass or such flat material

II

THE REEVING LINE BEND

III

is a form of the Half Granny

NOTE

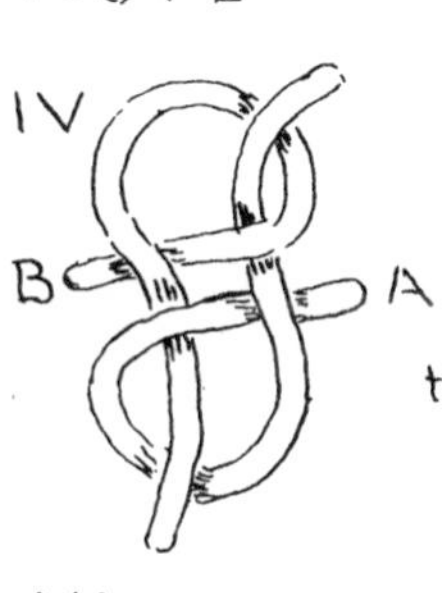
IV
B
A

V
A
B

In the Half Granny Fig. IV by interchanging the ends A & B the knot passes into the Oblique Granny

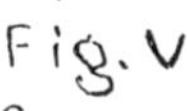

Fig. V

VI

D C

The Half Granny must not be confused with Fig. VI, which slips and which, by interchanging C and D, passes into the Thief (Oblique Reef) Knot Fig. VII

C
VII
D

THE GRANNY

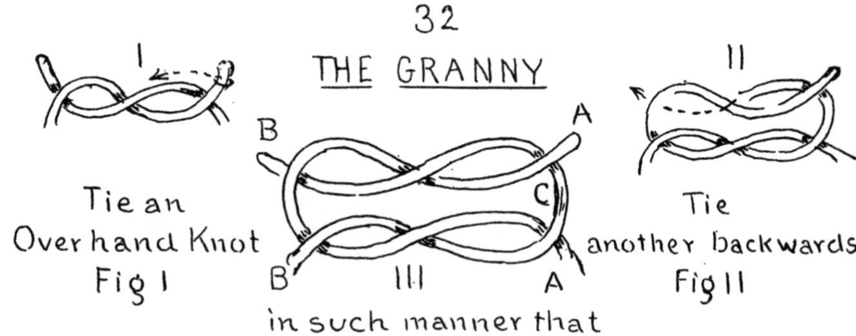
I
II
B
A
C
B
III
A

Tie an Overhand Knot Fig I

Tie another backwards Fig II

in such manner that the ends A A lie on opposite sides of the bight C

GRANNY and CLOVE HITCH

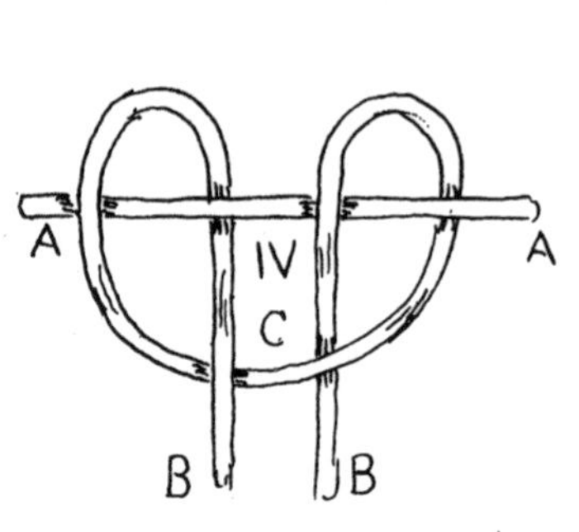
A
A
IV
C
B
B

See page 5, Fig. II

Straighten the line A A, Fig III
The parts BB-C become a Clove Hitch around the line A A

A Granny, therefore, may be tied as follows.

Tie a Clove Hitch around the line A A Fig. IV

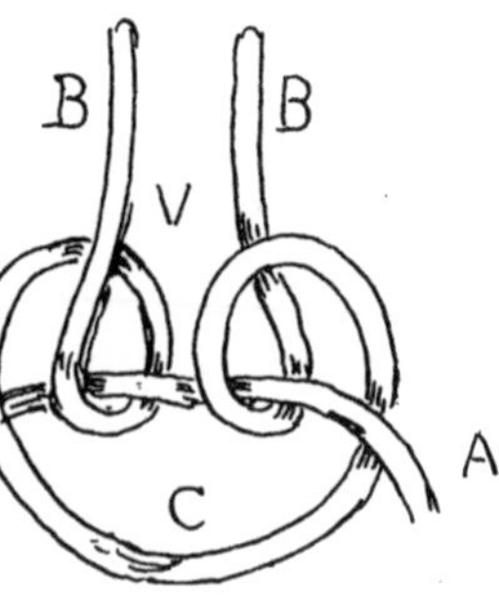
B
B
V
A
A
C

Turn the ends BB up around A and pull BB and C Fig. V

OBLIQUE GRANNY

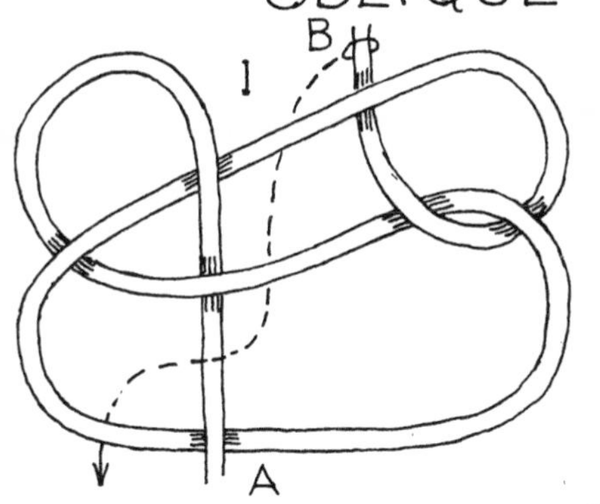
B
I
A

Fig I is the Half Granny. Pass the end B down under two strands and over the strand A. The knot becomes Fig II The Oblique Granny

II

When this knot is pulled taut, it slips apart and will not hold.

pull

pull

M

B A

But, by bringing the ends A & B together Fig. II, by holding A & B in one hand and the part M in the other, Fig II becomes a reliable Loop.

See page 5

The Japanese method of tying this Loop is shown on page 148.

BUNTLINE HITCH AND OBLIQUE GRANNY

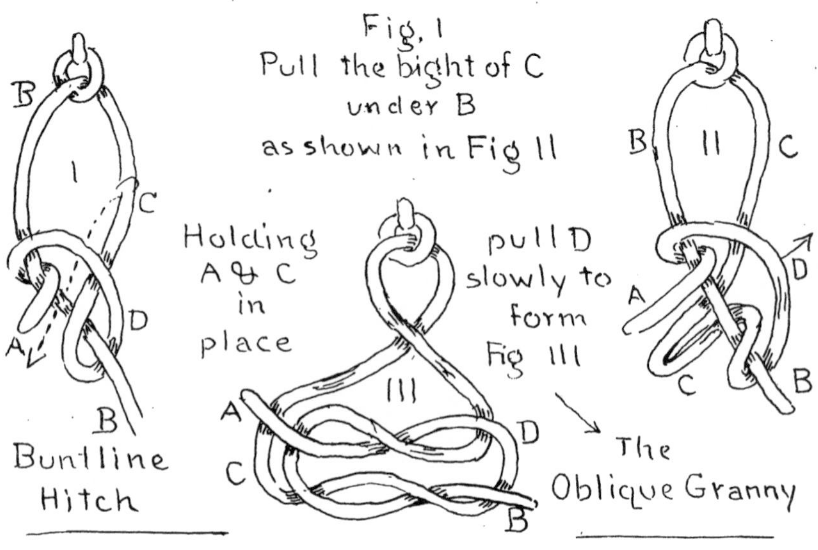
Fig. I
Pull the bight of C
under B
as shown in Fig II
B
I
C
A
D
B
Buntline
Hitch
Holding
A & C
in
place
III
A
C
D
B
pull D
slowly to
form
Fig III
The
Oblique Granny
B
II
C
A
D
C
B

FOUR-IN-HAND TIE

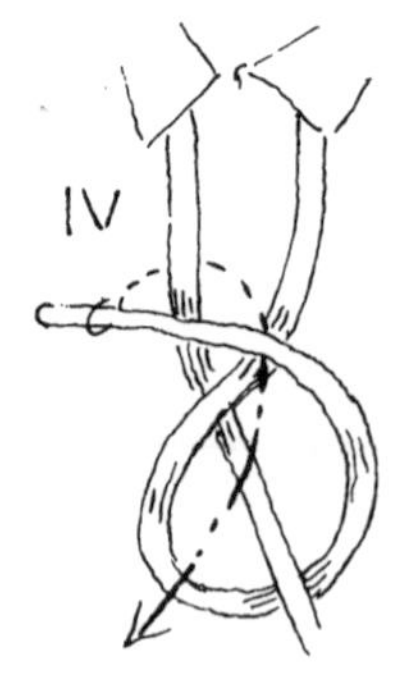
IV

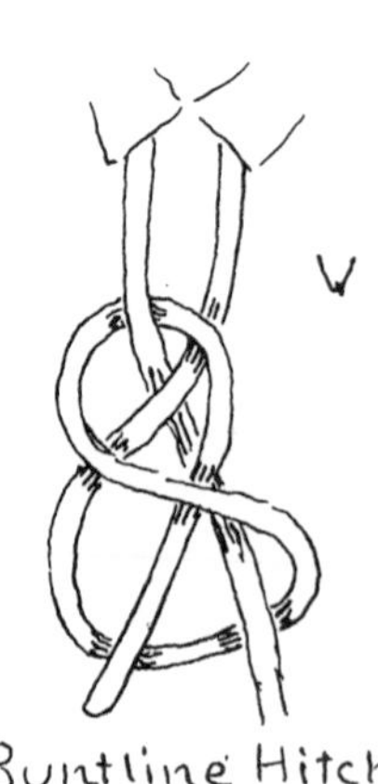
V

Buntline Hitch

SINGLE CARRICK BEND

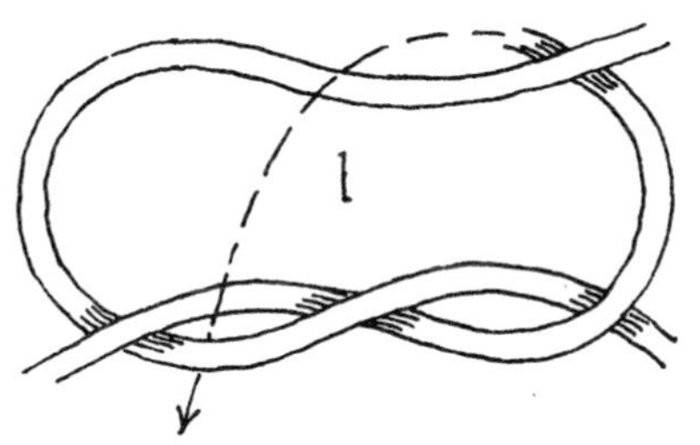
I
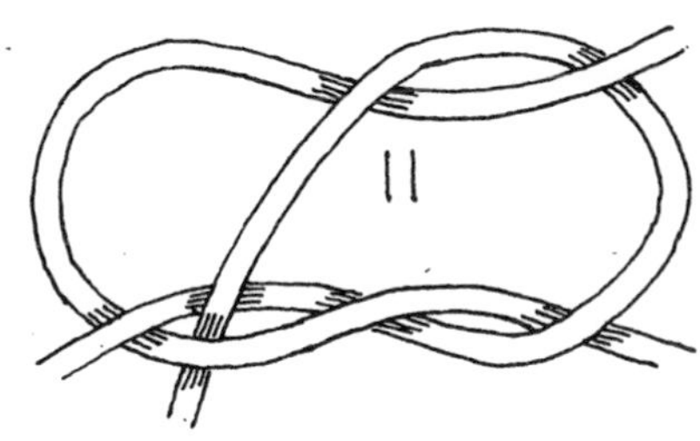
II

The two bights that form the finished knot, lie on planes perpendicular to each other.
The lay of the strands resembles that of the four strand Round Braid.

III

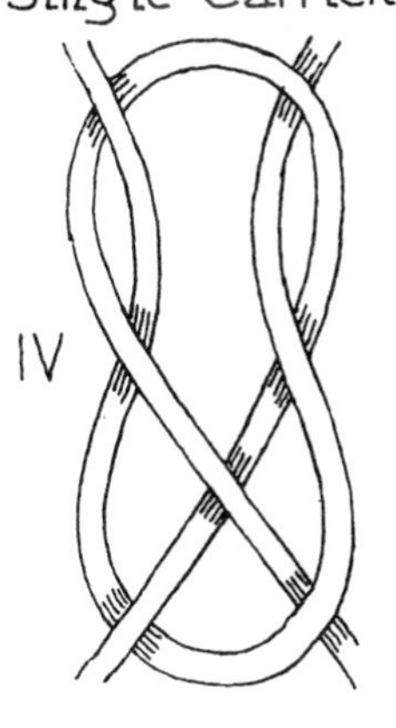
Single Carrick
IV

Fig. IV
Single Carrick
and Fig. V
Half Carrick
are very much alike.
They differ in the braiding of their strands,
alternately over and under in Fig V
very irregular in Fig IV

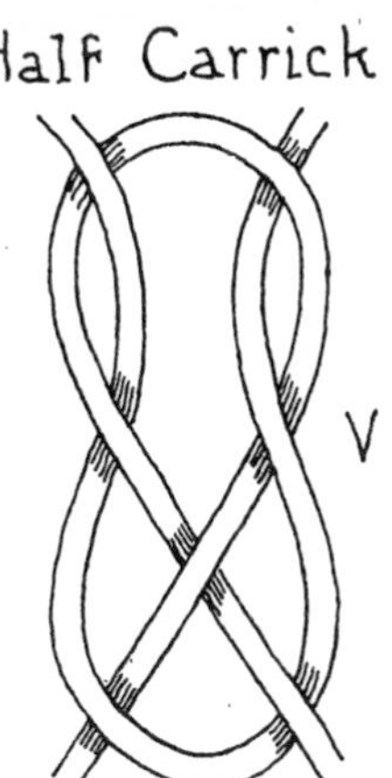
Half Carrick
V

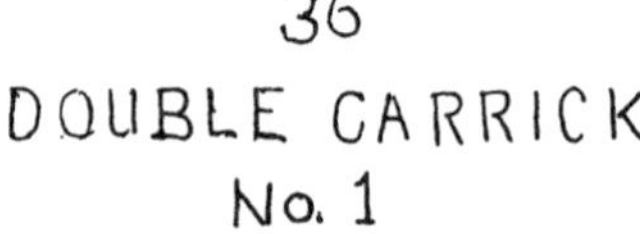

DOUBLE CARRICK No. 1

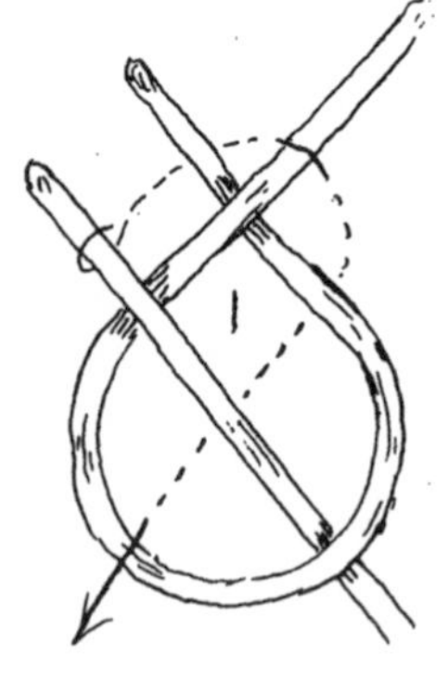
I

This Knot differs from the Double Carrick No 2 by the irregular braiding of the strands

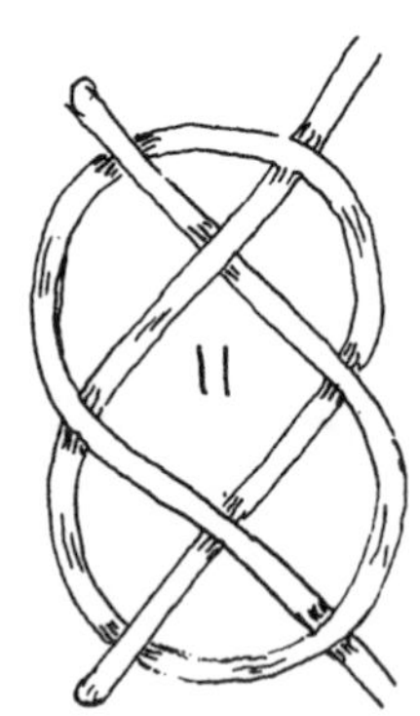
II

III

Fig. V begins with an Overhand Knot Fig. IV

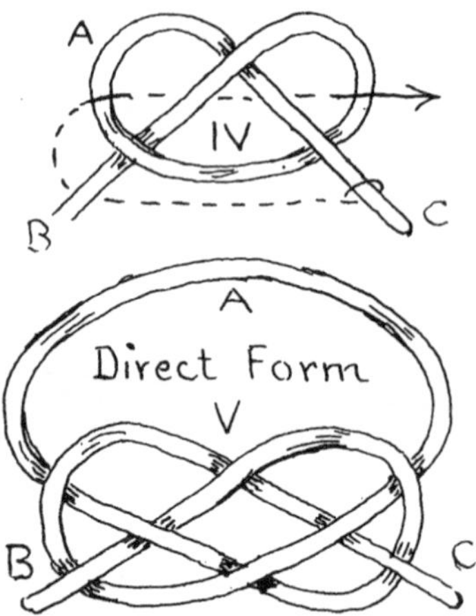
A
IV
B
C
A
Direct Form
V
B
C

Fig. VII begins with the Miller's Knot Fig. VI

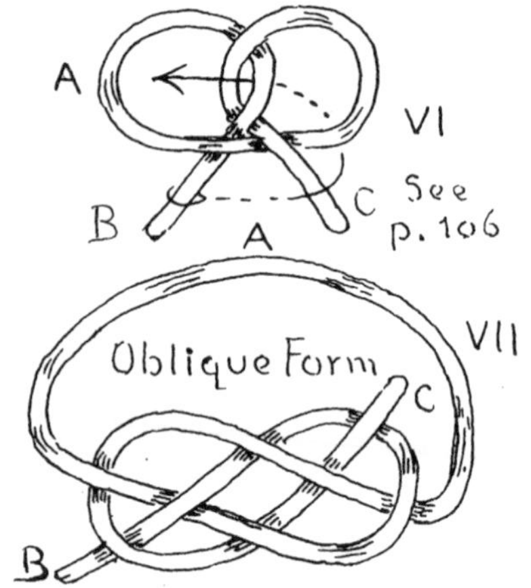
A
VI
B
C
See p. 106
A
VII
Oblique Form
C
B

HALF CARRICK

This is Nameless-2 of the first edition

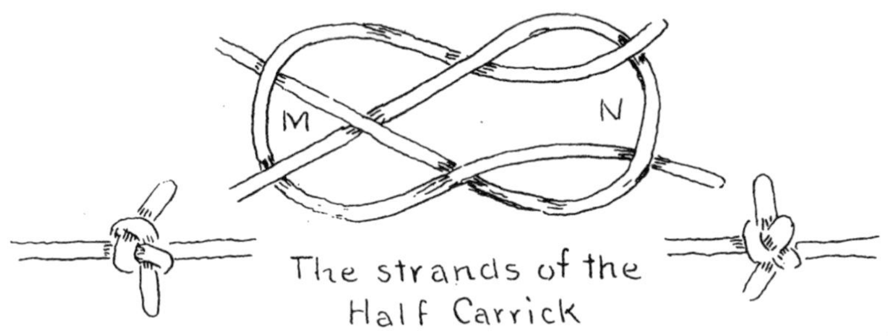
M
N

The strands of the Half Carrick in one half (M) of the knot, have the lay characteristic of the Double Carrick-No. 2. The strands of the other half (N) correspond with the lay of the Granny.

So far as I know this knot is not in use

I
II
III
IV-a
obverse
IV-b
reverse

OBLIQUE HALF CARRICK

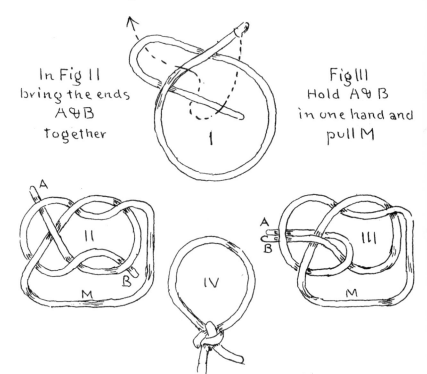

In Fig II bring the ends A&B together

Fig III Hold A&B in one hand and pull M

I

A

II

B

M

IV

A

B

III

M

HALF CARRICK and MILLER'S KNOT

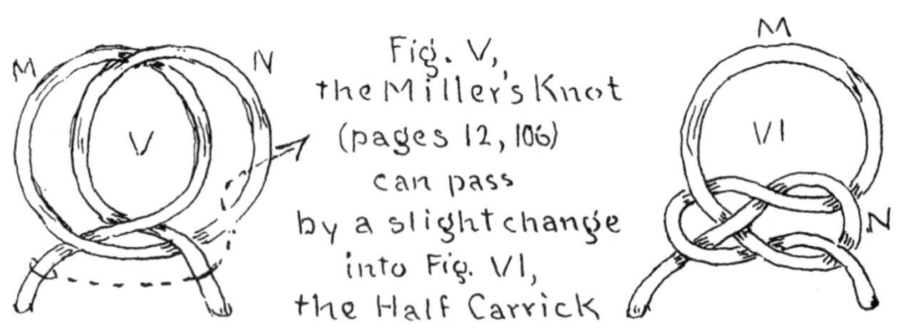
M
N
V
M
VI
N

Fig. V, the Miller's Knot (pages 12, 106) can pass by a slight change into Fig. VI, the Half Carrick

DOUBLE CARRICK
No. 2

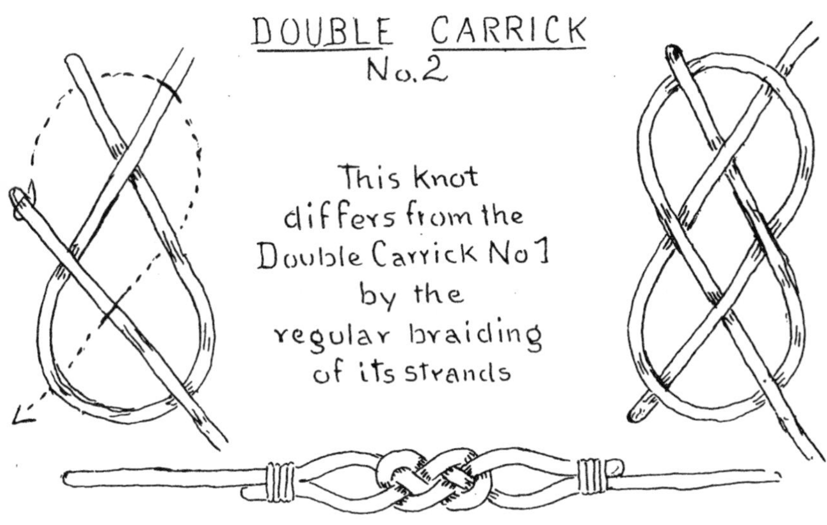

This knot differs from the Double Carrick No 1 by the regular braiding of its strands

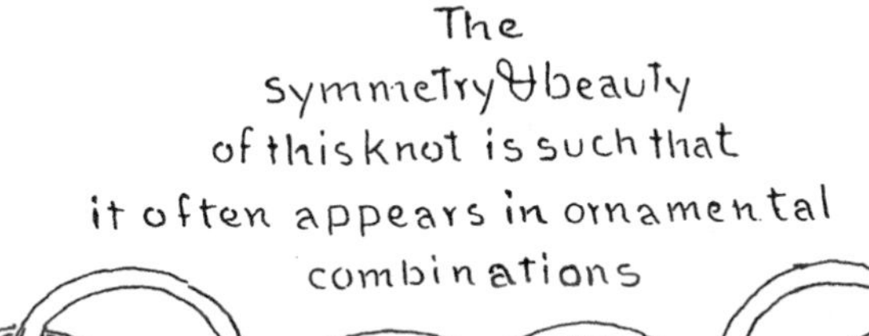

The symmetry & beauty of this knot is such that it often appears in ornamental combinations

See pages 143, 147, 188 &c.

OBLIQUE DOUBLE CARRICK No. 2

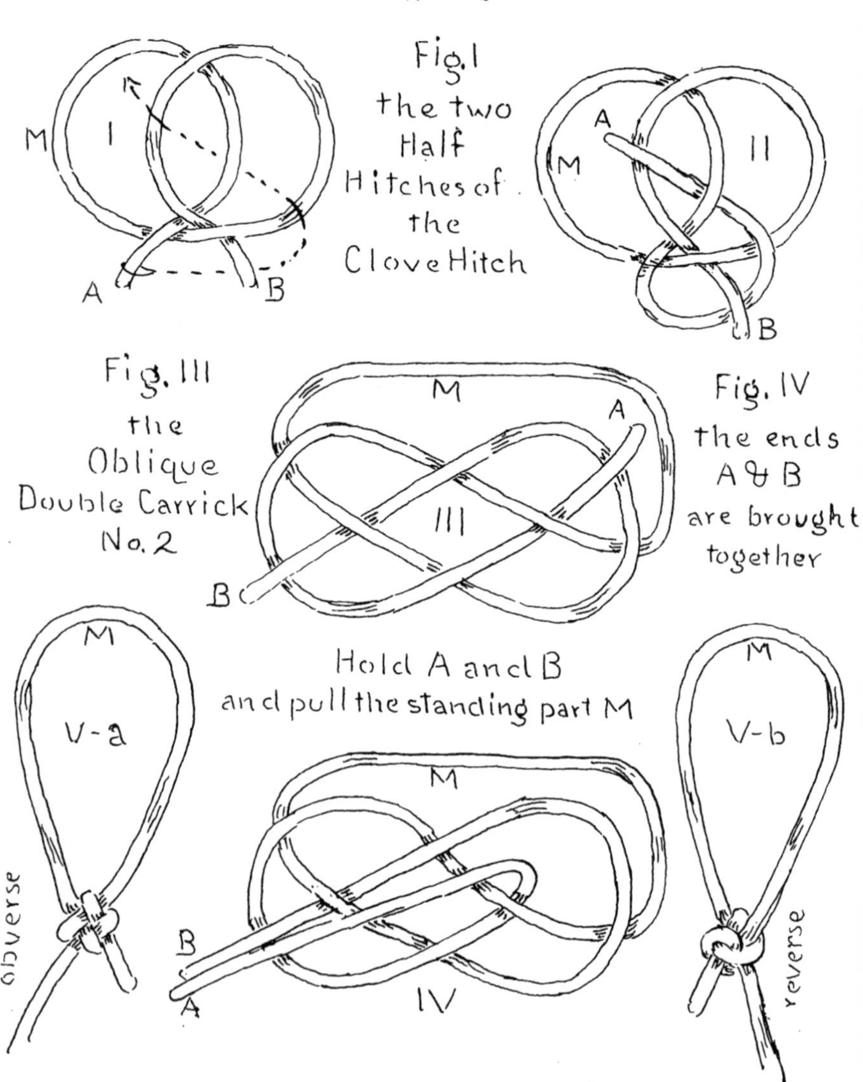
M
I
A
B
Fig. I
the two Half Hitches of the Clove Hitch
A
M
II
B
Fig. III
the Oblique Double Carrick No. 2
M
A
III
B
Fig. IV
the ends A & B are brought together
M
V-a
obverse
Hold A and B and pull the standing part M
M
B
A
IV
M
V-b
reverse

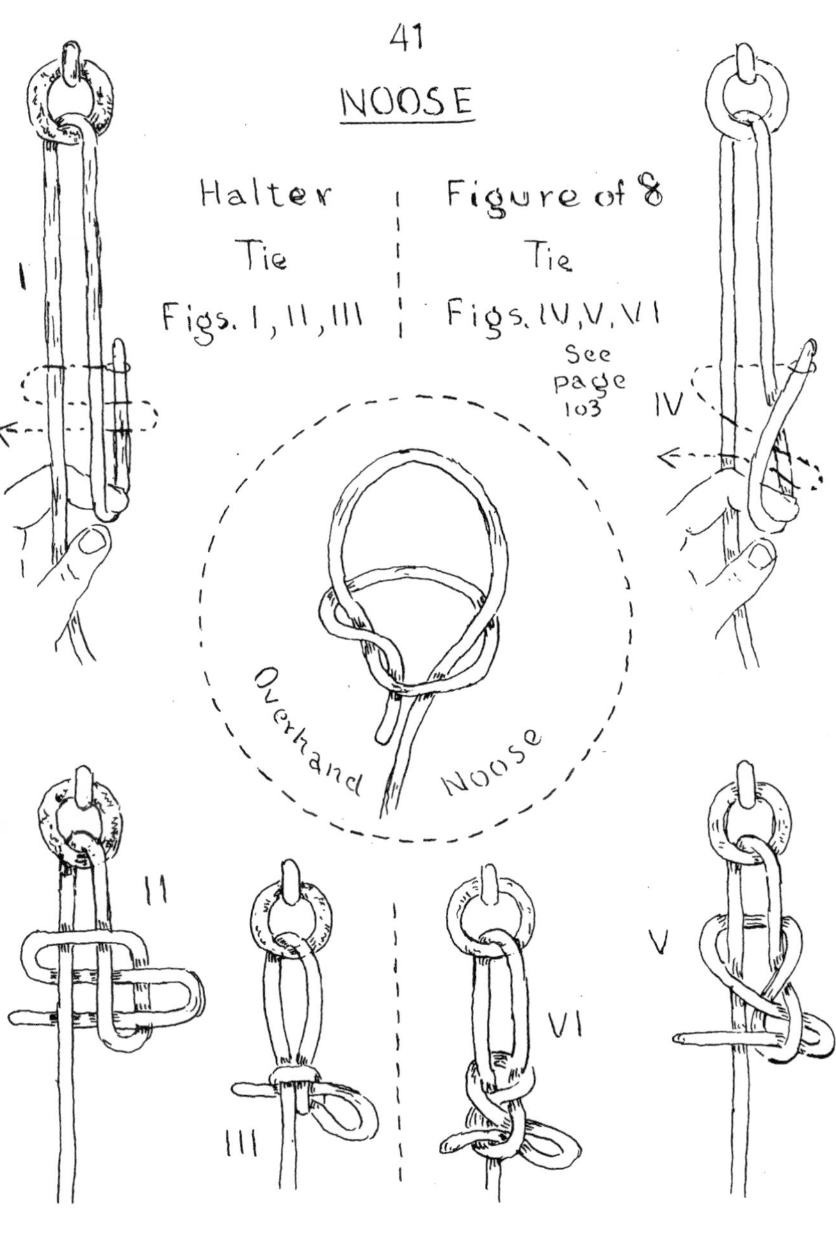
41
NOOSE
Halter
Tie
Figs. I, II, III
Figure of 8
Tie
Figs. IV, V, VI
See
page
103
I
IV
Overhand
Noose
II
III
VI
V

DOUBLE NOOSE

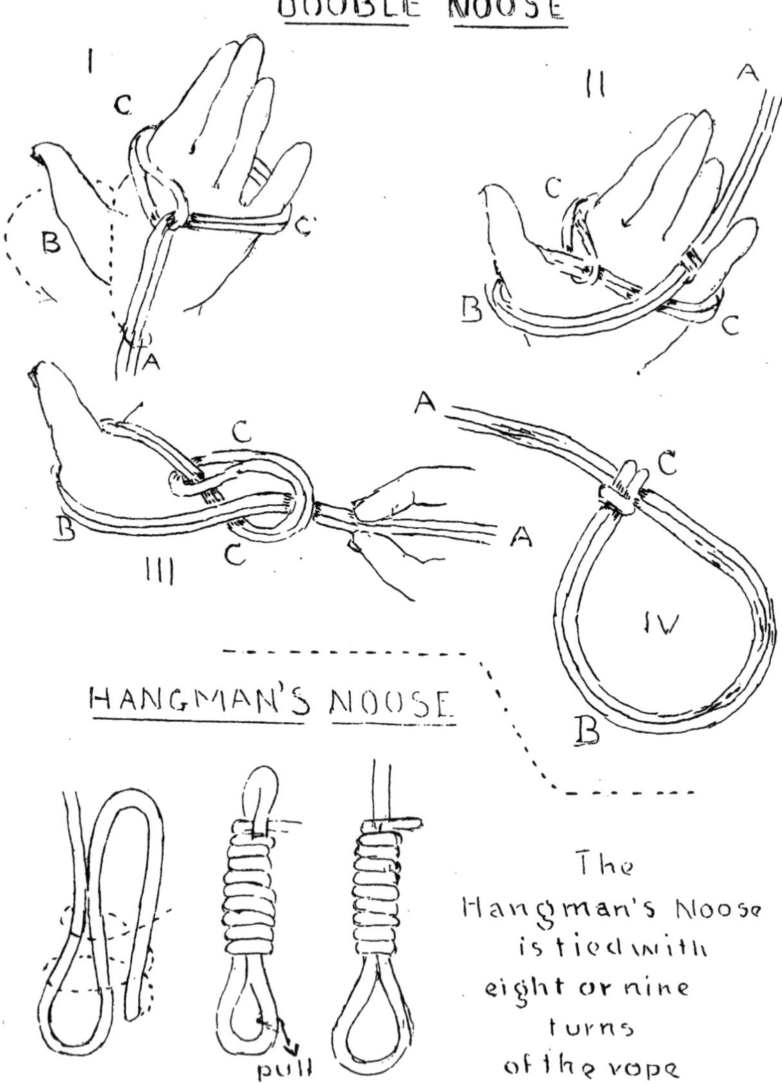
I
C
B
C
A
II
A
C
B
C
A
C
B
C
III
A
C
IV
B
pull

HANGMAN'S NOOSE

The Hangman's Noose is tied with eight or nine turns of the rope

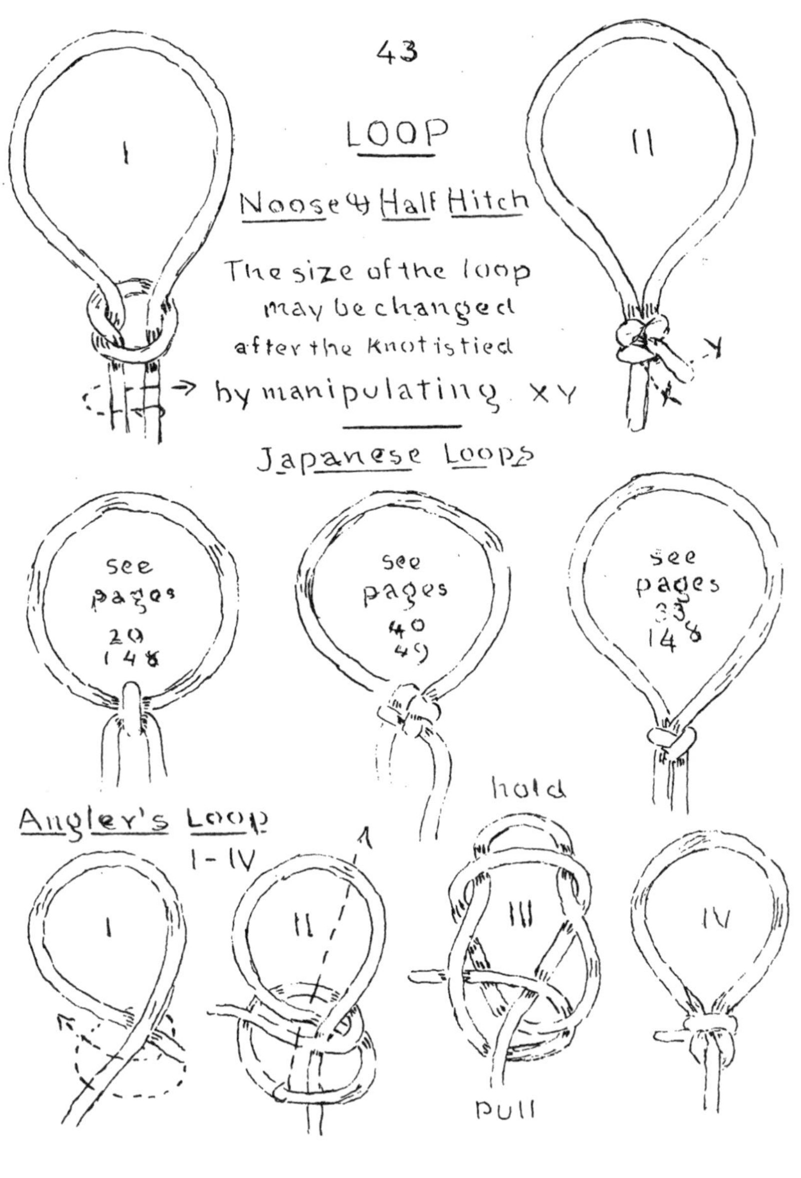
LOOP
Noose & Half Hitch
I
II
The size of the loop
may be changed
after the knot is tied
by manipulating XY
Y
X
Japanese Loops
see pages 20 148
see pages 40 49
see pages 33 148
Angler's Loop
I - IV
I
II
III
IV
hold
pull

ARTILLERY or MAN-HARNESS KNOT

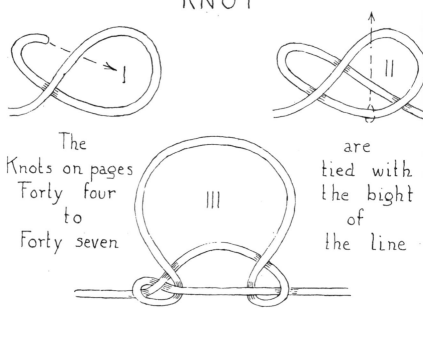

The Knots on pages Forty four to Forty seven are tied with the bight of the line.

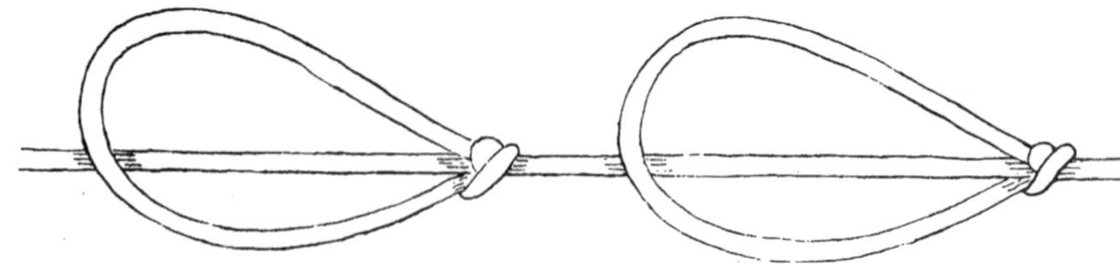

LINEMAN'S KNOT

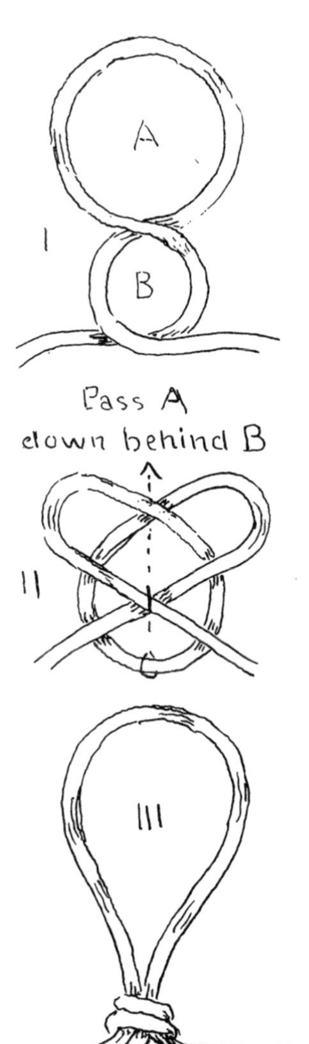
A
I
B
Pass A
down behind B
II
III

LOOP

beginning with an Overhand Knot

Fig. 1

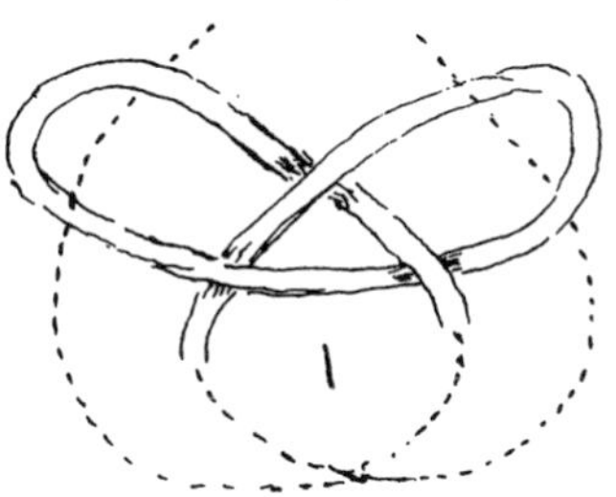
I

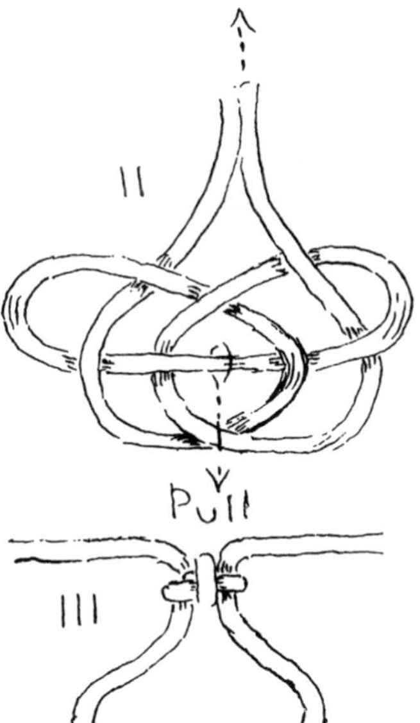
Pull
II
Pull
III

DOUBLE LOOP

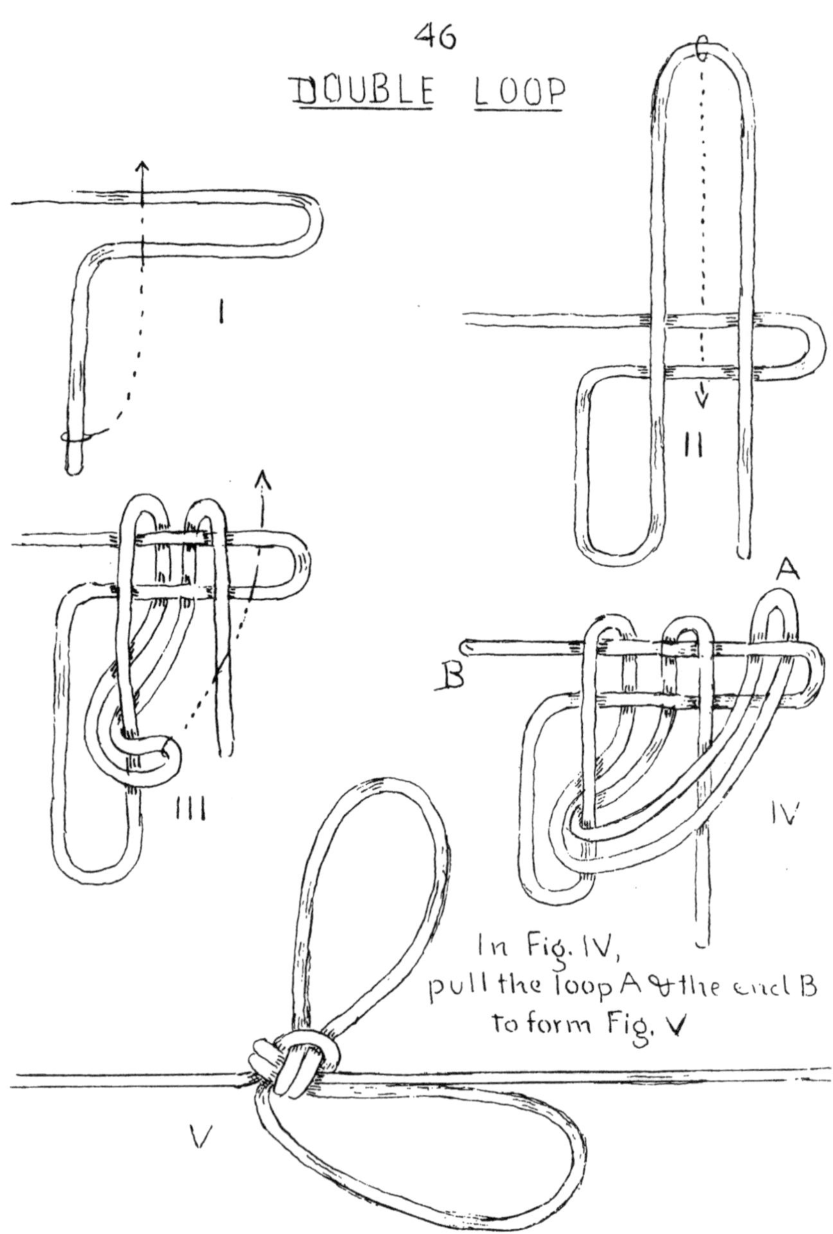
I
C
II
III
A
B
IV
V

In Fig. IV, pull the loop A & the end B to form Fig. V

DOUBLE LOOPS

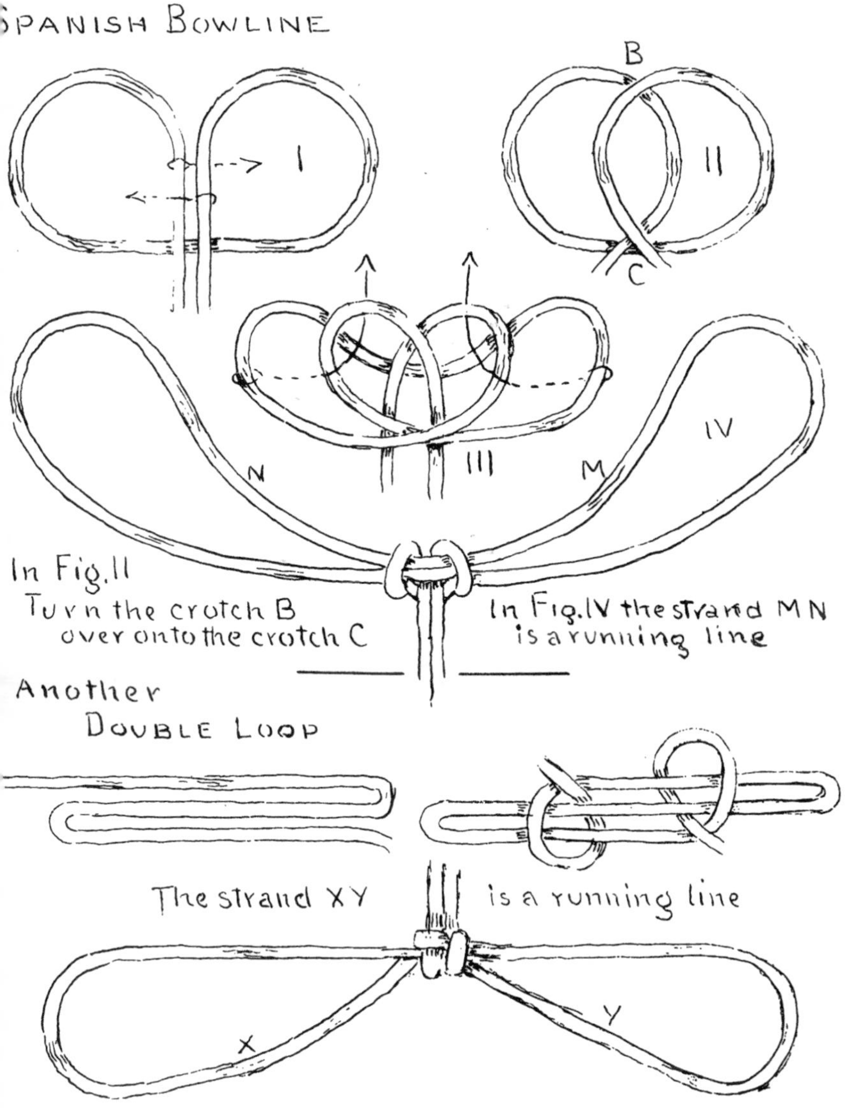
SPANISH BOWLINE
I
B
II
C
III
N
M
IV
In Fig. II
Turn the crotch B
over onto the crotch C
In Fig. IV the strand MN
is a running line
Another
DOUBLE LOOP
The strand XY
is a running line
X
Y

STOPPER KNOTS

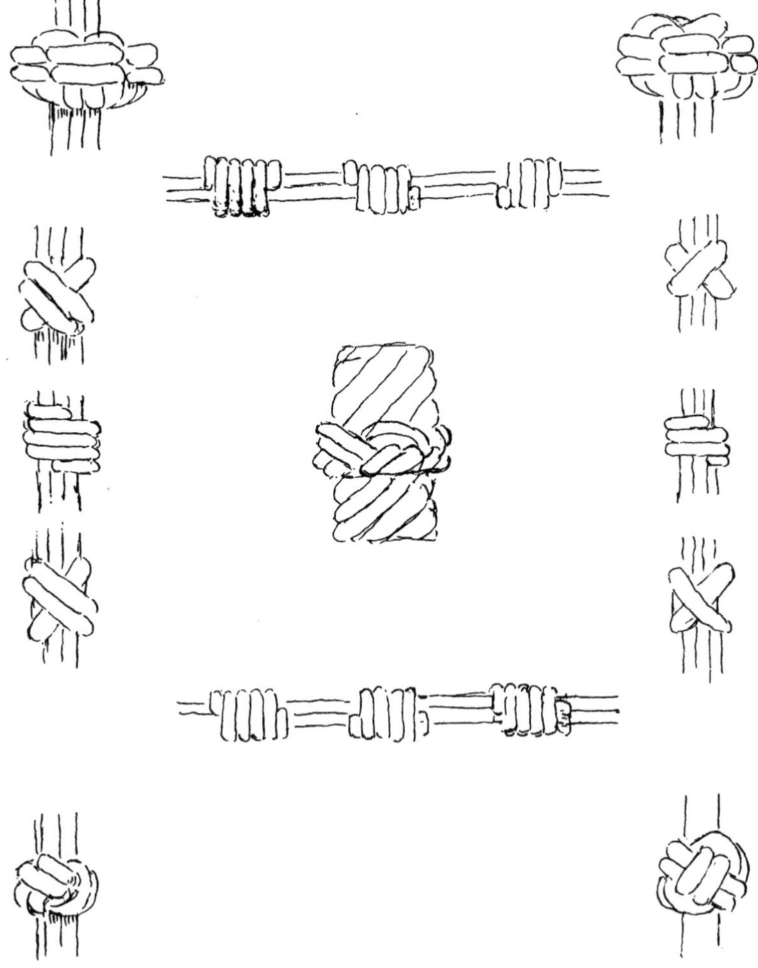

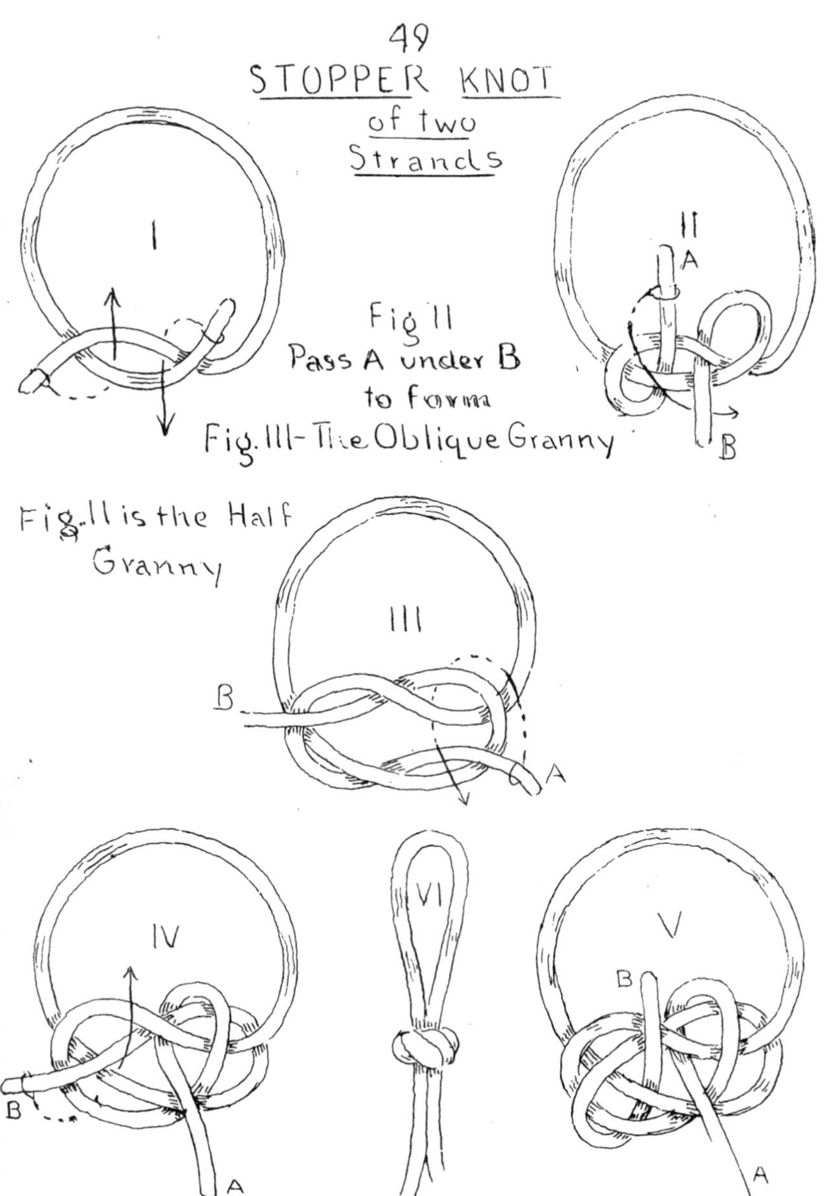
49
STOPPER KNOT
of two
Strands
I
II
A
Fig II
Pass A under B
to form
Fig. III - The Oblique Granny
B
Fig. II is the Half
Granny
III
B
A
IV
B
A
VI
V
B
A

WALL KNOT

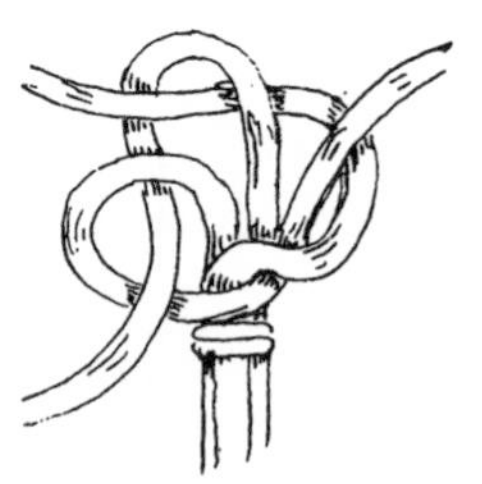

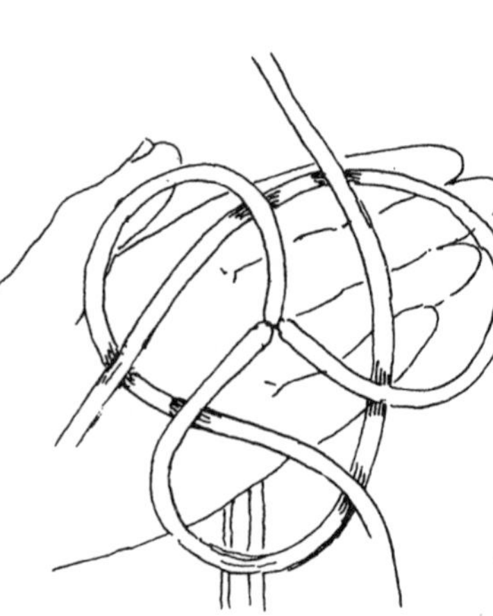

With 3 cords the Wall may be tied to the right or to the left

With a rope the Wall must follow the lay of the strands

CROWN KNOT

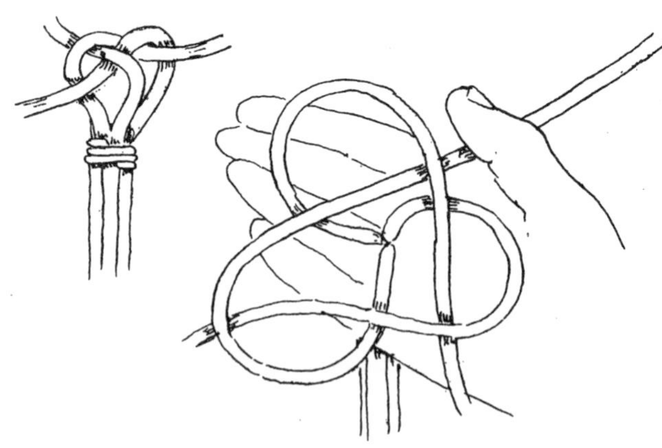

MAN-ROPE KNOT

A combination of the Wall & Crown with the strands doubled

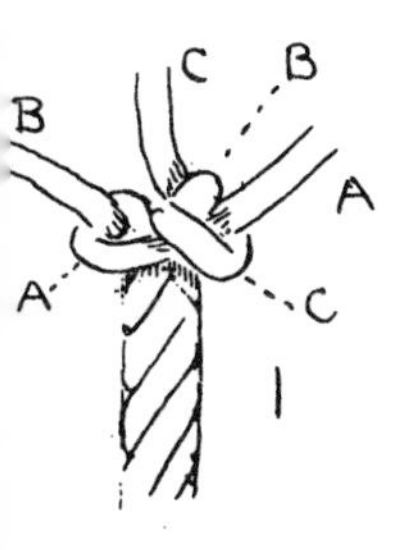
C
B
B
A
A
C
I

Single Wall

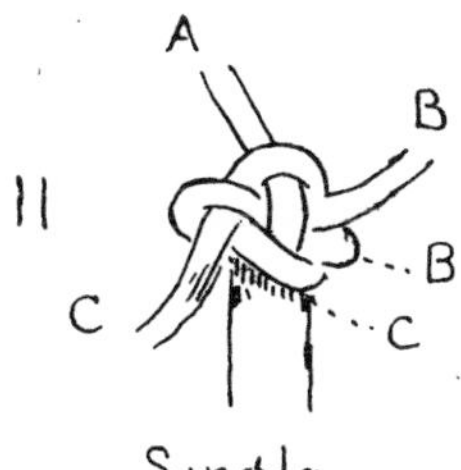
A
B
II
B
C
C

Single Wall & Crown

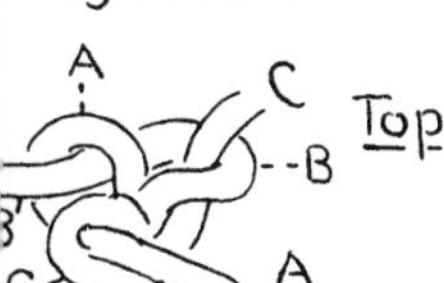
A
C
B
C
A
Top

A
Top
B
C

In doubling each strand follows its own lay

V

The Crown Fig. II brings each end against its own part

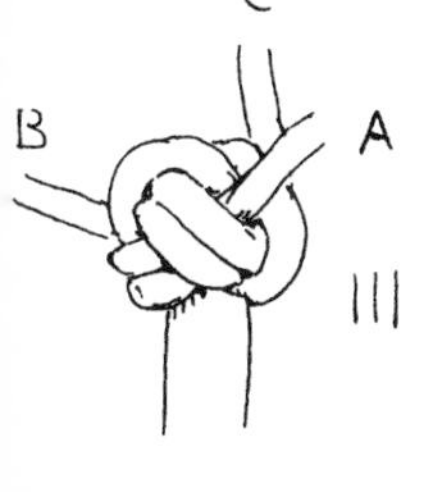
C
B
A
III

Double Wall & Single Crown

The 3 ends A B C Fig III are passed down through the center of the Knot Fig. IV and are cut off

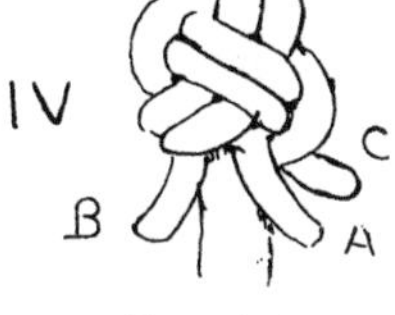
IV
C
B
A

Double Wall & Crown

TWIN WALL KNOT

Wall A & B together
around C & D
Fig I, II

C & D are
walled Together
Following the dotted lines

53
DIAMOND KNOT

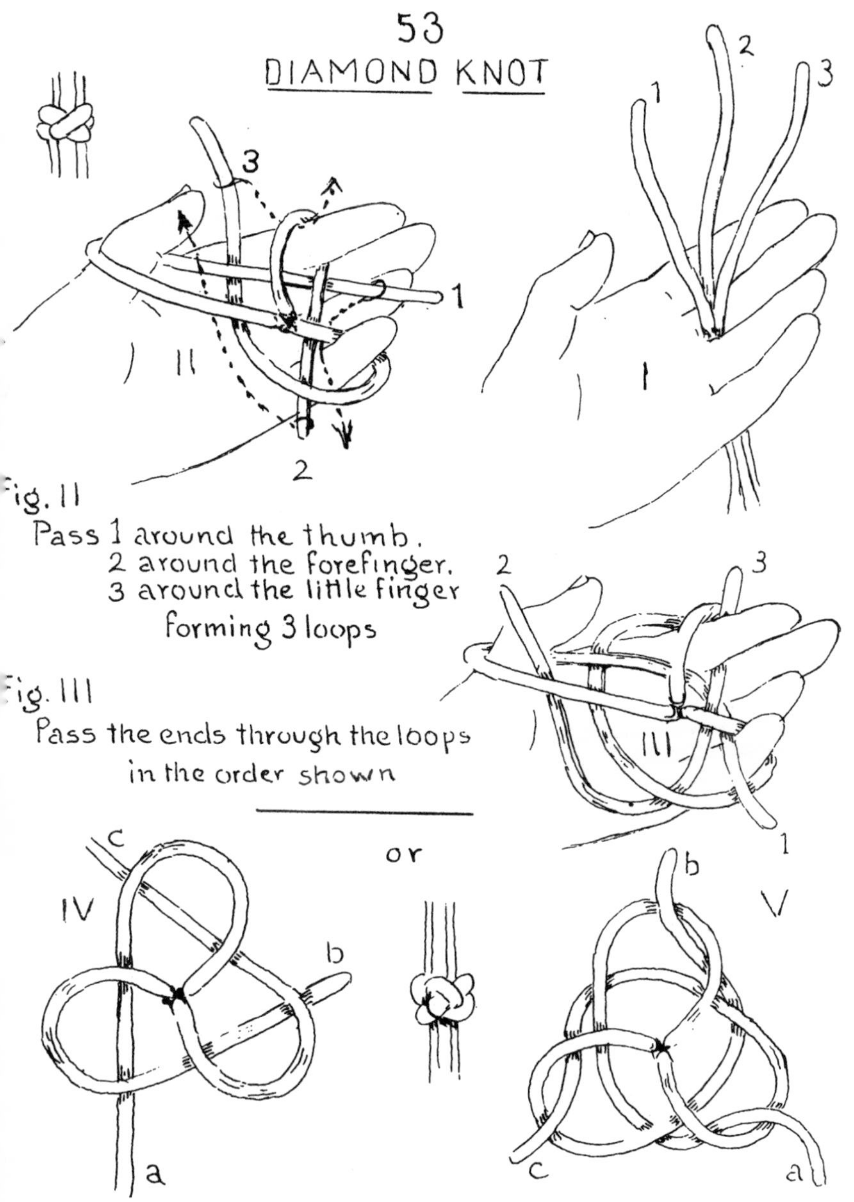

1
2
3
I
II
III
IV
V
a
b
c
or

Fig. II
Pass 1 around the thumb.
2 around the forefinger.
3 around the little finger
forming 3 loops

Fig. III
Pass the ends through the loops
in the order shown

DIAMOND KNOT
of
Four
Strands

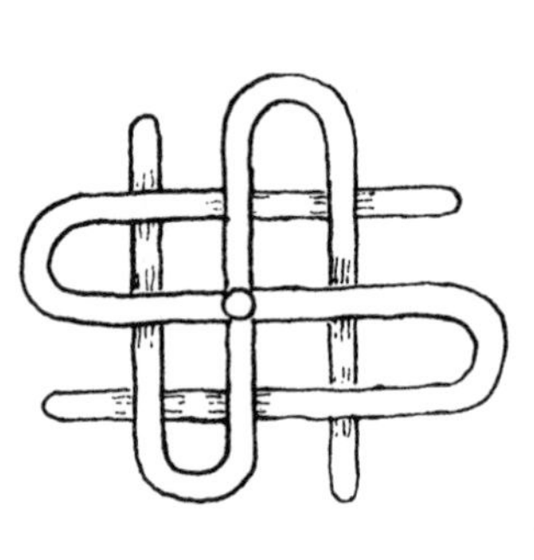

III

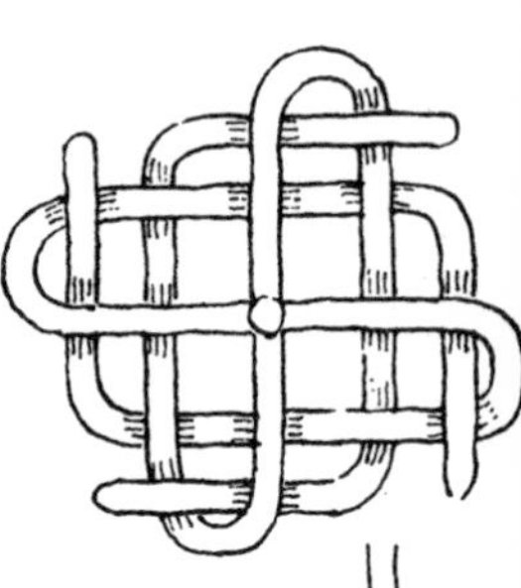

II

DIAMOND
of
Two Strands

Fig IV
The
Oblique
Double Carrick
No 2
See page 40
Fig III

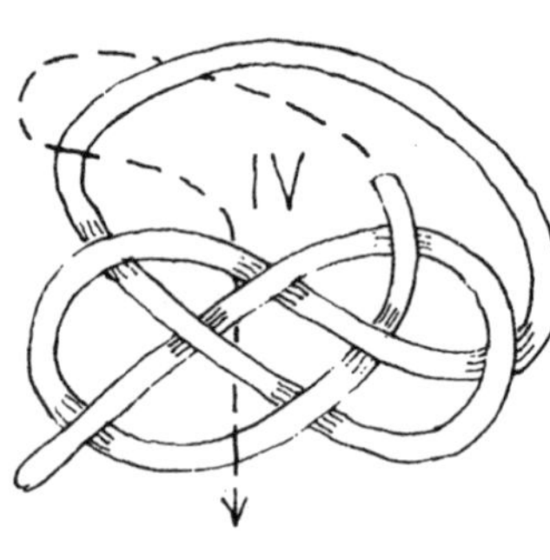

IV

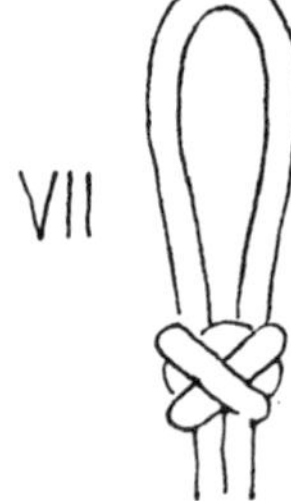

VII

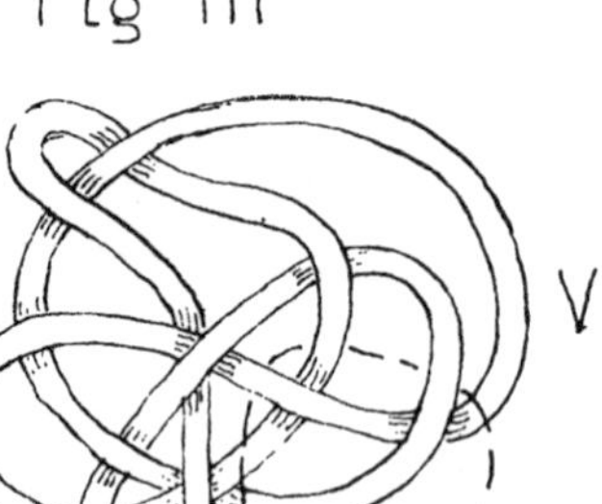

V

VI

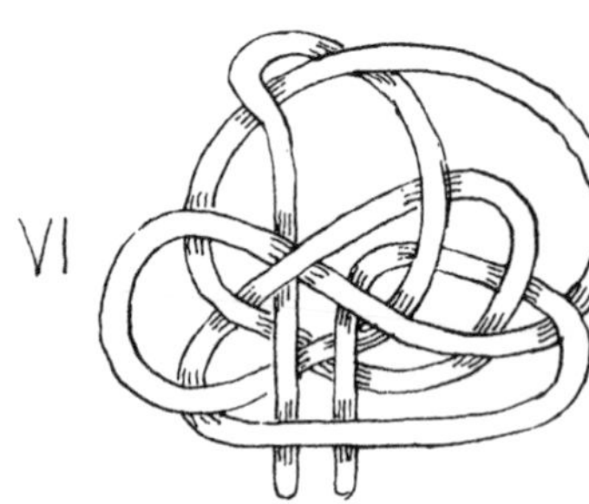

DOUBLE DIAMOND

C I B A A B C

Fig I is the Diamond Knot

In doubling each strand follows its own lay

For practise with this, and with the various Stopper Knots, the construction is more easily followed if the strands are of different colors.

II A B C

First stage.

In Fig. I

- pass A over C & under B
- pass B over A & under C
- pass C over B & under A

to form Fig II

III

Second stage

In Fig. II

- pass A over both strands of C & under both Strands of B
- pass B over both strands of A & under both strands of C
- pass C over both strands of B & under both strands of A

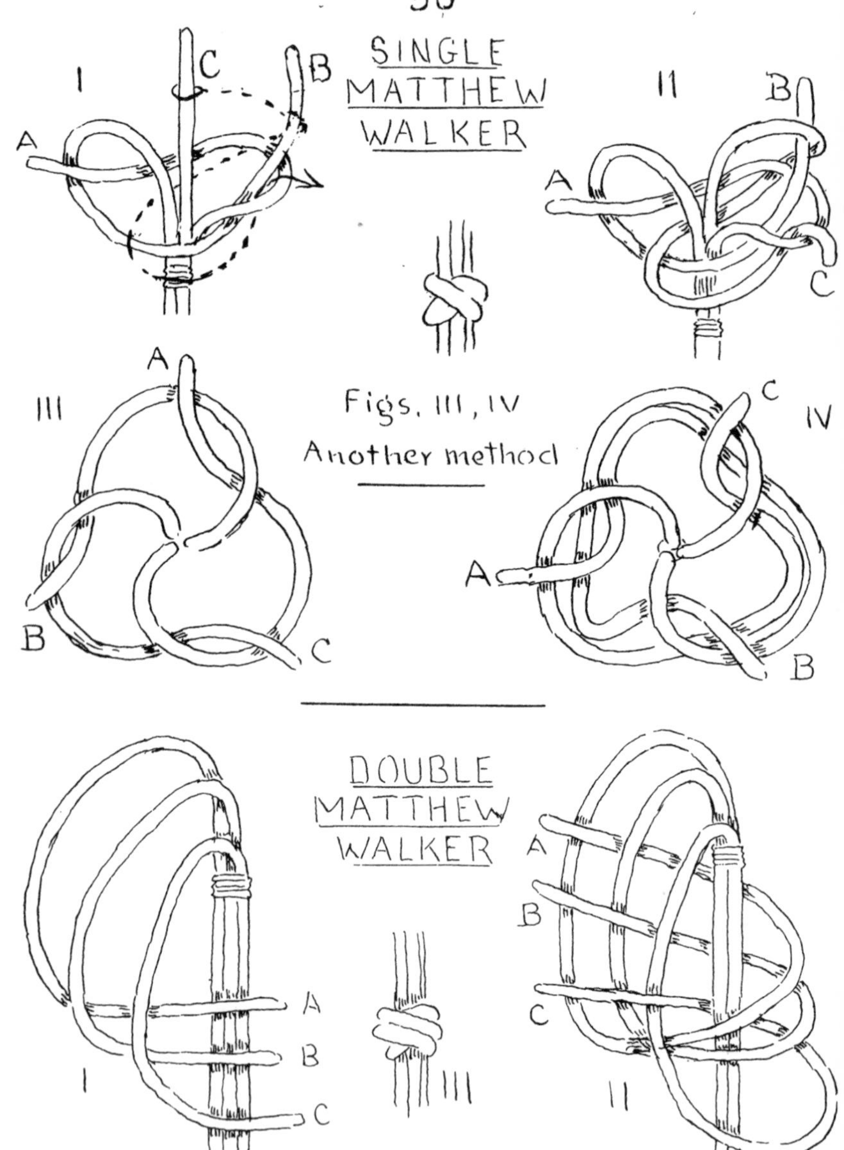
SINGLE
MATTHEW
WALKER
I
A
C
B
II
A
B
C
III
A
B
C
Figs. III, IV
Another method
IV
A
C
B
DOUBLE
MATTHEW
WALKER
I
A
B
C
III
II
A
B
C

INVERTED WALL KNOT

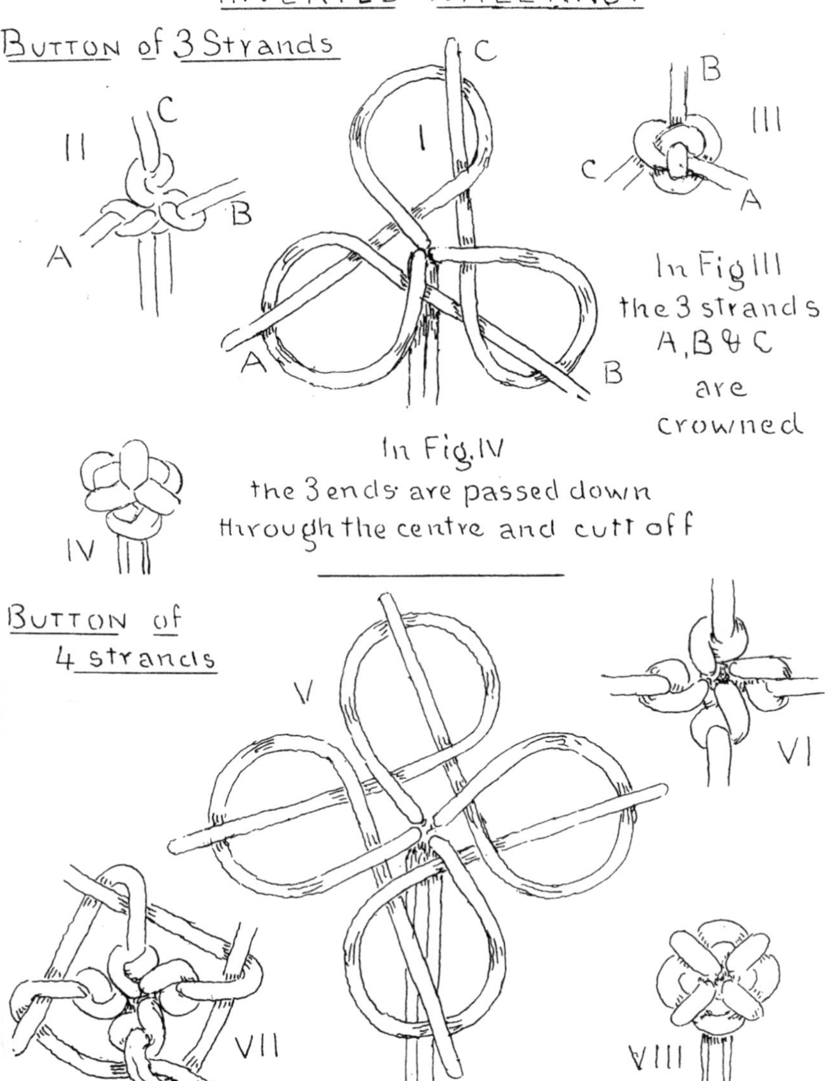
Button of 3 Strands
C
II
C
B
A
I
A
B
B
III
C
A
In Fig III
the 3 strands
A, B & C
are
crowned
In Fig. IV
the 3 ends are passed down
through the centre and cutt off
IV
Button of
4 strands
V
VI
VII
VIII

STAR KNOT

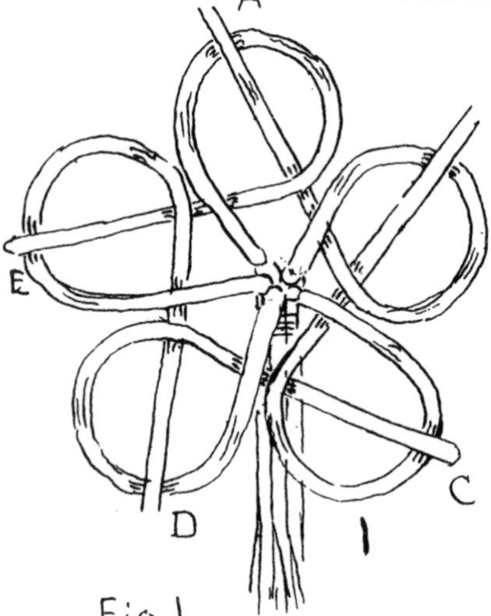

A
B
E
D
C
I
B
C
A
D
E
II

Fig. I
Inverted Wall Knot
of 5 strands

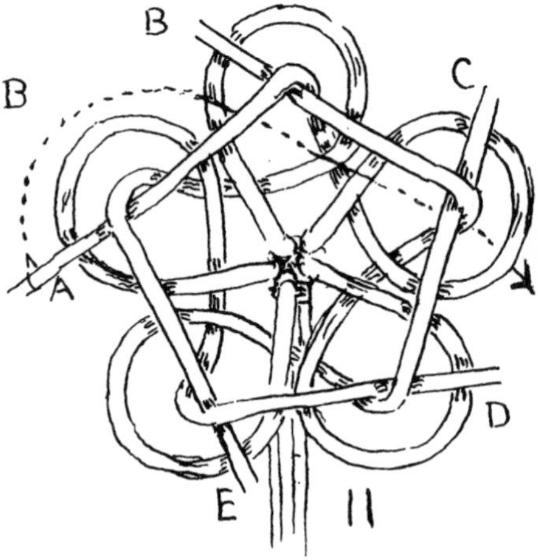

Fig. II
The 5 strands
A, B, C, D, E
are crowned

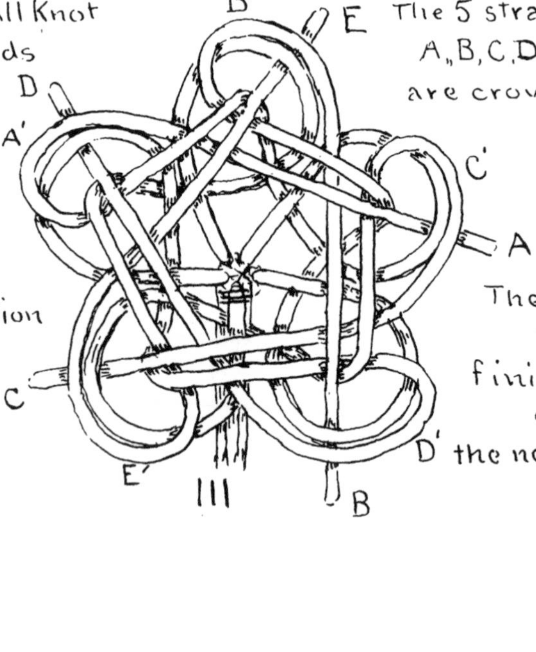

B'
E
D
A'
C'
A
C
E'
III
B
D'

Fig. III
A'A, B'B, C'C
D'D & E'E
show
the next position
of the
5 strands

The knot
is
finished
on
the next page

STAR KNOT

Continued

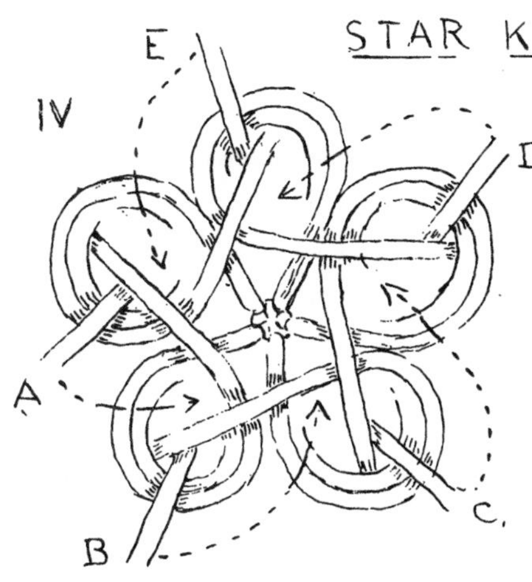
IV
E
D
A
B
C

Fig IV
is
the reverse side of
Fig. III
with some of the strands
omitted
to avoid confusion

Fig V
(reverse side)
The ends A, B, C, D and E
following the arrows in Fig IV
pass up through
the bights and the center of the
knot

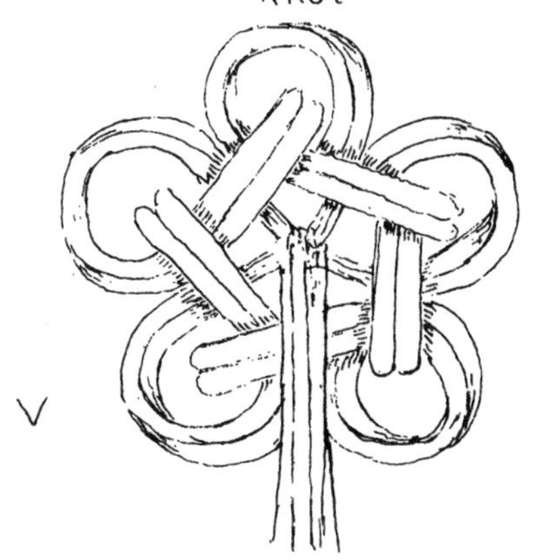
V

VI

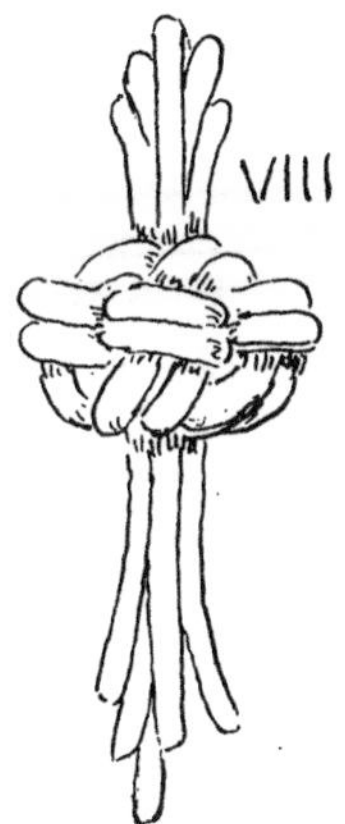
VIII

TURK'S HEAD

A Turk's Head may be defined as a complex of like interlacing circles so united as to form a single line, and whose centers are the angles of a regular polygon of 3,4,5 or of any convenient number of sides.

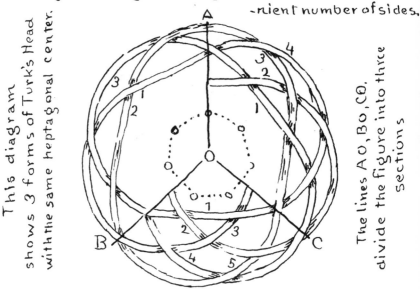

This diagram shows 3 forms of Turk's Head with the same heptagonal center.

The lines AO, BO, CO, divide the figure into three sections

The section AOB represents a heptagonal Turk's Head of three strands

the section AOC	the section BOC
of 4 strands	of 5 strands

TURK'S HEAD

Triangular Center

Two strands

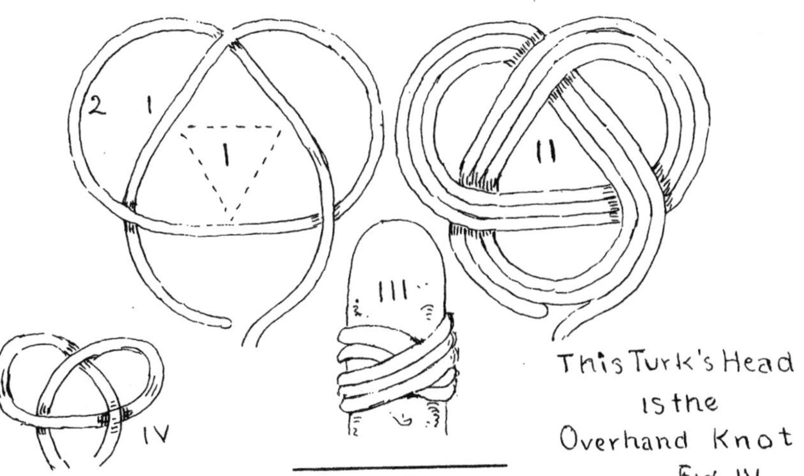
2
1
I
II
III
IV

This Turk's Head is the Overhand Knot Fig. IV

A Triangular Turk's Head with 4 Strands

In this Turk's Head the circles are Joined in one line by means of loops a, b, c.

On account of the crowded interlacing at the center of the Knot this method is not practicable for centers of four or more sides

TURK'S HEAD

Quadrangular Center

Three strands

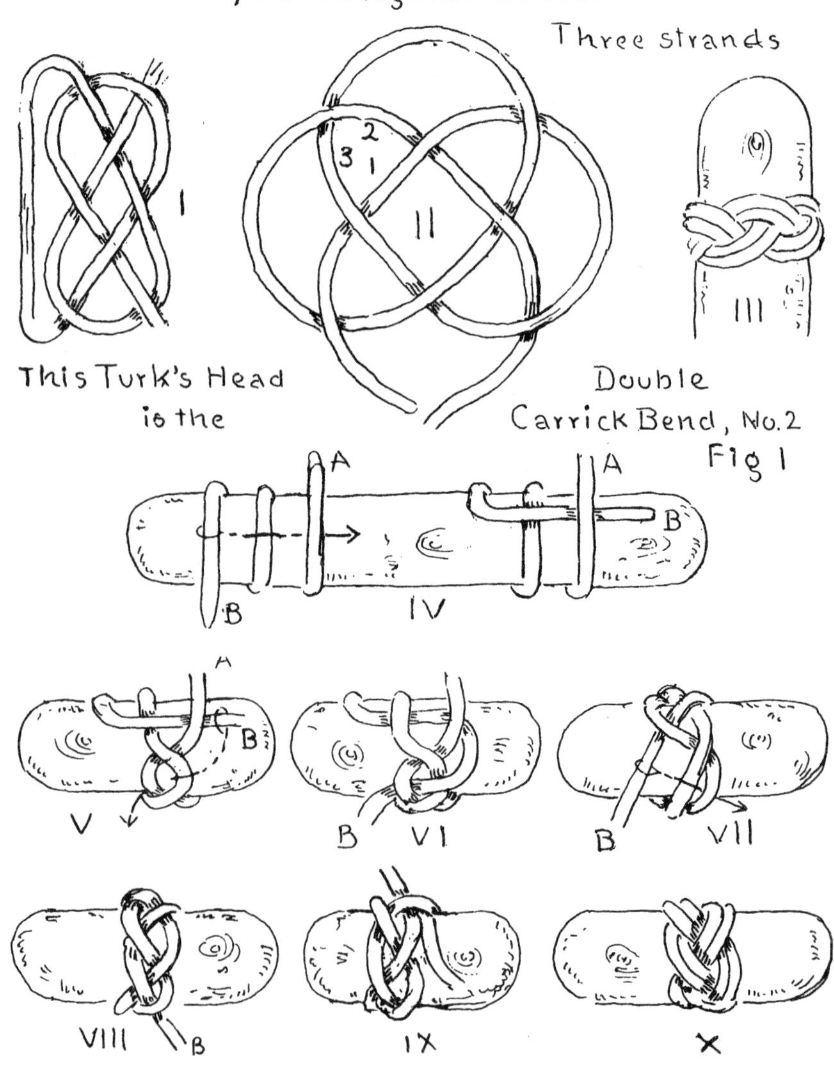
I
2
3
1
II
III
This Turk's Head
is the
Double
Carrick Bend, No. 2
Fig 1
A
A
B
B
IV
A
B
V
B
VI
B
VII
VIII
B
IX
X

TURK'S HEAD of 3 strands and pentangular center

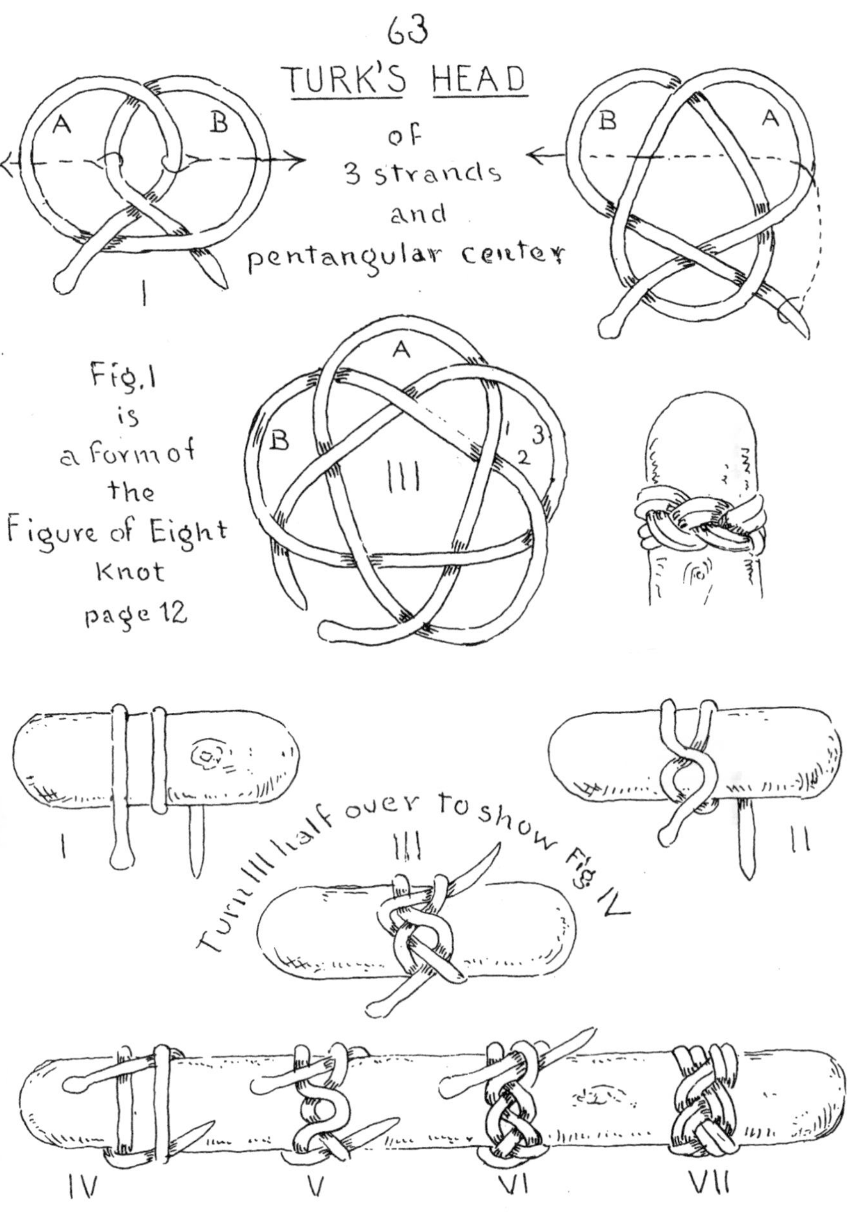
A
B
I
B
A
Fig.1 is a form of the Figure of Eight Knot page 12
A
B
1
3
2
III
I
II
Turn III half over to show Fig. IV
III
IV
V
VI
VII

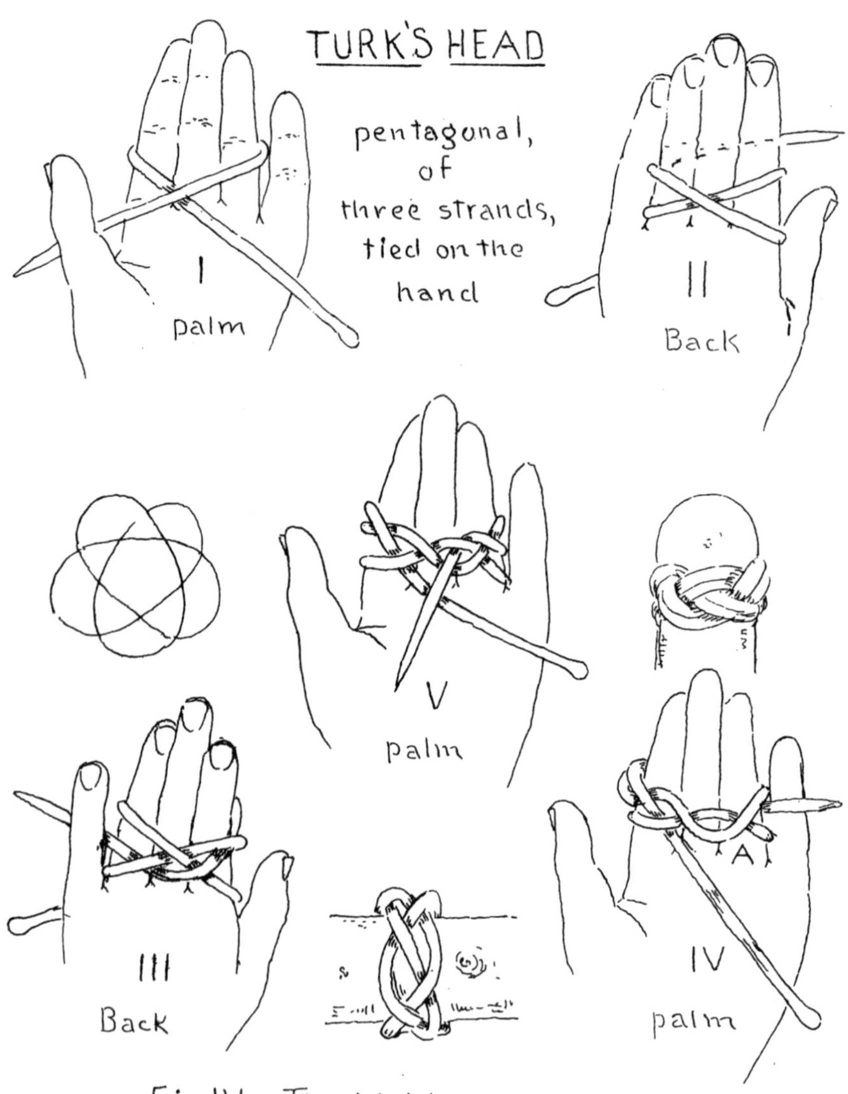
TURK'S HEAD
pentagonal,
of
three strands,
tied on the
hand
I
palm
II
Back
V
palm
III
Back
A
IV
palm

Fig IV – The bights are crossed at A

TURK'S HEAD
of
four strands
and pentangular center

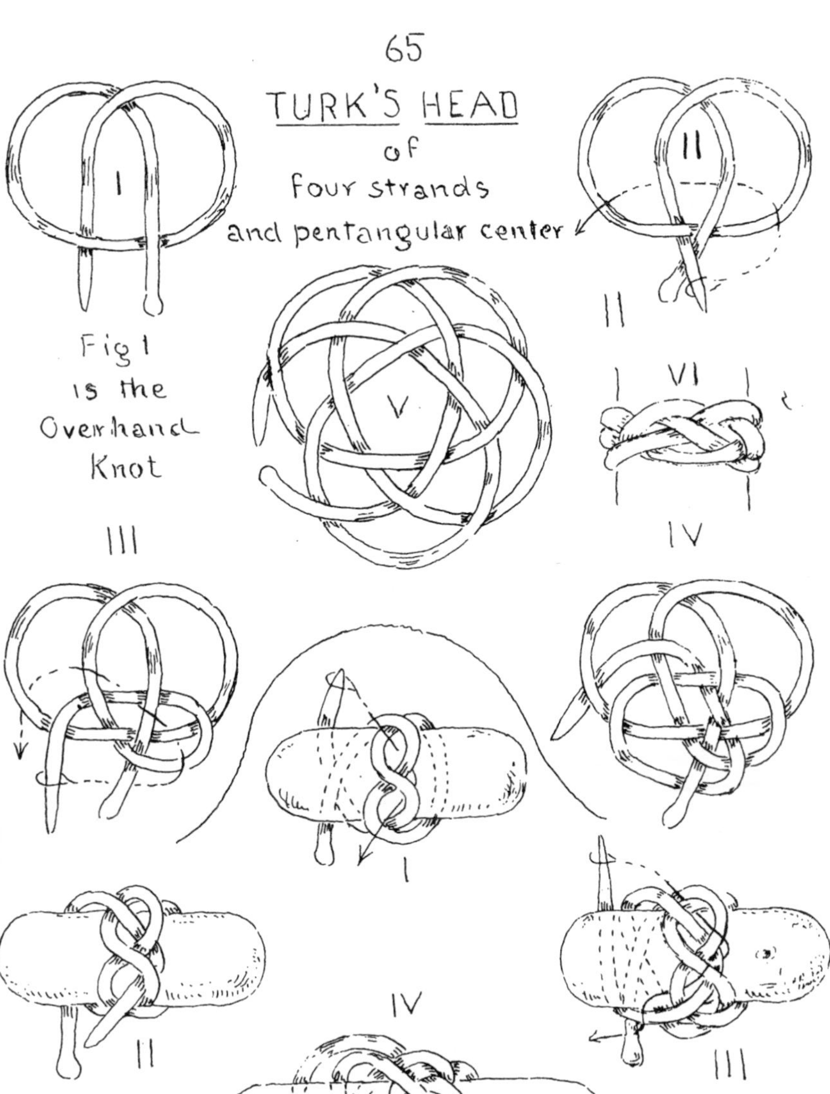
I
II
II
VI
V
Fig 1
is the
Overhand
Knot
III
IV
I
II
III
IV

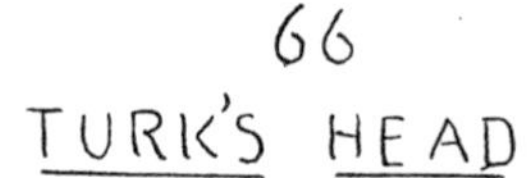

TURK'S HEAD

as a
Stopper
Knot

I II III IV

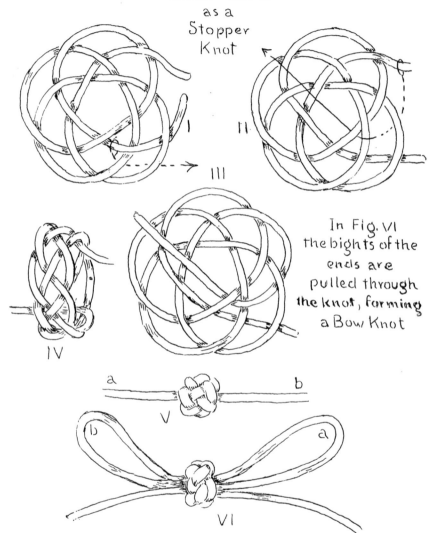

In Fig. VI the bights of the ends are pulled through the knot, forming a Bow Knot

a b
V

b a
VI

TURK'S HEAD as a BUTTON

I

Fig. I- Turk's Head

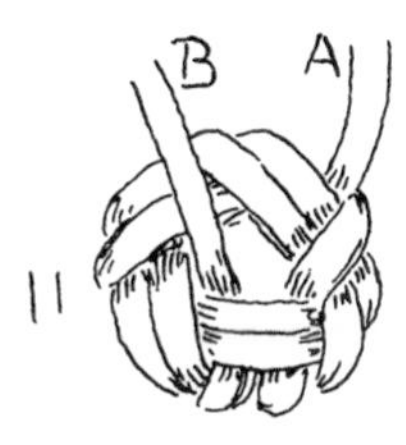
B
A
II

Fig. II-The strands are double

B
III
A

Fig. III
End A carried down through the Knot

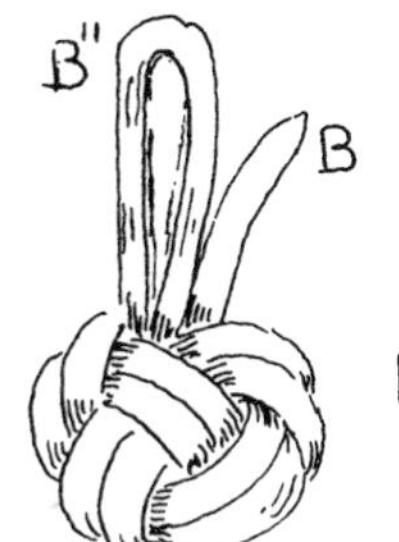
B''
B
IV
B'
A

Fig. IV
End B is carried down and back through the Knot forming two loops B' and B''

Top of knot

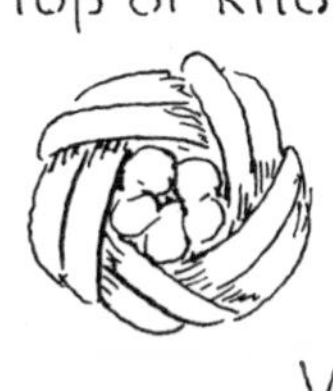
V

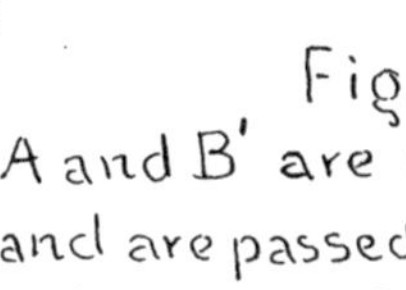
VI

Fig. V
A and B' are crowned and are passed up through the centre of the crown coming out alongside of B-B''
All ends are cut off except one loop
Fig. VI

SENNIT

Plaiting with an uneven number of strands

I
II

The outer strands in alternate order pass over 2 strands, Fig 1, 3 strands, Fig 2, (or any convenient number) meeting in a "herring-bone" central line

---

FRENCH SENNIT

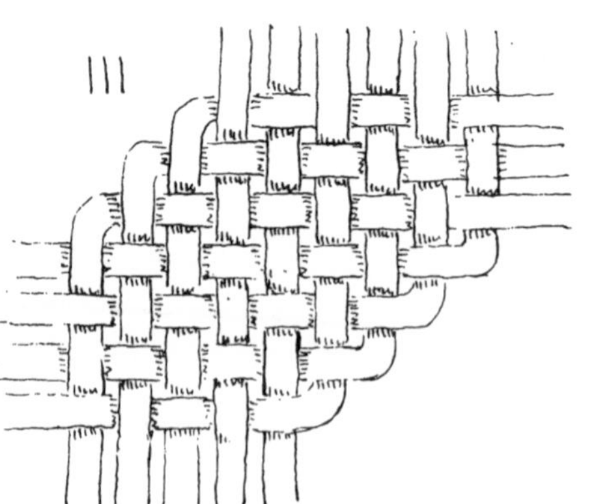
III

The strands in this method may be odd or even in number

SENNIT

Of Five Strands

Of Seven Strands

Of Nine Strands

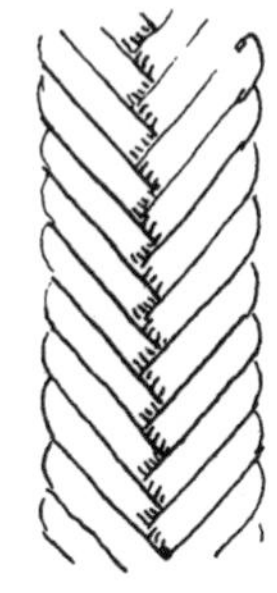
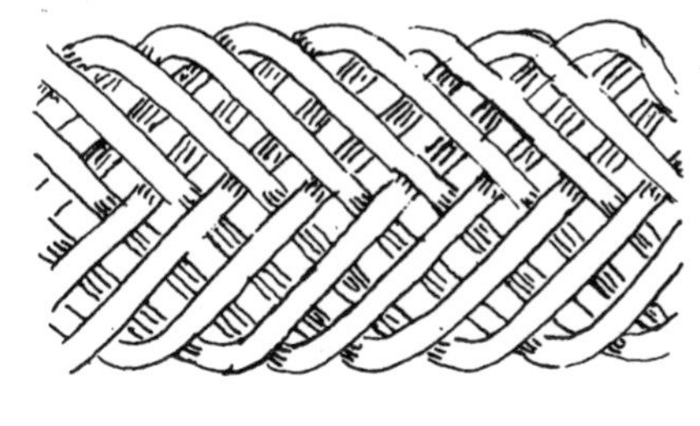
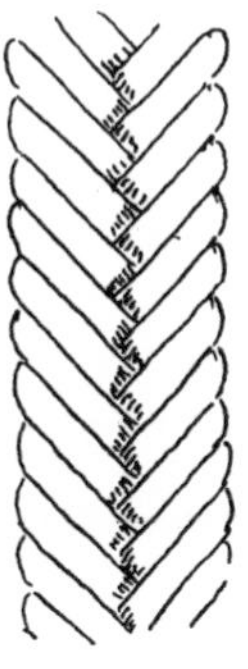

SENNIT

of three Strands forming a Ring

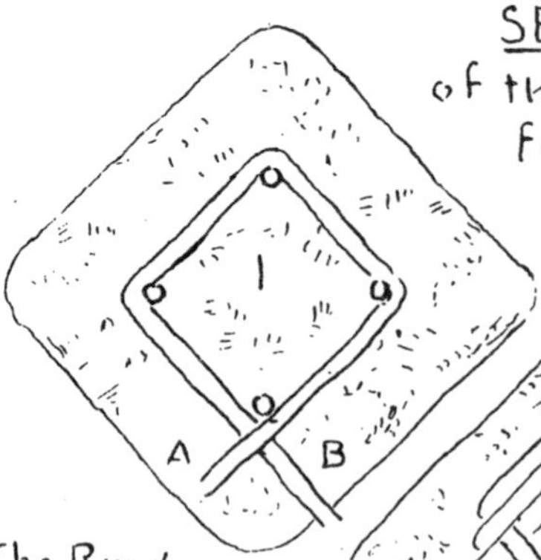

I

A B

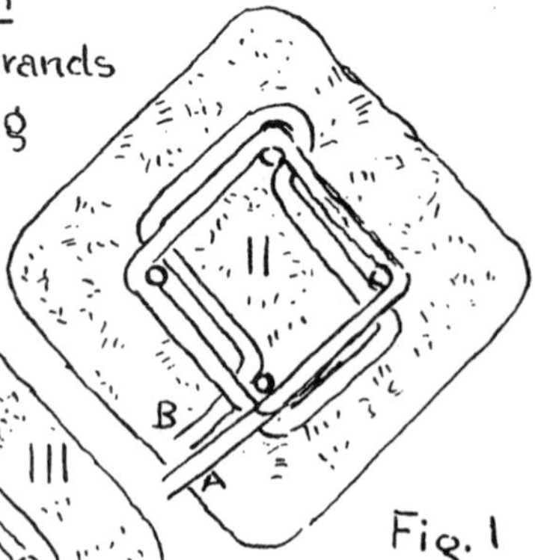

II

B A

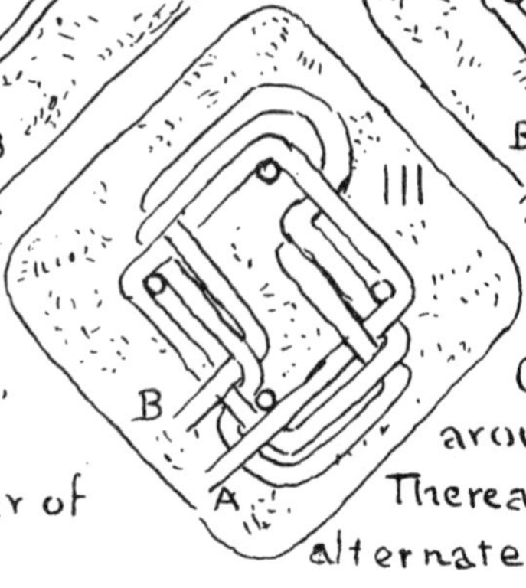

III

B A

The Ring may be tied around 4, 6, 8, or any even number of pins

Fig. I
Begin at A. Carry the line A B around outside of pins Thereafter the line lies alternately outside and inside of the pins - Fig. II, III

Fig. IV
The strands of Fig. III are thrown over a post. The strands may be doubled or tripled

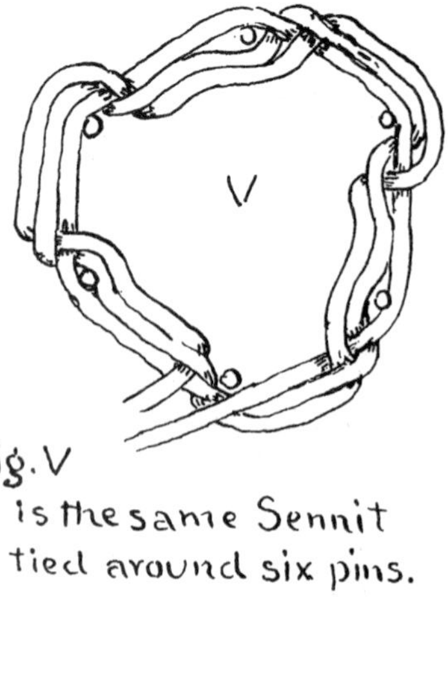

IV

V

Fig. V
is the same Sennit tied around six pins.

SENNIT

of Five and Seven Strands forming Rings

In addition to the four fixed pins, others are needed to hold the work in place

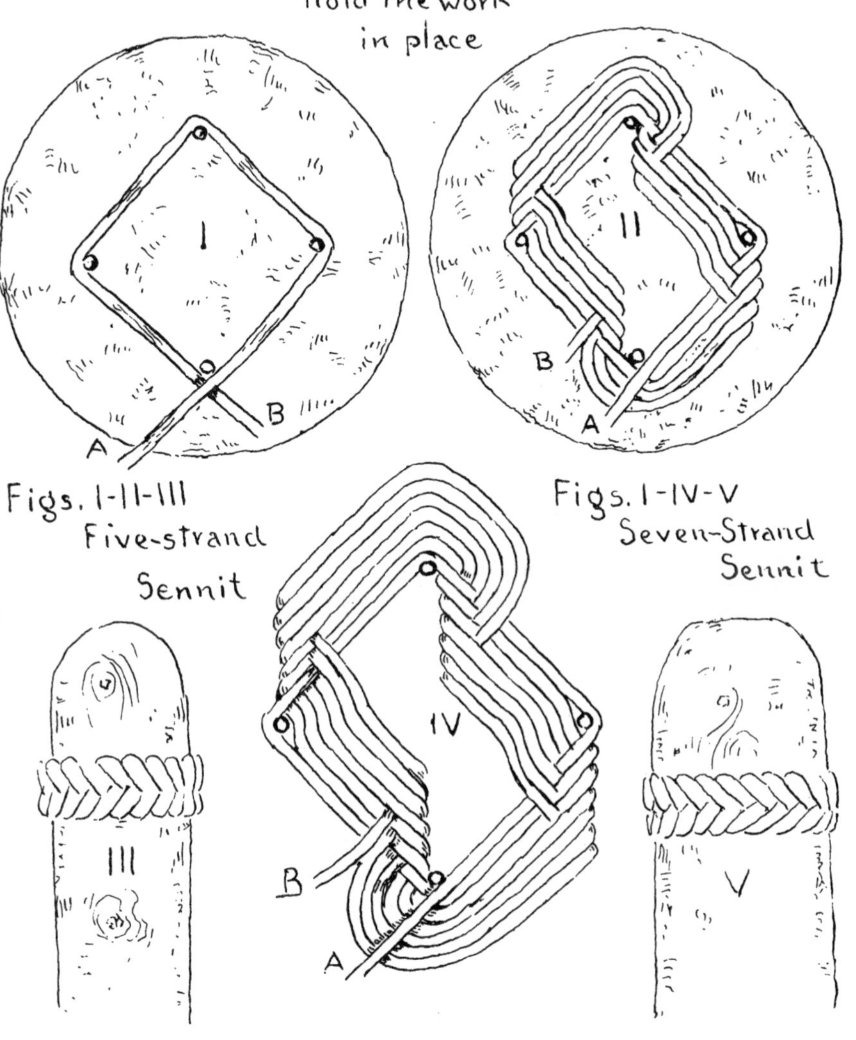
I
A
B
II
B
A
IV
B
A
III
V

Figs. I-II-III Five-strand Sennit

Figs. I-IV-V Seven-Strand Sennit

THREE-STRAND SENNTS

tied with one line

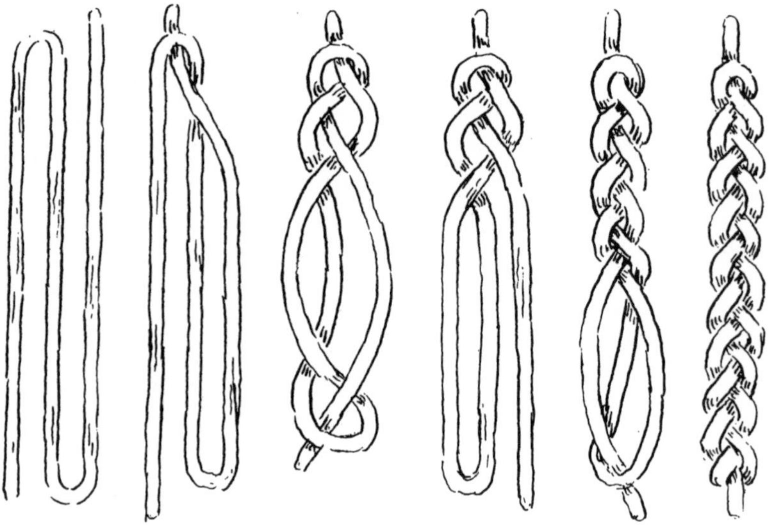

Overhand Knot — Figure of Eight Knot

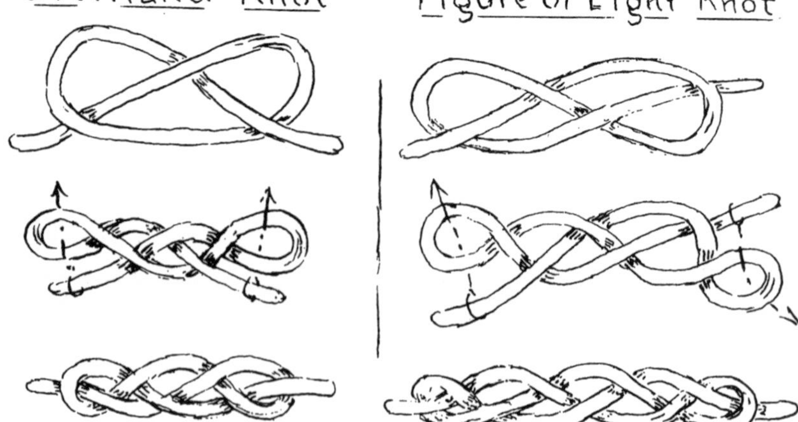

TRIANGULAR BRAID OF TWO STRANDS

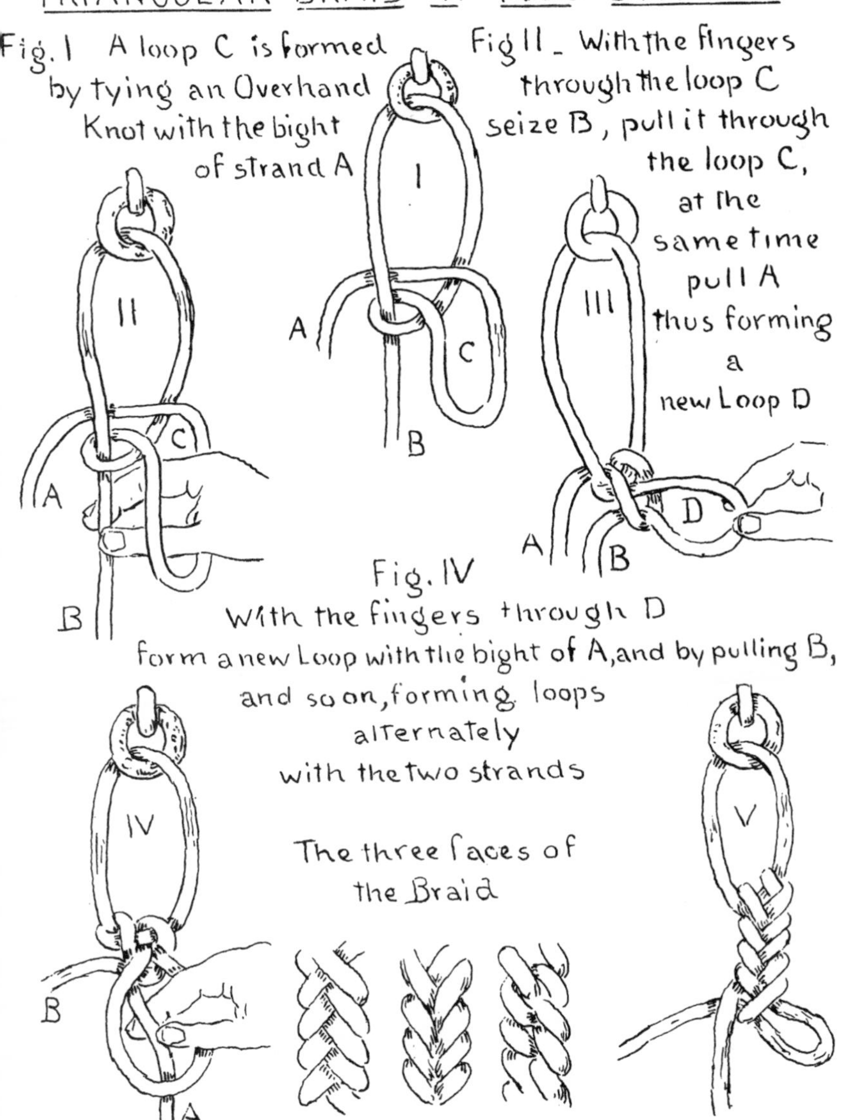
Fig. I A loop C is formed by tying an Overhand Knot with the bight of strand A
Fig II _ With the fingers through the loop C seize B, pull it through the loop C, at the same time pull A thus forming a new Loop D
I
II
III
IV
V
A
B
C
D
Fig. IV
With the fingers through D form a new Loop with the bight of A, and by pulling B, and so on, forming loops alternately with the two strands
The three faces of the Braid

SINGLE STRAND SQUARE BRAID

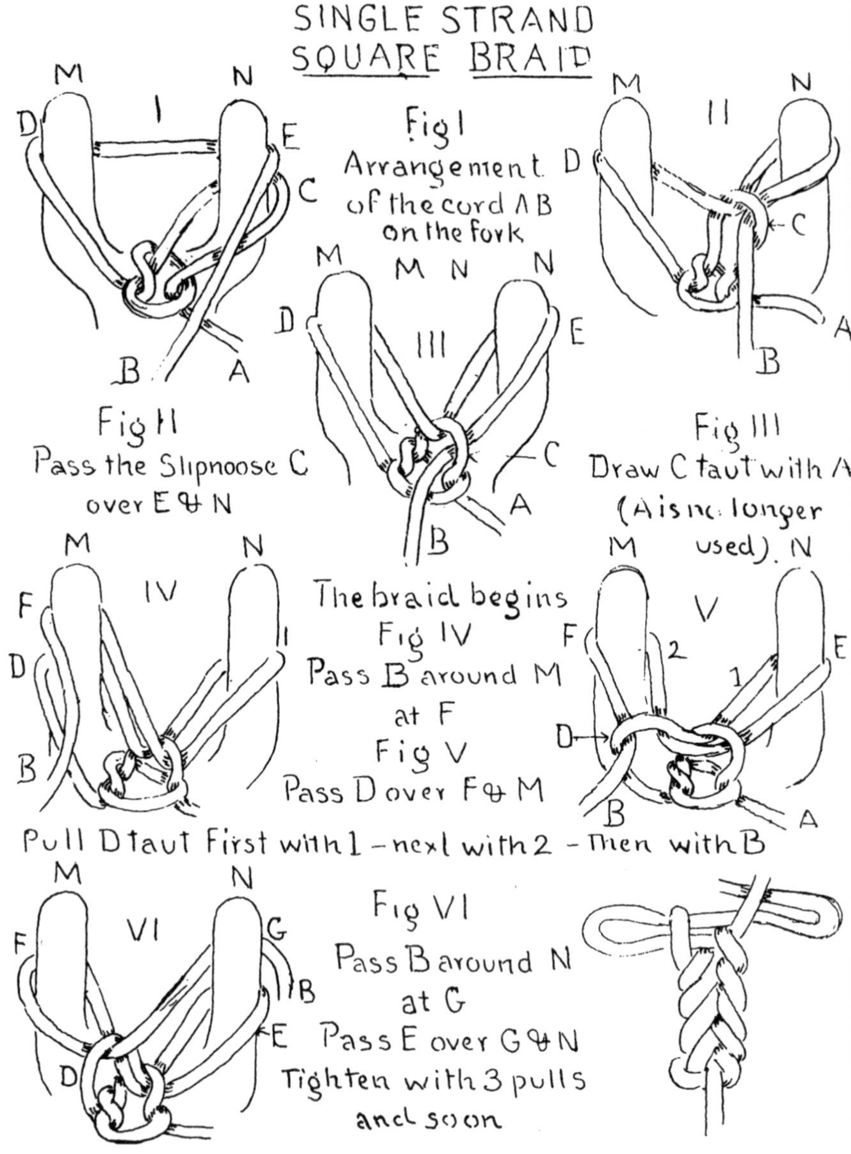
Fig I
Arrangement of the cord AB on the fork
Fig II
Pass the Slipnoose C over E & N
Fig III
Draw C taut with A (A is no longer used).
The braid begins
Fig IV
Pass B around M at F
Fig V
Pass D over F & M
Pull D taut First with 1 - next with 2 - Then with B
Fig VI
Pass B around N at G
Pass E over G & N
Tighten with 3 pulls and so on

BRAID OF THREE STRANDS

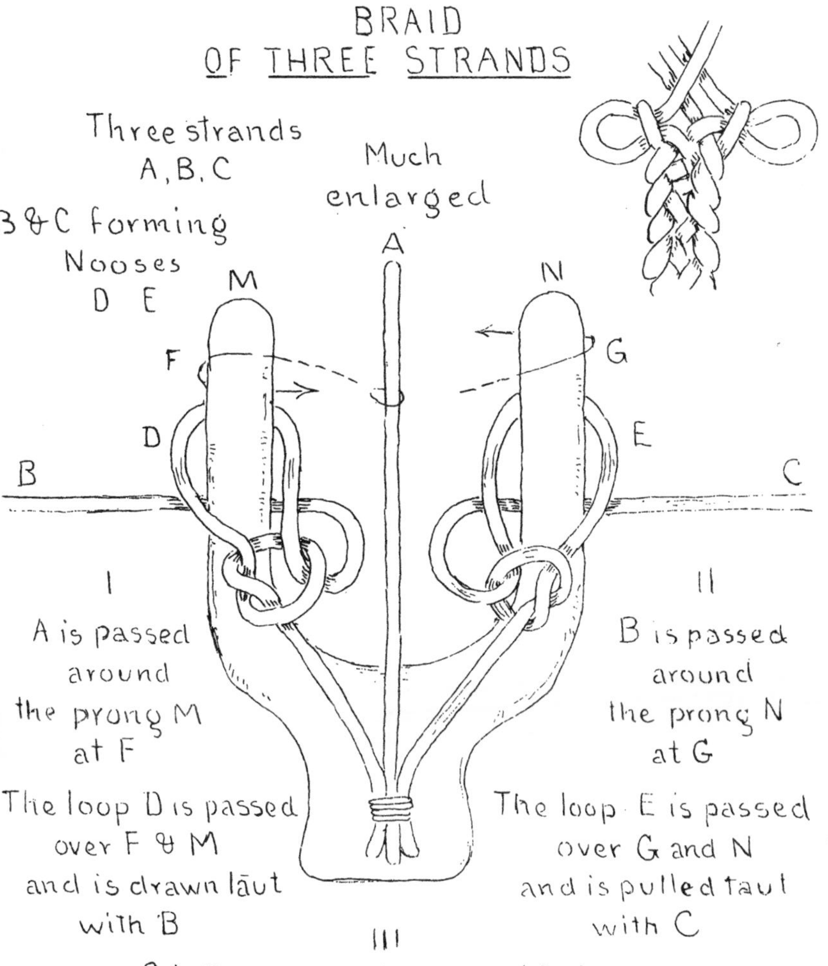
Three strands
A, B, C
B & C forming
Nooses
D E
Much
enlarged
A
M
N
F
G
D
E
B
C
I
II
A is passed
around
the prong M
at F
B is passed
around
the prong N
at G
The loop D is passed
over F & M
and is drawn taut
with B
The loop E is passed
over G and N
and is pulled taut
with C

III

C is then passed around M etc.

The strand that pulls its loop taut forms the next new loop

The arrows at F & G indicate the lay of the strands that form the new loops.

FOUR-STRAND ROUND BRAID

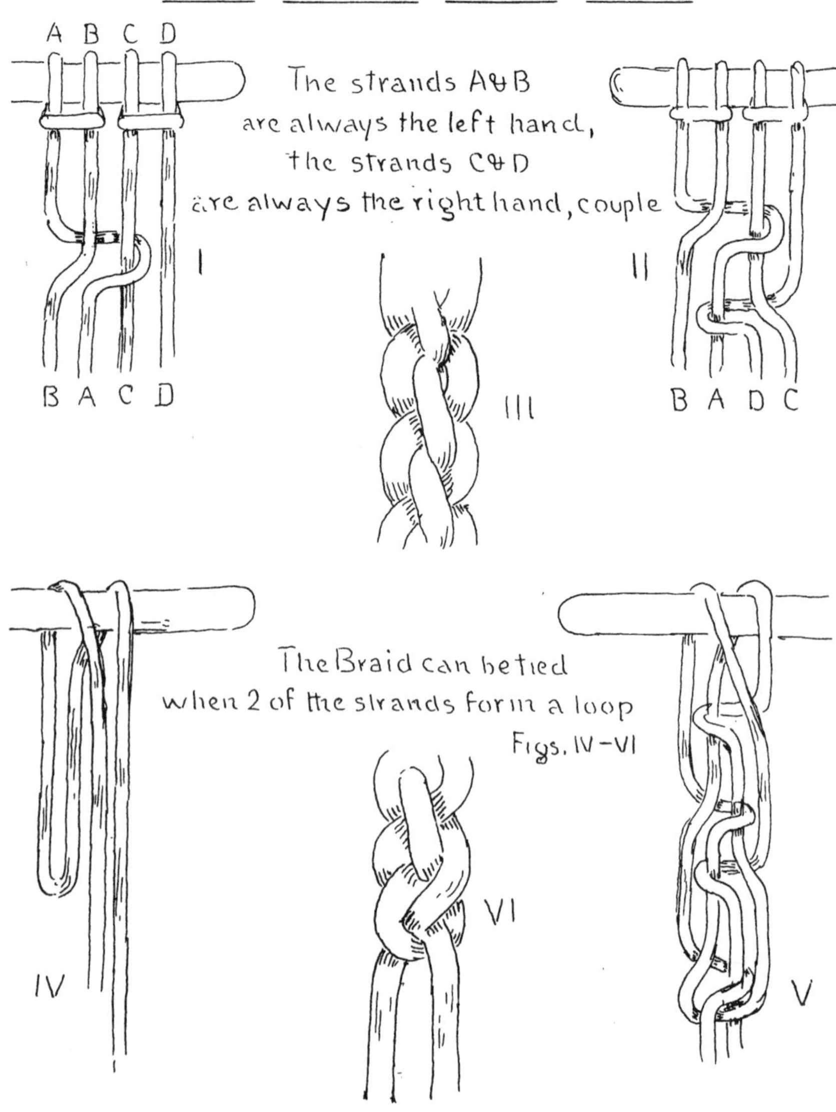
A B C D
The strands A&B
are always the left hand,
the strands C&D
are always the right hand, couple
I
II
B A C D
B A D C
III
The Braid can be tied
when 2 of the strands form a loop
Figs. IV–VI
VI
IV
V

77

ROUND BRAID

tied with a doubled strand

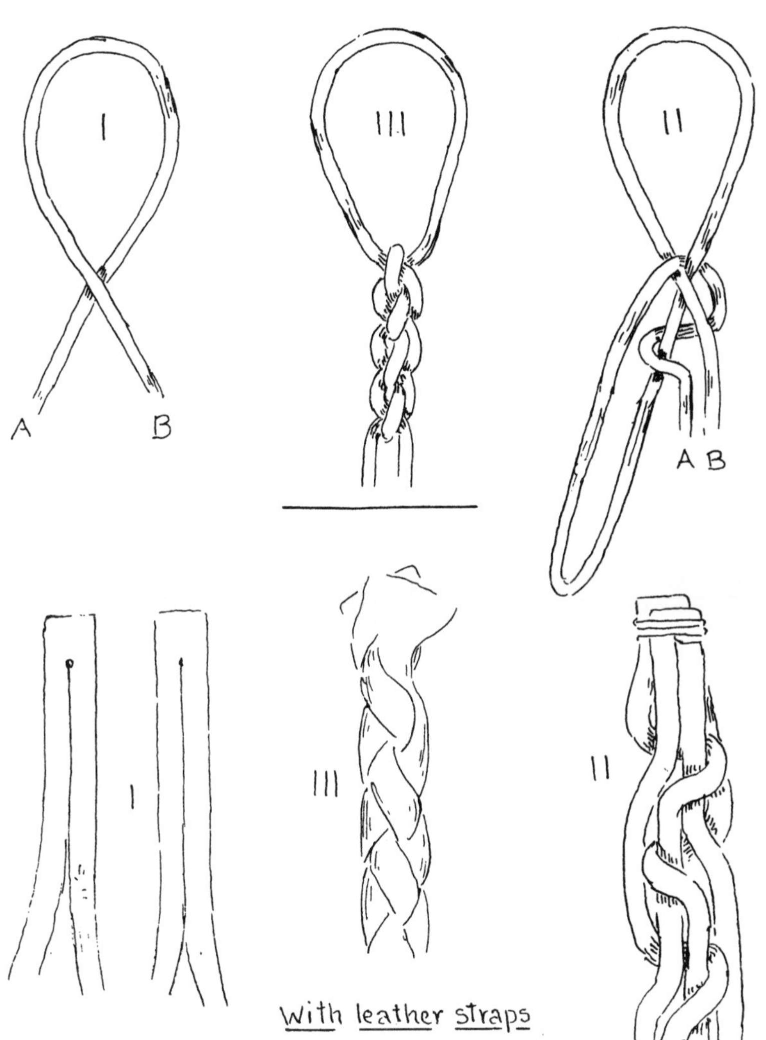

I
III
II
A
B
A B
I
III
II

With leather straps

FOUR-STRAND FLAT BRAID

I
III
II

Joining two Strands
A and B

IV

Figs. IV, V
the
Carrick Bend

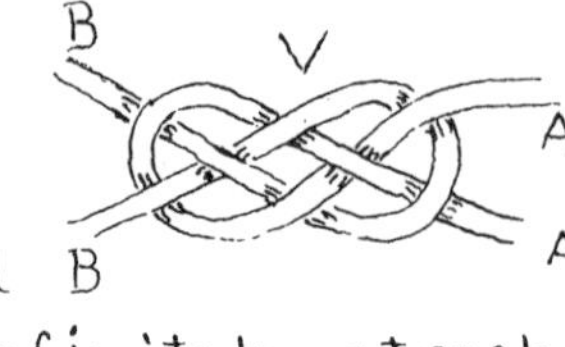
B
V
A
A
B

The Braid can be extended indefinitely at each end or at both ends Figs. VI, VII, VIII

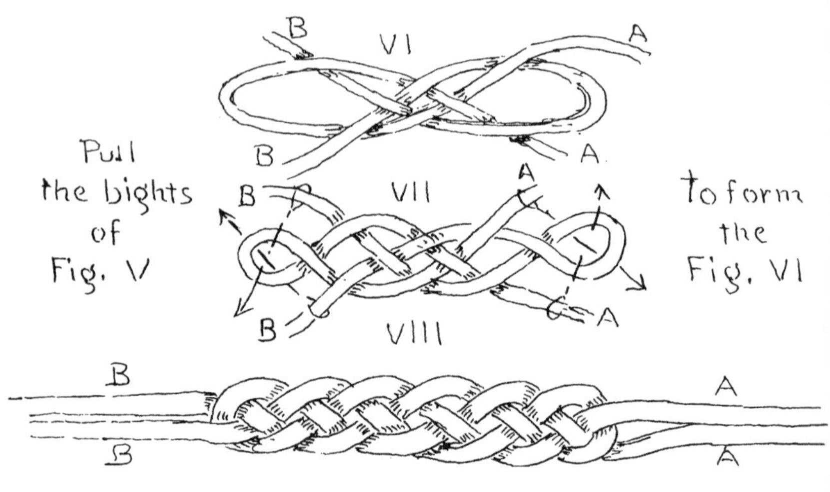
B
VI
A
B
A
B
VII
A
B
A
VIII
B
A
B
A

Pull the bights of Fig. V

To form the Fig. VI

A SIX-STRAND AND EIGHT-STRAND BRAID

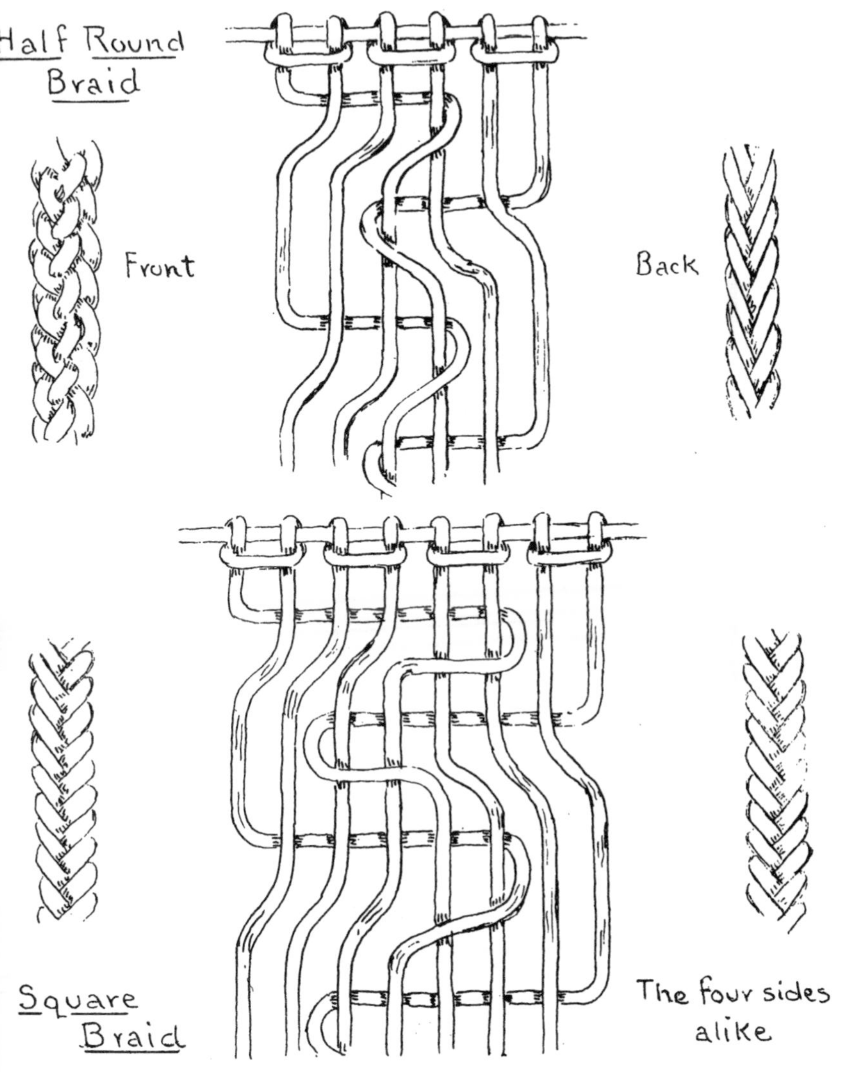
Half Round
Braid
Front
Back
Square
Braid
The four sides
alike

SQUARE BRAID

of ten strands

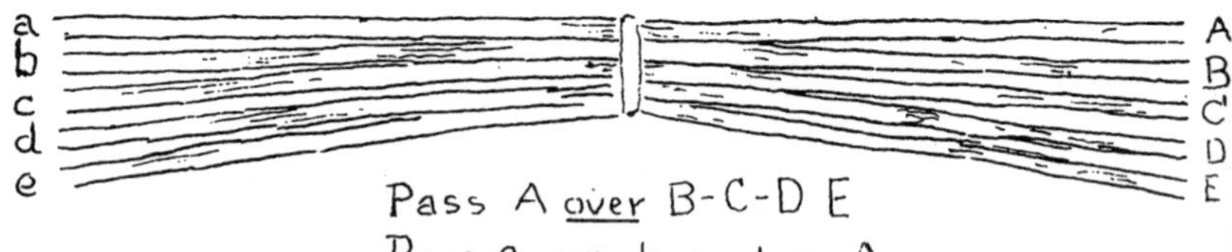
a
b
c
d
e
A
B
C
D
E

Pass A over B-C-D E

Pass a over b-c-d-e-A

Pass b under c-d-e-A   Pass B under C-D-E-a-b

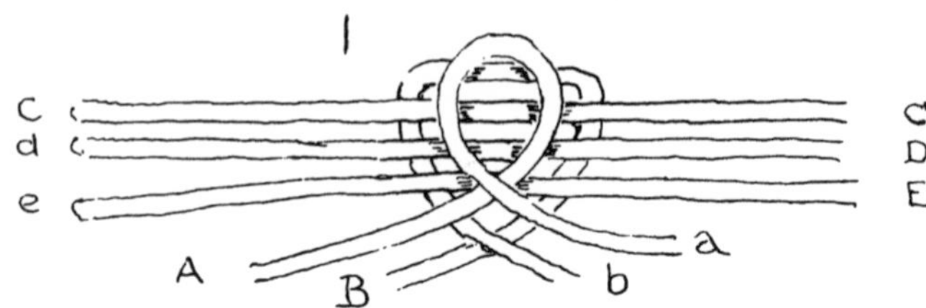
I
c
d
e
C
D
E
A
B
b
a

Pass C over D-E-a-b   Pass c over d-e-A-B-C

Pass d under e-A-B-C   Pass D under E-a-b-c-d

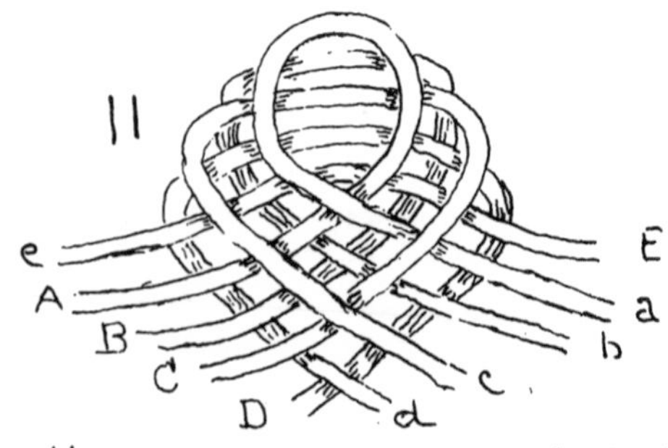
II
e
A
B
C
D
d
c
b
a
E

Fig. II repeats the method of Fig. I and its repetition forms the Braid.

CROWN BRAID

This is the Crown Knot repeated in superposed layers

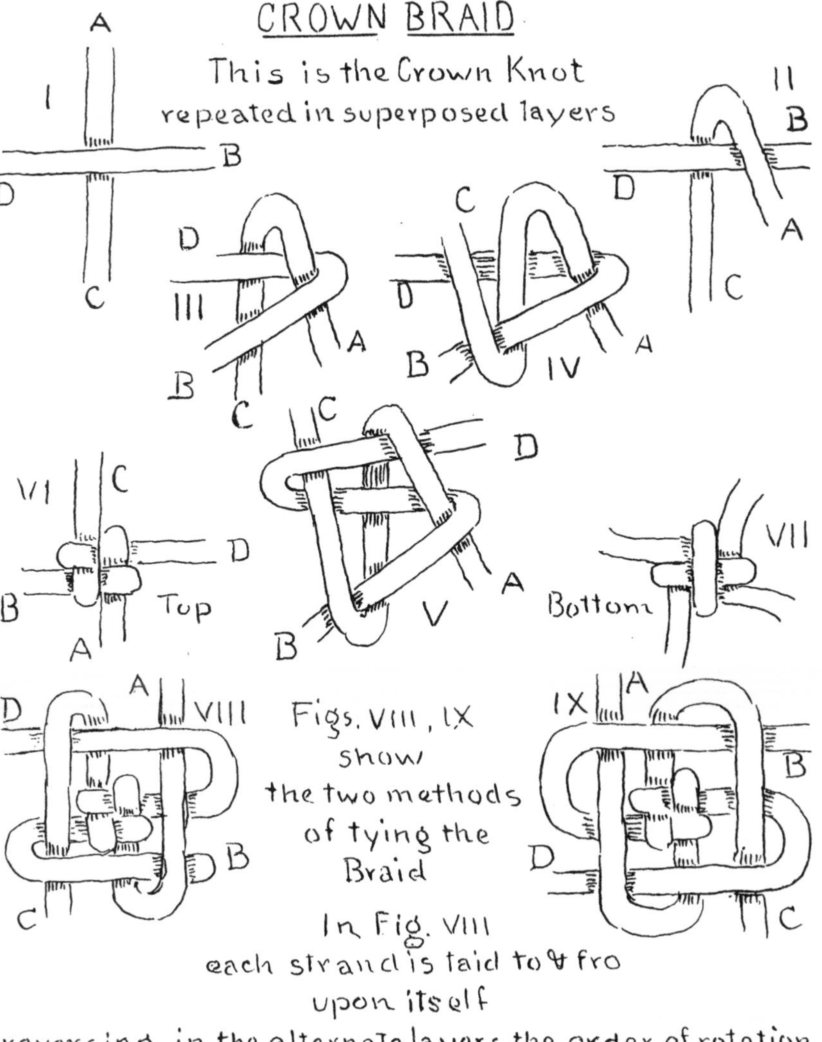
A
I
B
D
C
II
B
D
A
C
D
III
A
B
C
C
D
B
IV
A
C
D
VI
C
D
B
Top
A
A
V
B
Bottom
VII
D
A
VIII
B
C
IX
A
B
D
C

Figs. VIII, IX show the two methods of tying the Braid

In Fig. VIII each strand is laid to & fro upon itself reversing, in the alternate layers, the order of rotation

In Fig. IX the order of rotation is always the same

CROWN BRAID

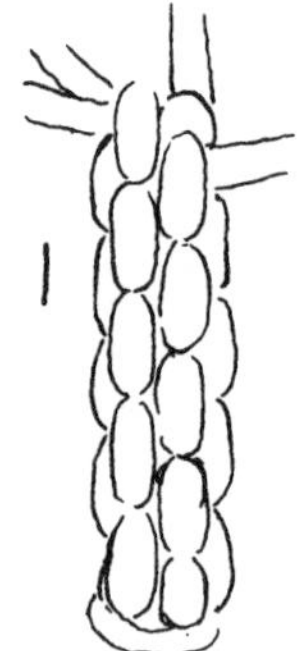
I

Fig. I
is the Braid tied by the method of
Fig. VIII on the last page

Fig. II
is the Braid tied by the method of
Fig. IX, on the last page

II

Six-Strand Braid

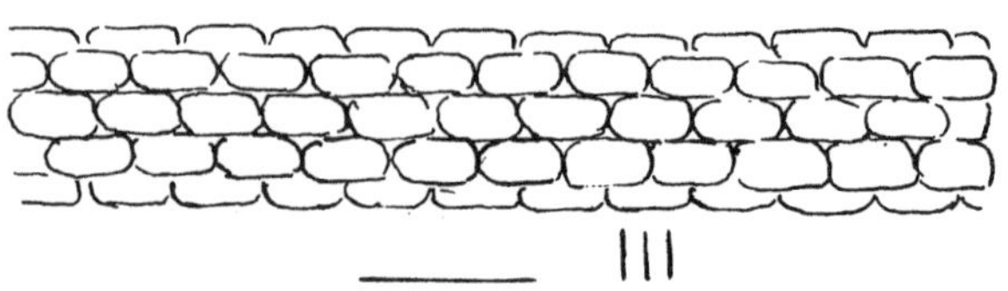

III

The Braid may be tied around a Core, Fig. IV

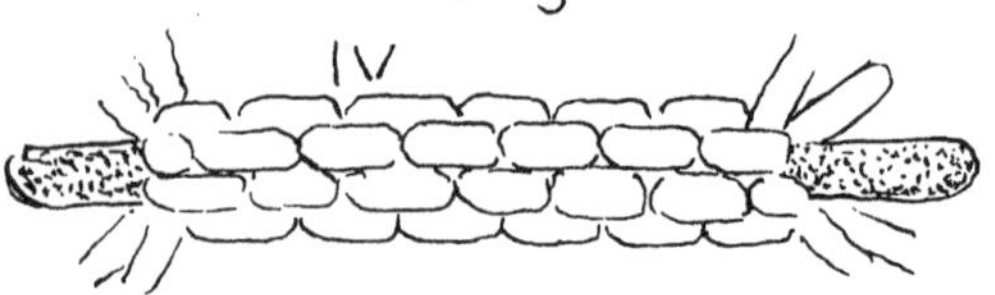
IV

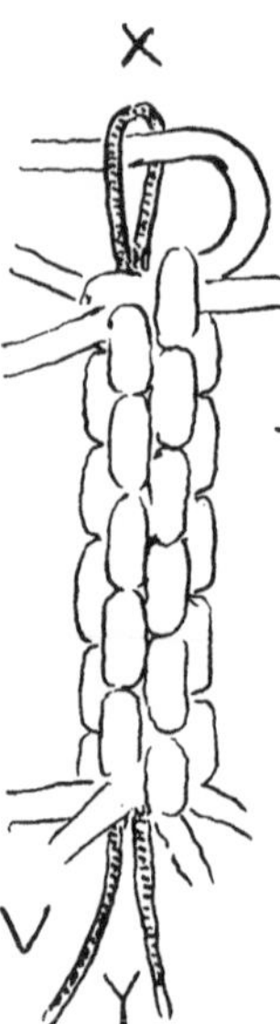
X
V
Y

The Core may be pulled out
Fig. V
and, with a copper wire X-Y,
the strands
at each end of the Braid
can be drawn
through the centre, Fig. VI, so as
to form
a neat finish at both ends

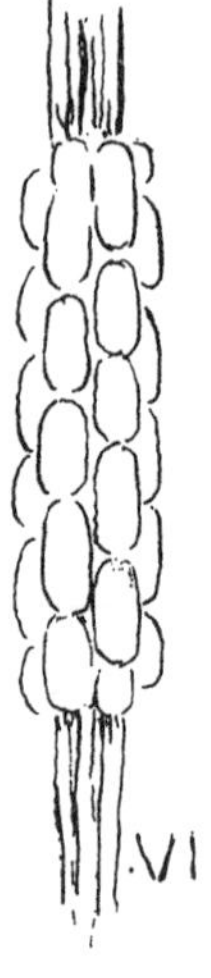
VI

CHAIN BRAID

Single

tied with the Bight

A

Double

tied with the End

B

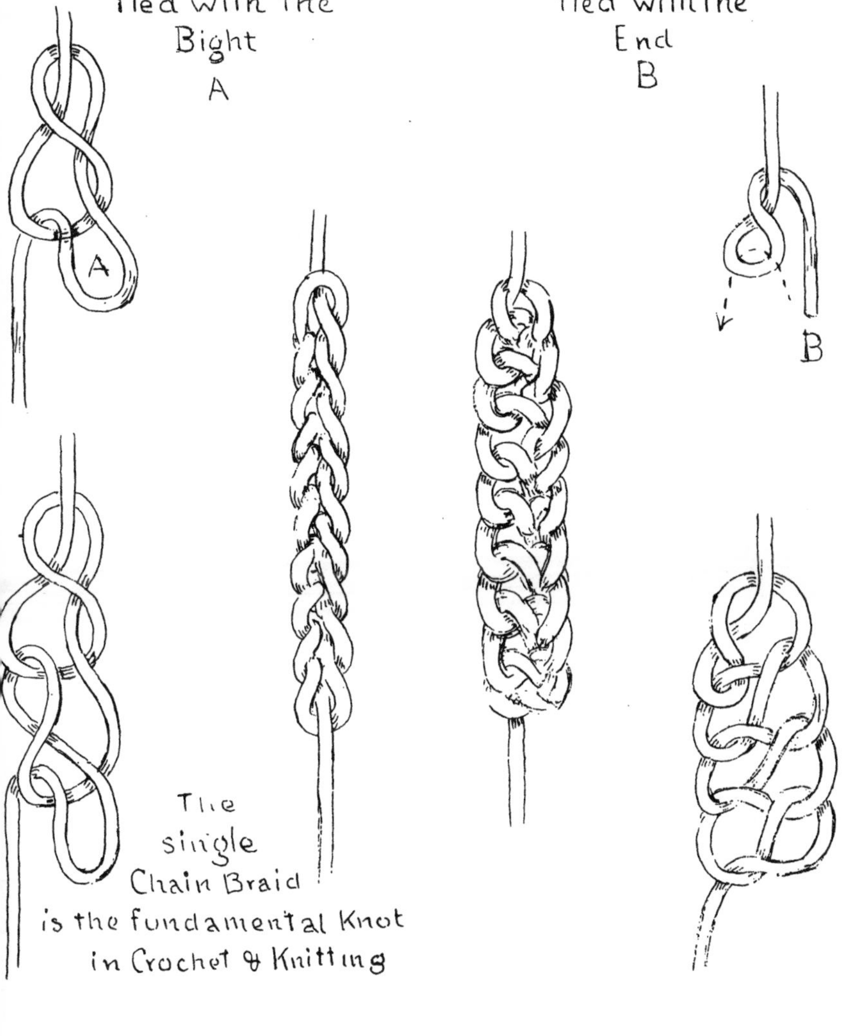

A

B

The single Chain Braid is the fundamental Knot in Crochet & Knitting

84

FALSE BRAID in Leather

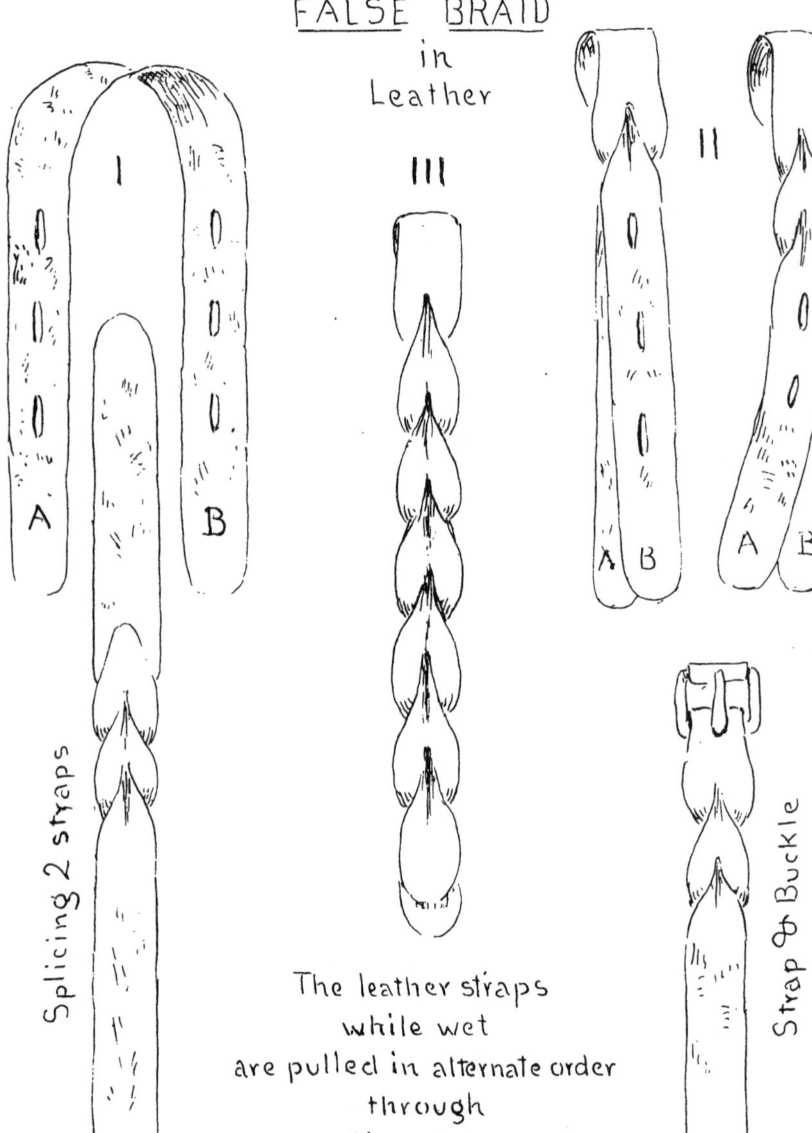
I
A
B
III
II
A
B
A
B
Splicing 2 straps
Strap & Buckle

The leather straps while wet are pulled in alternate order through the slots

85
FALSE BRAID

Three straps may unite in a False Braid as shown in Fig I

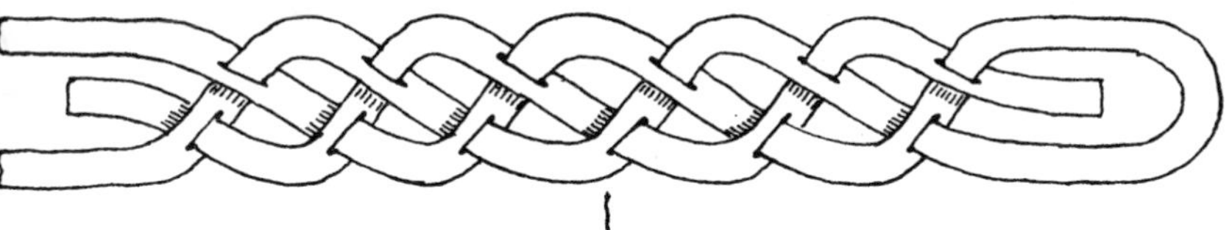

I

Four straps may also be combined as shown in Fig II

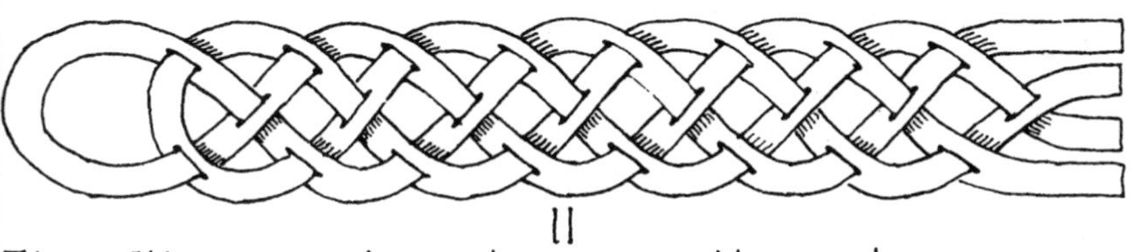

II

The slits are cut one by one as the work progresses

The Braid will be square in cross section when, with 2 straps, the width of the strap is twice its thickness—with 3 straps, 3 times, & with 4 straps, 4 times the thickness.

The 3 methods may combine to form a Leash or Quirt

III

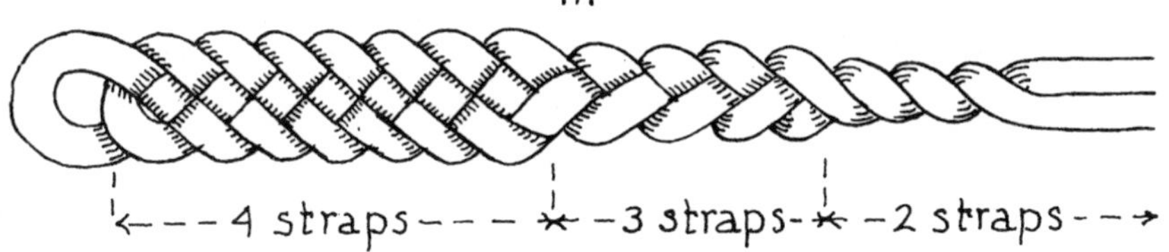
←---4 straps---→←-3 straps-→←-2 straps--→

TRICK BRAID

Fig. I – Leather strap with two slits and three strands

Fig. II – A over B and C over A
Pass M through X
to form Fig. III

Fig IV
B over C, A over B
M through Y.
Repeat
as desired

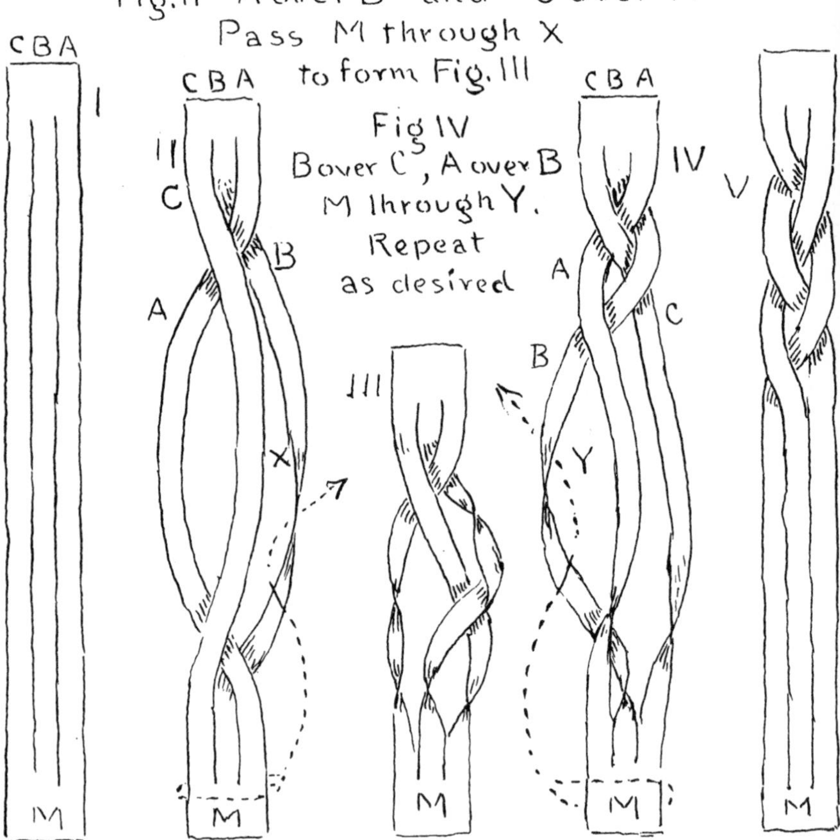

C B A
I
M
C B A
II
C
B
A
X
M
III
M
C B A
IV
A
C
B
Y
M
V
M

VI

SAILORS KNOTS

REEVING LINE

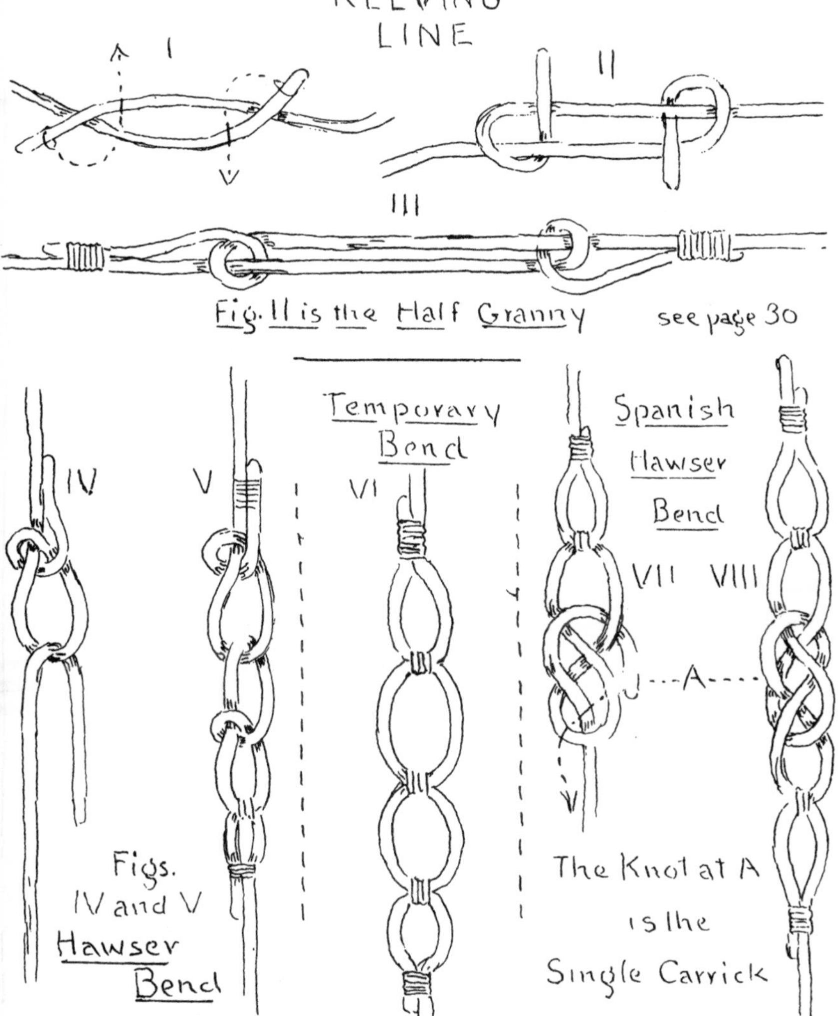
I
II
III
Temporary
Bend
IV
V
VI
Spanish
Hawser
Bend
VII
VIII
A
Figs.
IV and V
Hawser
Bend
The Knot at A
is the
Single Carrick

Fig. II is the Half Granny see page 30

HITCHES

Hook and Half Hitch

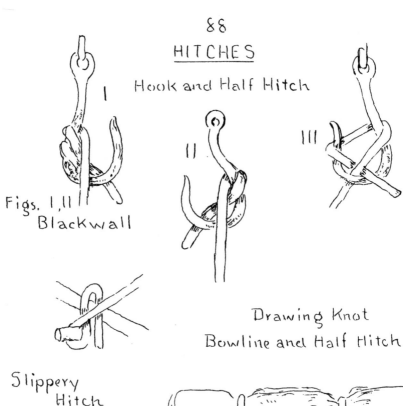

I

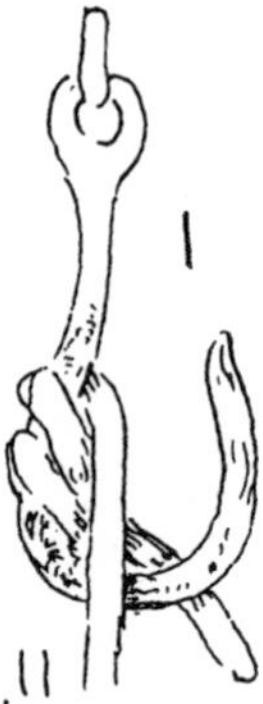

II

III

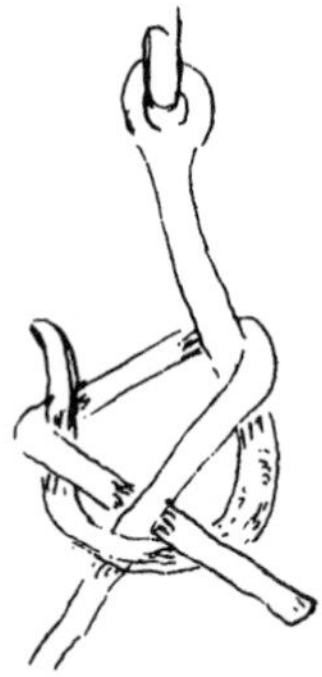

Figs. I, II
Blackwall

Drawing Knot
Bowline and Half Hitch

Slippery
Hitch

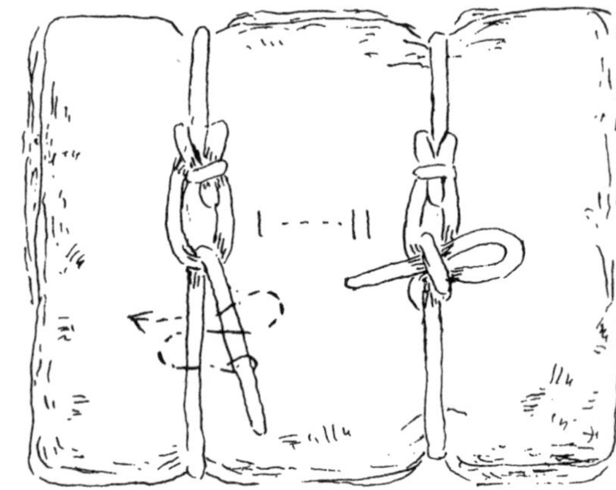
I----II

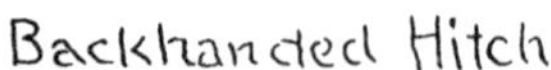

Backhanded Hitch

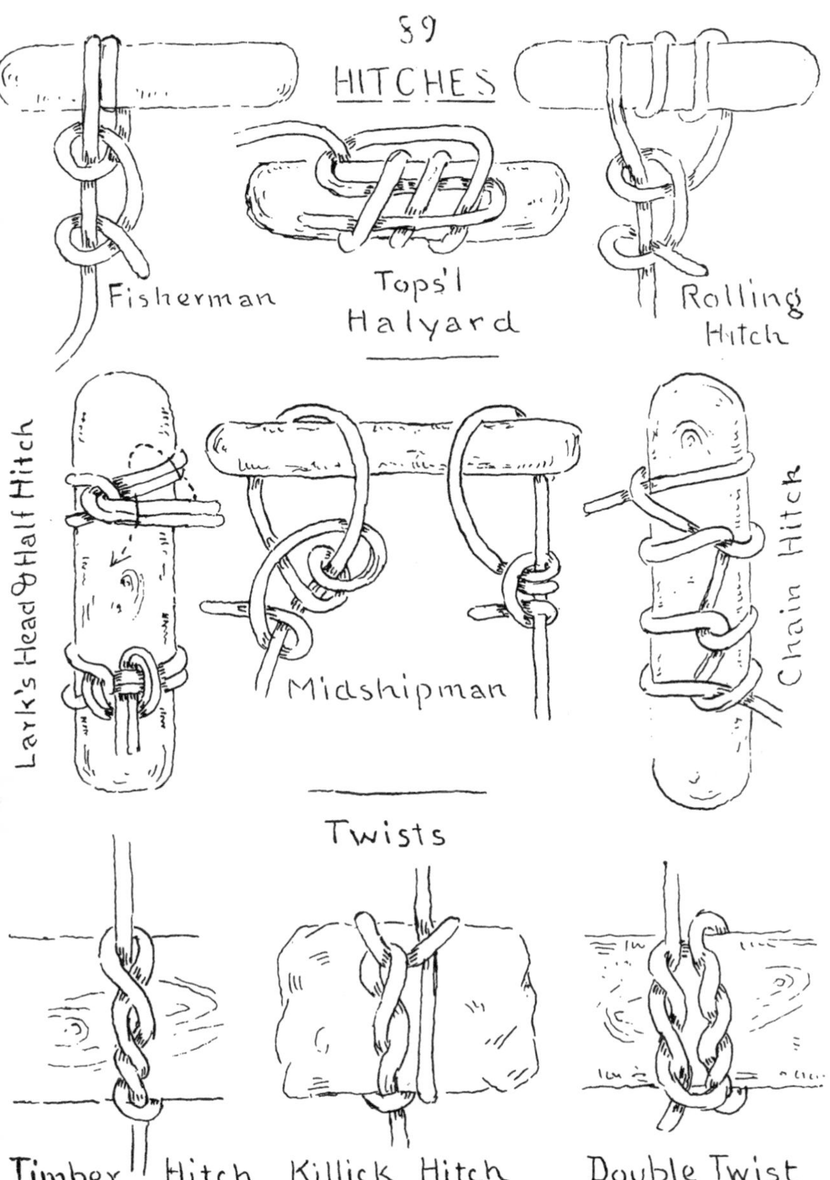

HITCHES
Fisherman
Tops'l
Halyard
Rolling
Hitch
Lark's Head & Half Hitch
Midshipman
Chain Hitch
Twists
Timber Hitch
Killick Hitch
Double Twist

CATSPAW

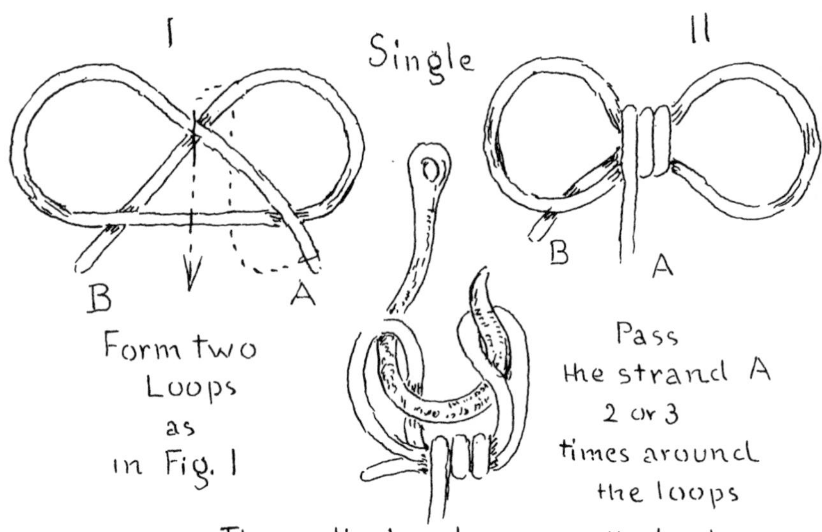
I
Single
II
B
A
B
A
Form two Loops as in Fig. I
Pass the strand A 2 or 3 times around the loops
Throw the two loops onto the hook

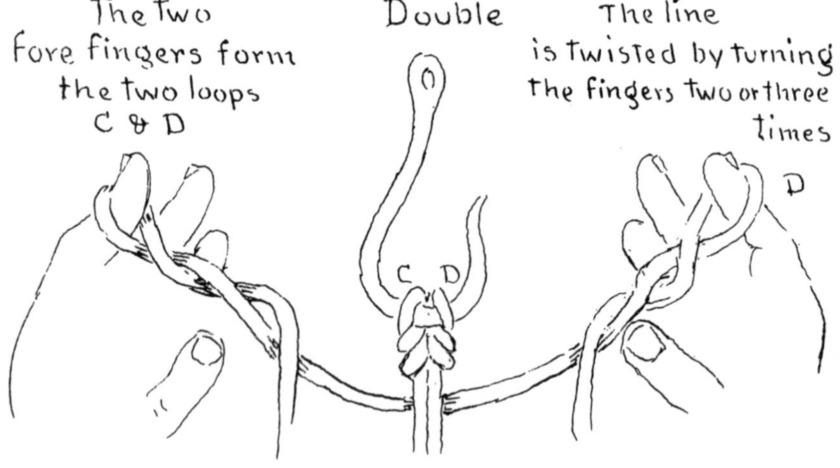
The Two Fore fingers form the two loops C & D
Double
The line is twisted by turning the fingers two or three times
D
C
D

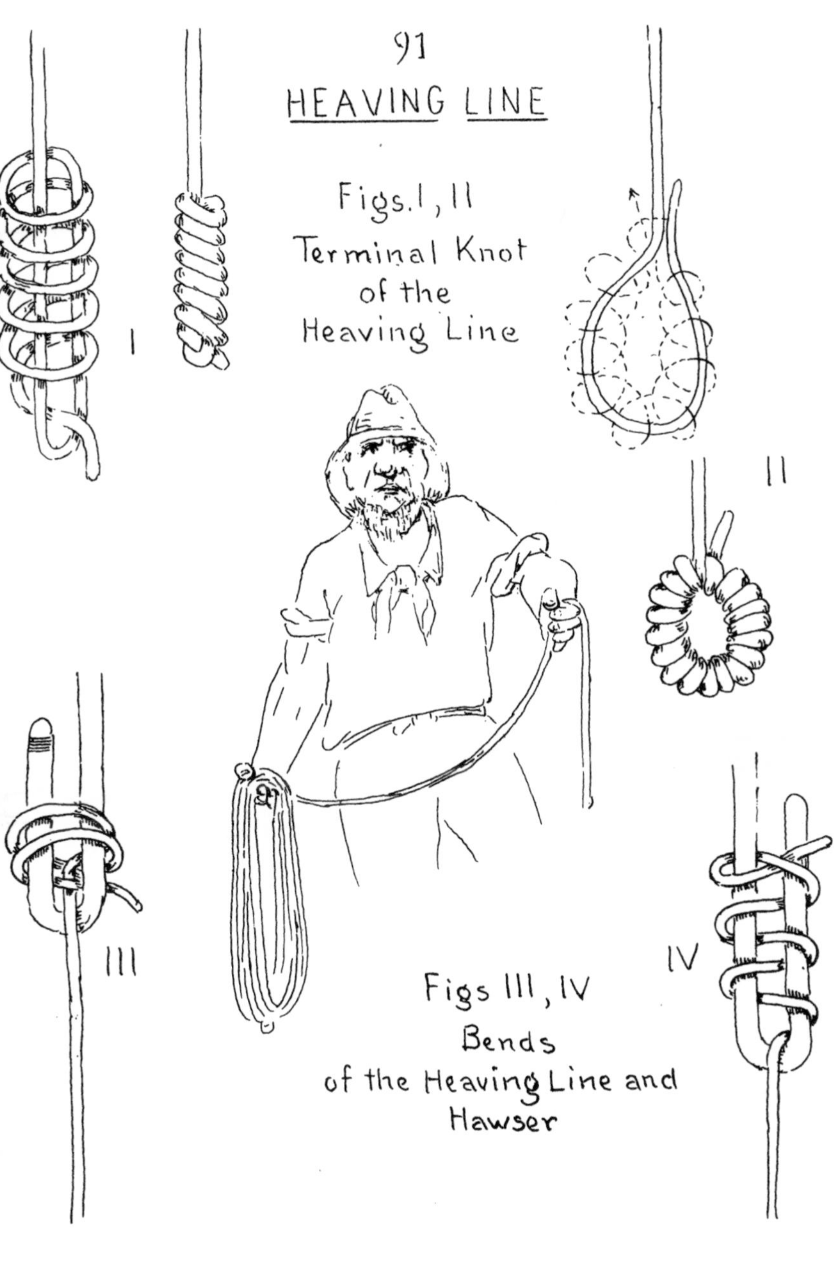
91
HEAVING LINE
Figs. I, II
Terminal Knot
of the
Heaving Line
I
II
III
IV
Figs III, IV
Bends
of the Heaving Line and
Hawser

THE TOGGLE

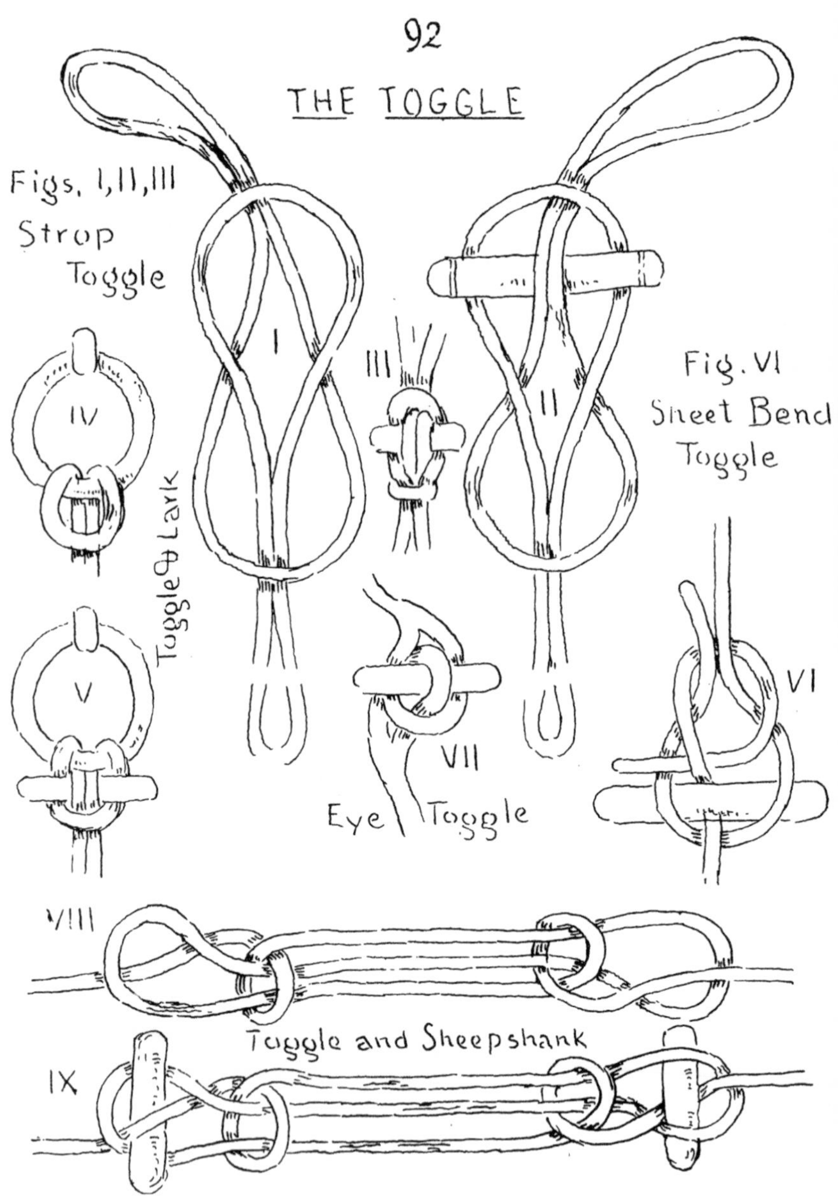
Figs. I, II, III
Strop
Toggle
I
II
III
Fig. VI
Sheet Bend
Toggle
IV
Toggle & Lark
V
VI
VII
Eye Toggle
VIII
Toggle and Sheepshank
IX

MOORING

Over a Post

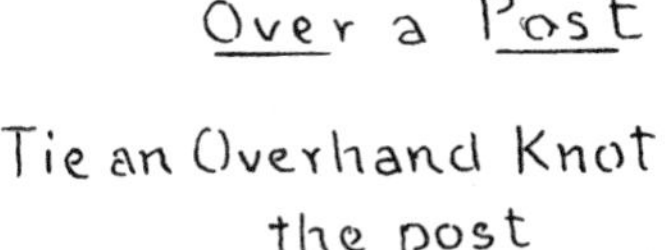

Tie an Overhand Knot on the post with the bight of the line and throw the loop A over the post

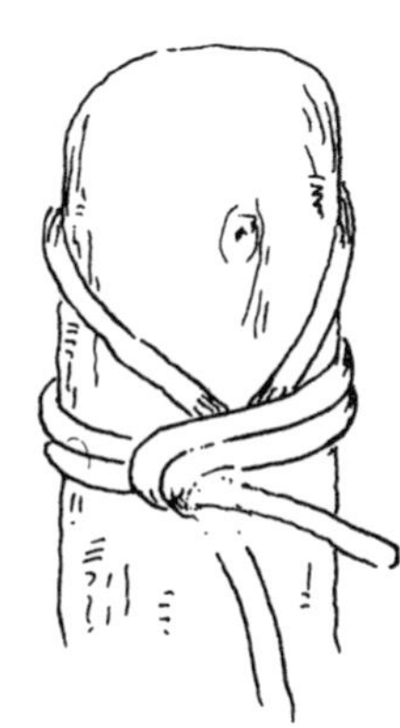

Through a Ring

In Fig I pass the bight of S through the loop E and pull the end E

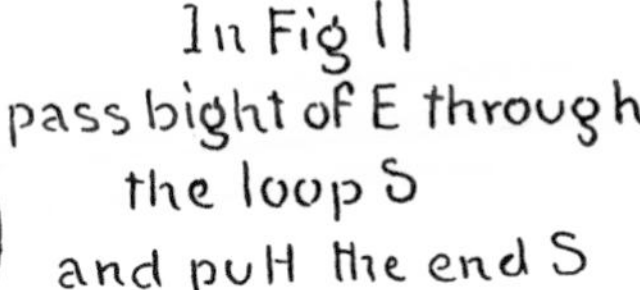

In Fig II pass bight of E through the loop S and pull the end S

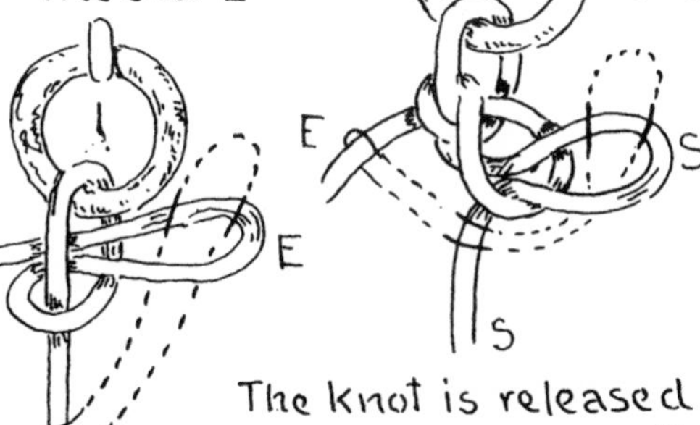
I
E
E
S
II
E
S
S

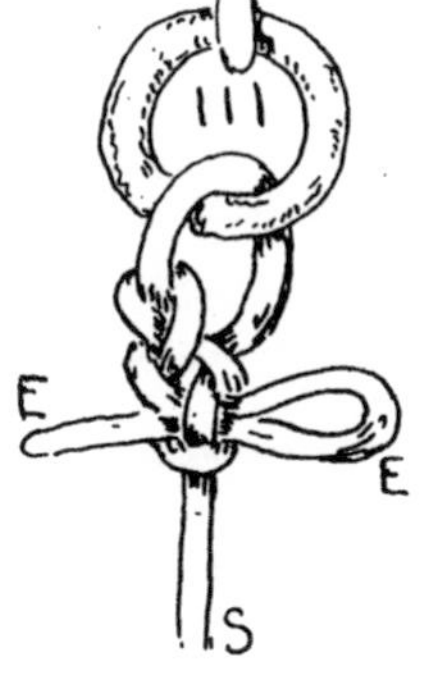
III
E
E
S

The knot is released by pulling the end E of III

MOORING

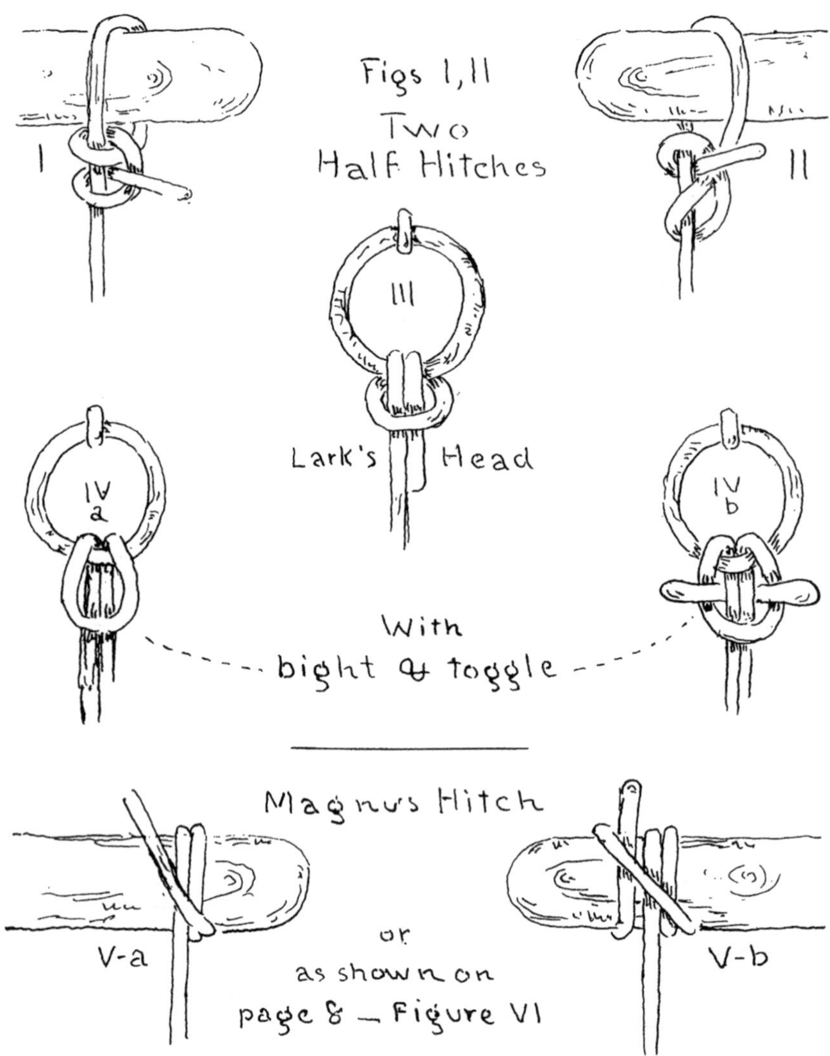

Figs I, II
Two
Half Hitches
I
II
III
Lark's Head
IV
a
IV
b
With
bight & toggle
Magnus Hitch
V-a
or
as shown on
page 8 – Figure VI
V-b

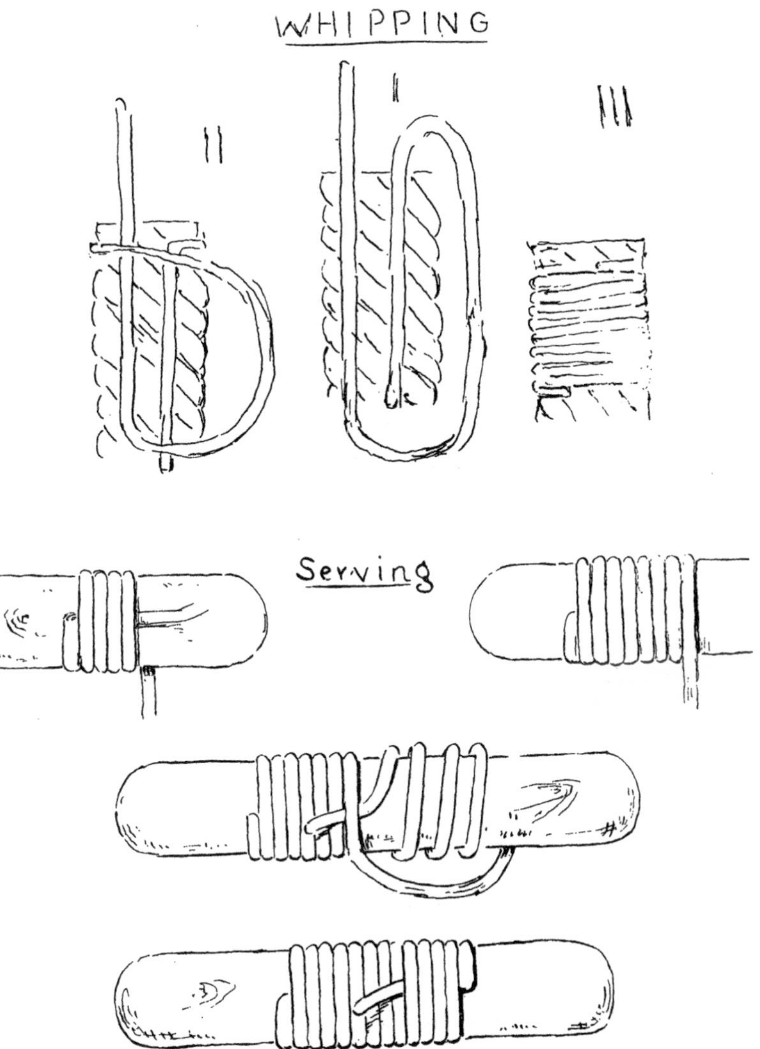
WHIPPING
II
I
III
Serving

SPLICING

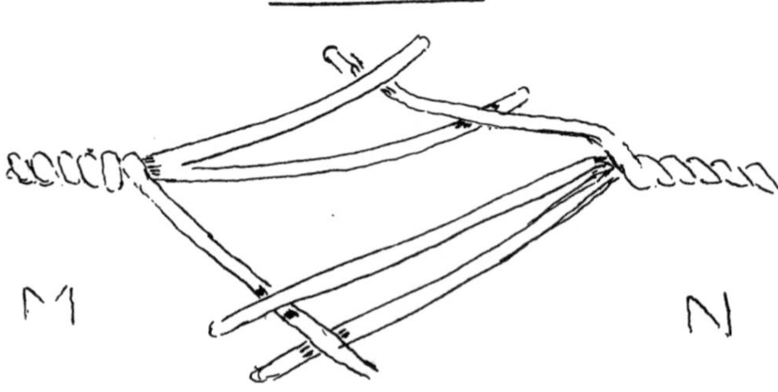
M
N

Unlay 7 or 8 strands of the two ropes M and N to be spliced Arrange them in such manner that each strand o M lies between two strands of N and each of N lies between two strands of M.

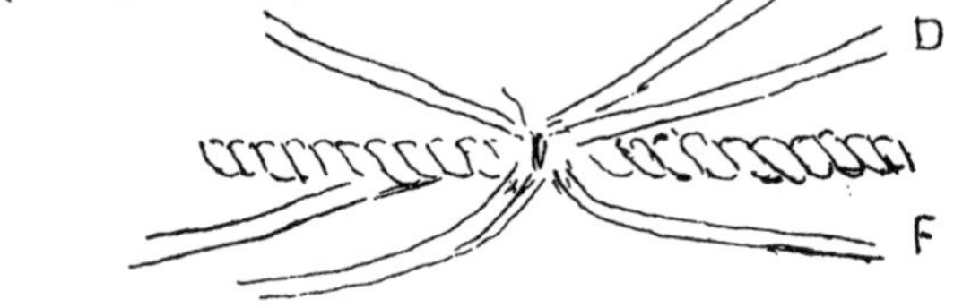
E
D
F

Push the six strands close together and bind them temporarily with twine

SHORT SPLICE

Braïding

Each strand passes over the next one and then under the second beyond.

SHORT SPLICE

Twisting the Strands

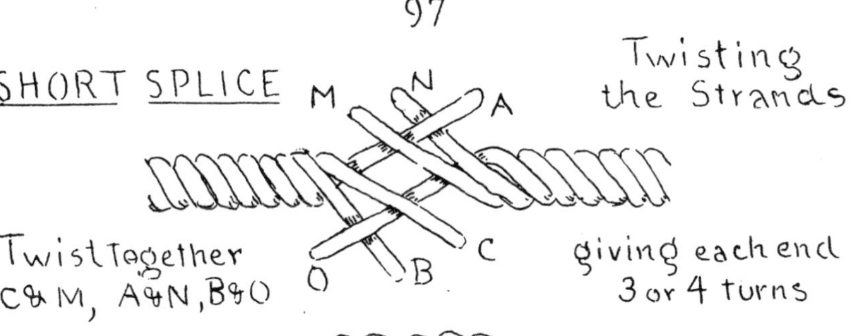
M
N
A
O
B
C

Twist together C&M, A&N, B&O

giving each end 3 or 4 turns

LONG SPLICE

Marry the strands as shown above

M N Y O

X C A B

Unlay C to X
and replace it with M
& similarly
unlay O to Y
and replace It wih B

Tie M & C together with an Overhand Knot
similarly tie together A&N and B&O
Taper the ends
and weave them into the strands of the rope

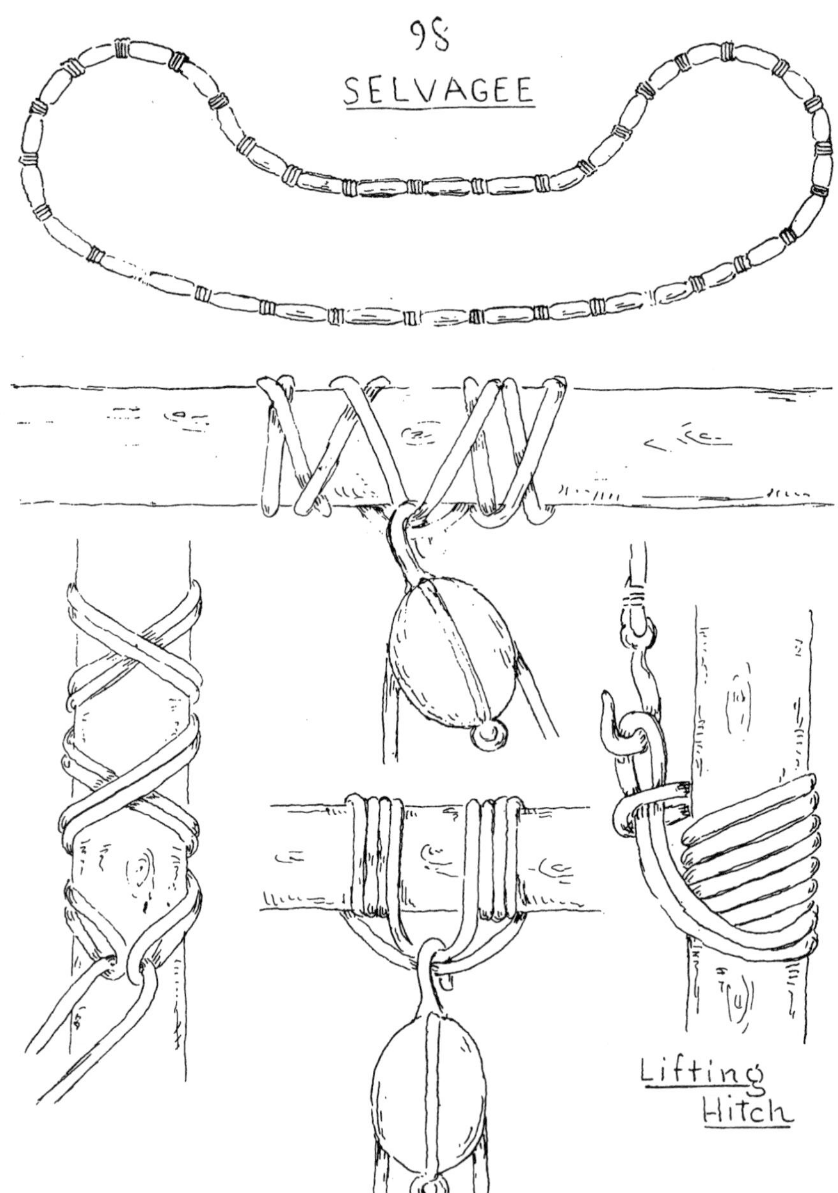
98
SELVAGEE
Lifting Hitch

GROMMET

Carefully unlay a single strand of rope twelve times the diameter of the Grommet

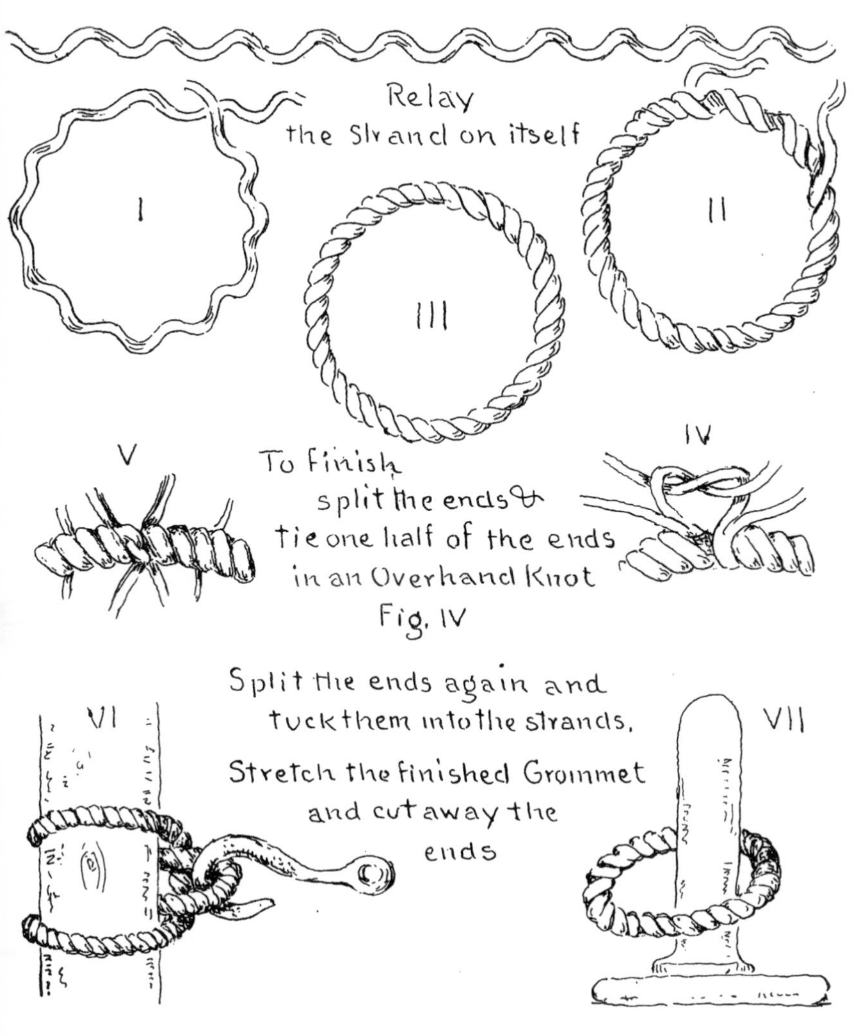
Relay
the Strand on itself
I
II
III
IV
V
To finish
split the ends &
tie one half of the ends
in an Overhand Knot
Fig. IV
Split the ends again and
tuck them into the strands.
Stretch the finished Grommet
and cut away the
ends
VI
VII

100

SHEEP SHANK

With both of the ends fast

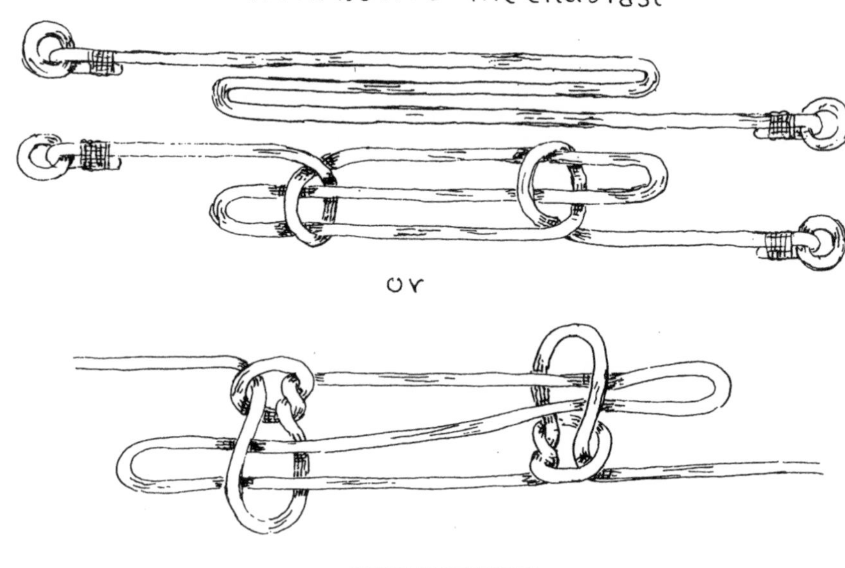
or

With the ends free

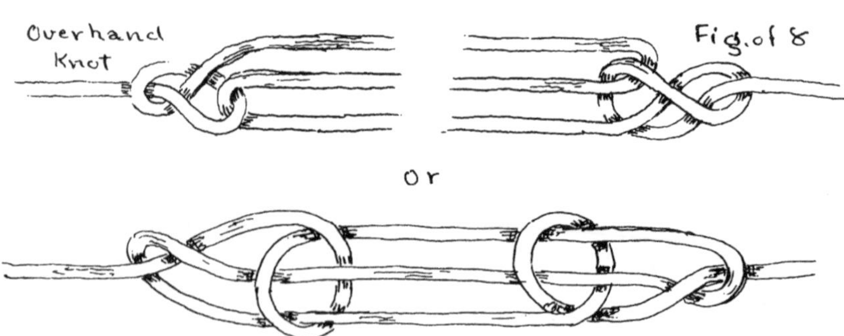
Overhand Knot
Fig. of 8
or

KNOTS OF THE RANCH AND FARM

LASSO

THE HONDA or Hondo

An Eyelet tied with two Overhand Knots

Lasso

HALTERS

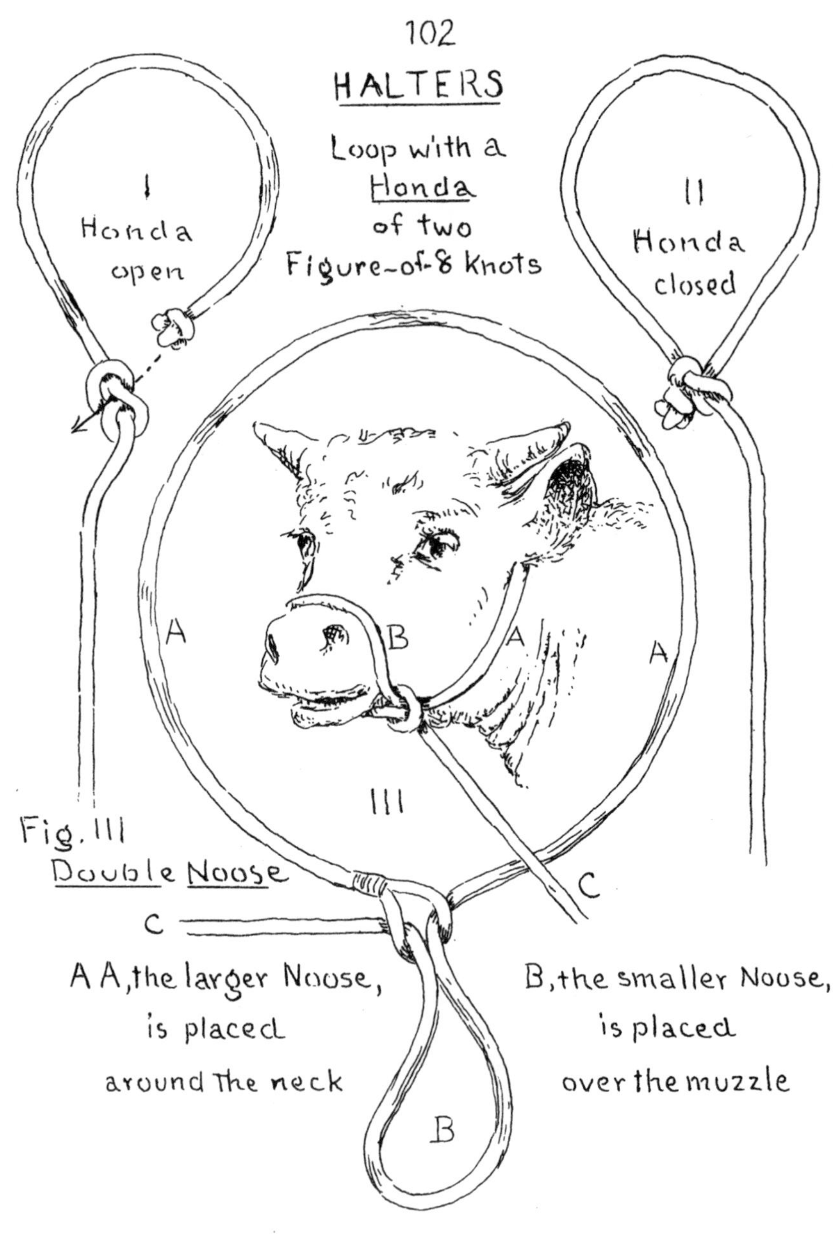
Loop with a
Honda
of two
Figure-of-8 Knots
I
Honda
open
II
Honda
closed
A
B
A
A
III
Fig. III
Double Noose
C
C
B

A A, the larger Noose, is placed around the neck

B, the smaller Noose, is placed over the muzzle

HALTER and MANGER KNOTS.

Figure-of-Eight Noose

See page 41

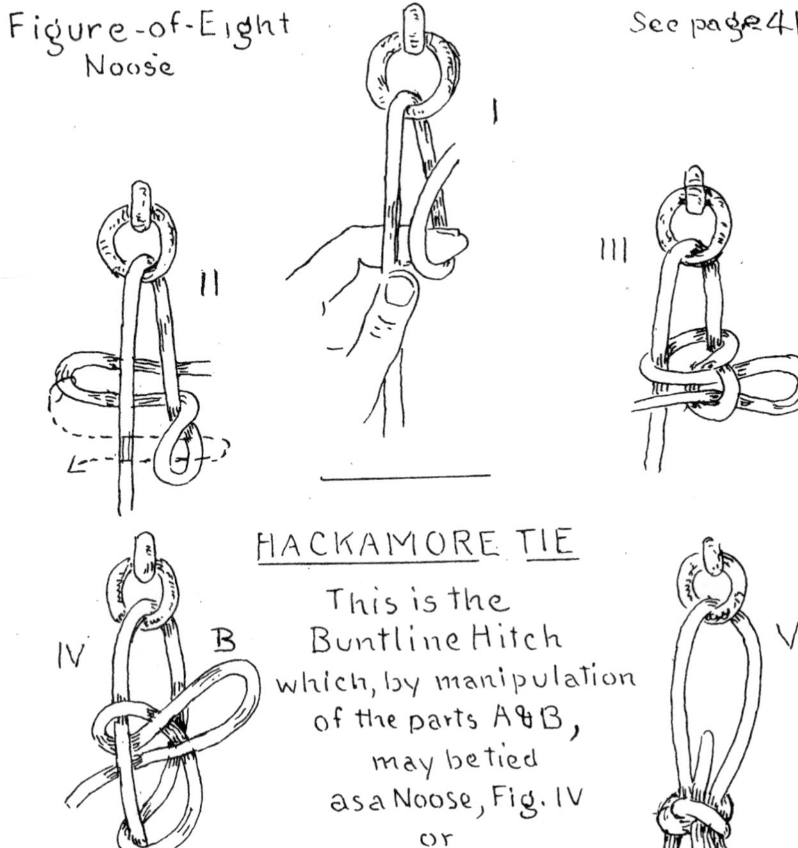
I
II
III
IV
B
A
V
A
B

HACKAMORE TIE

This is the Buntline Hitch which, by manipulation of the parts A & B, may be tied as a Noose, Fig. IV or as a Loop, Fig. V

see page 34

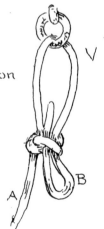

HALTER

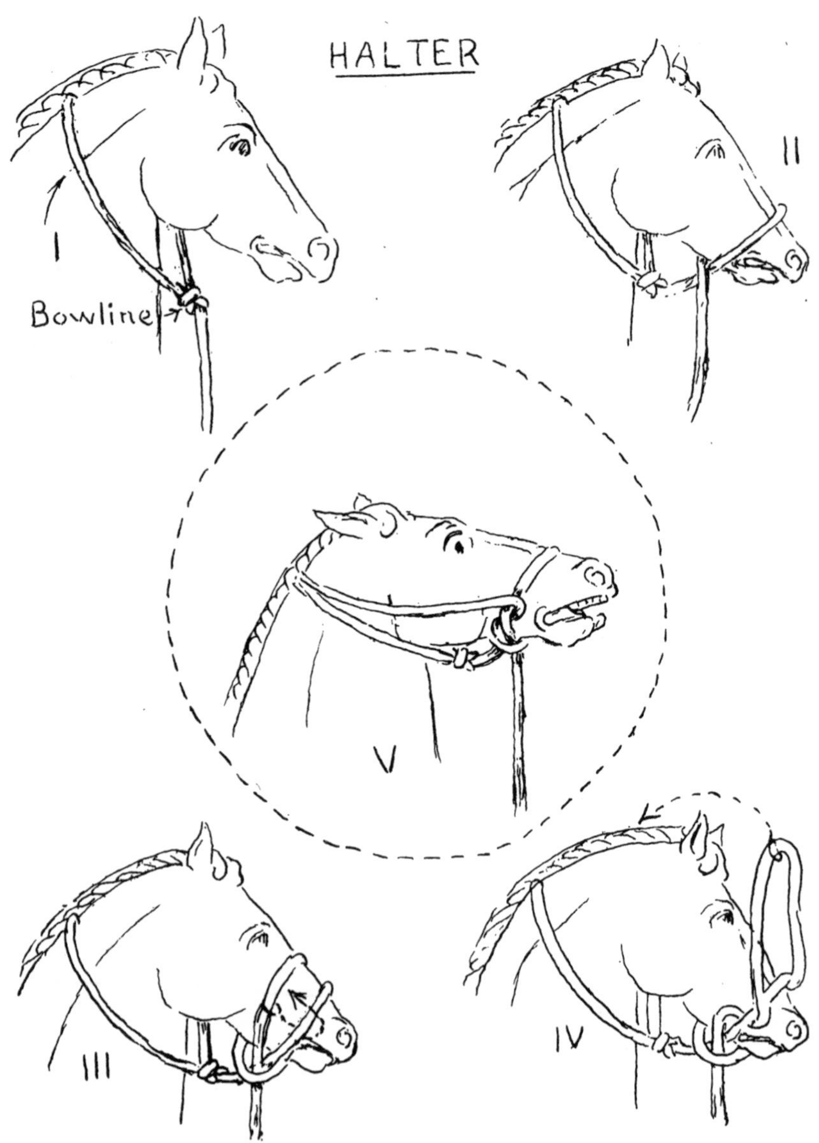
I
Bowline
II
V
III
IV

SACK KNOTS

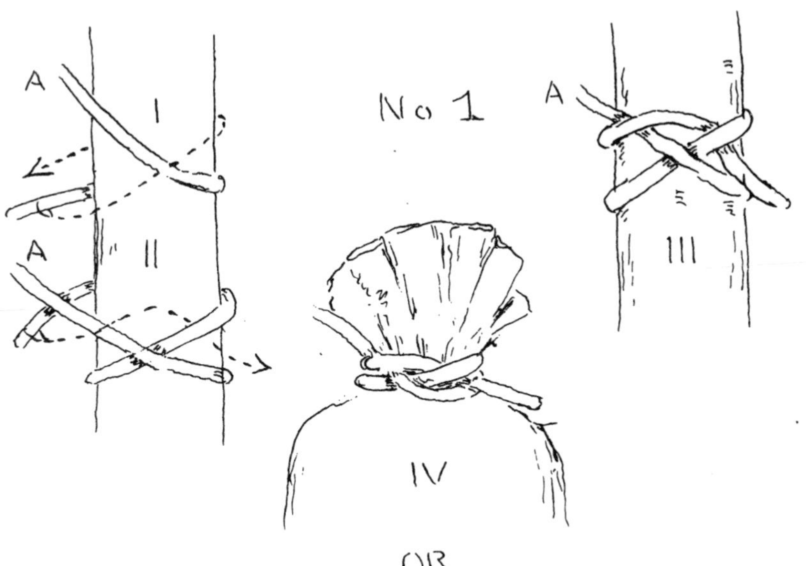
No 1
A
I
A
II
A
III
IV

OR

Tie an Overhand Knot Fig. V

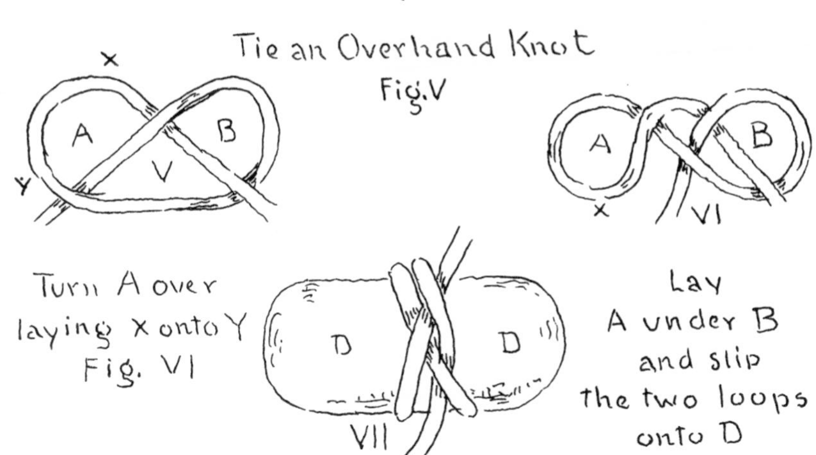
X
A
B
V
Y
A
B
X
VI
D
D
VII

Turn A over laying X onto Y Fig. VI

Lay A under B and slip the two loops onto D

SACK KNOTS

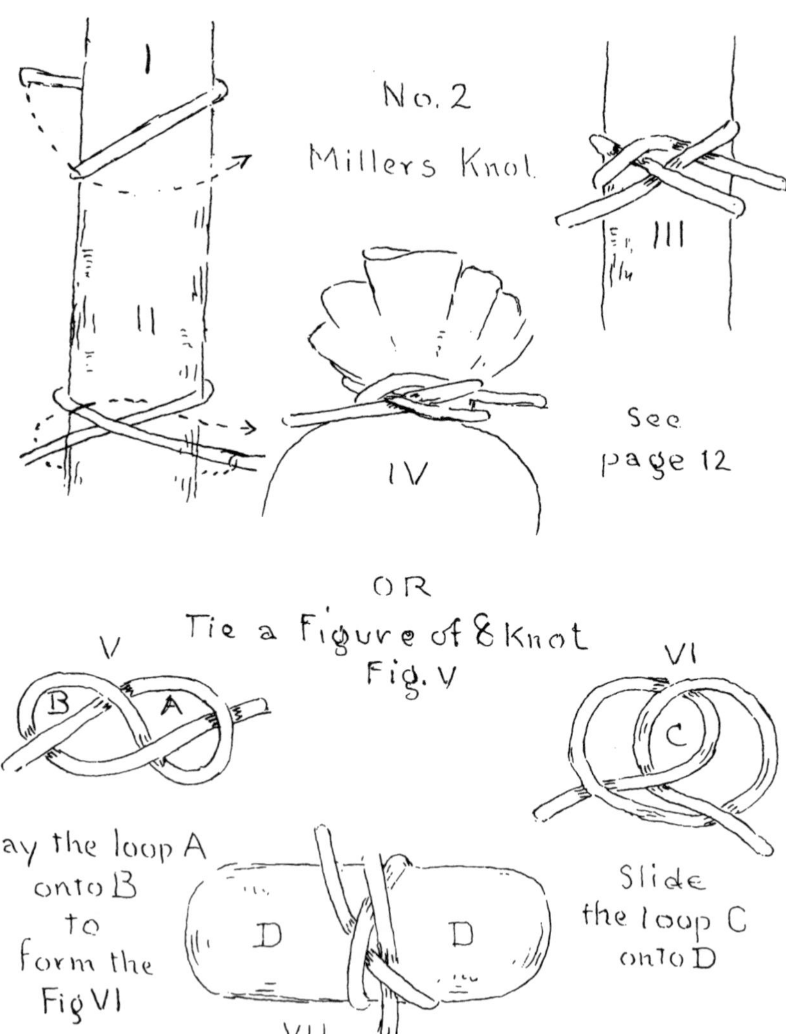
I
No. 2
Millers Knot
III
II
IV
See
page 12
OR
Tie a Figure of 8 Knot
Fig. V
V
B
A
VI
C
Lay the loop A
onto B
to
form the
Fig VI
D
D
VII
Slide
the loop C
onto D

SACK KNOTS

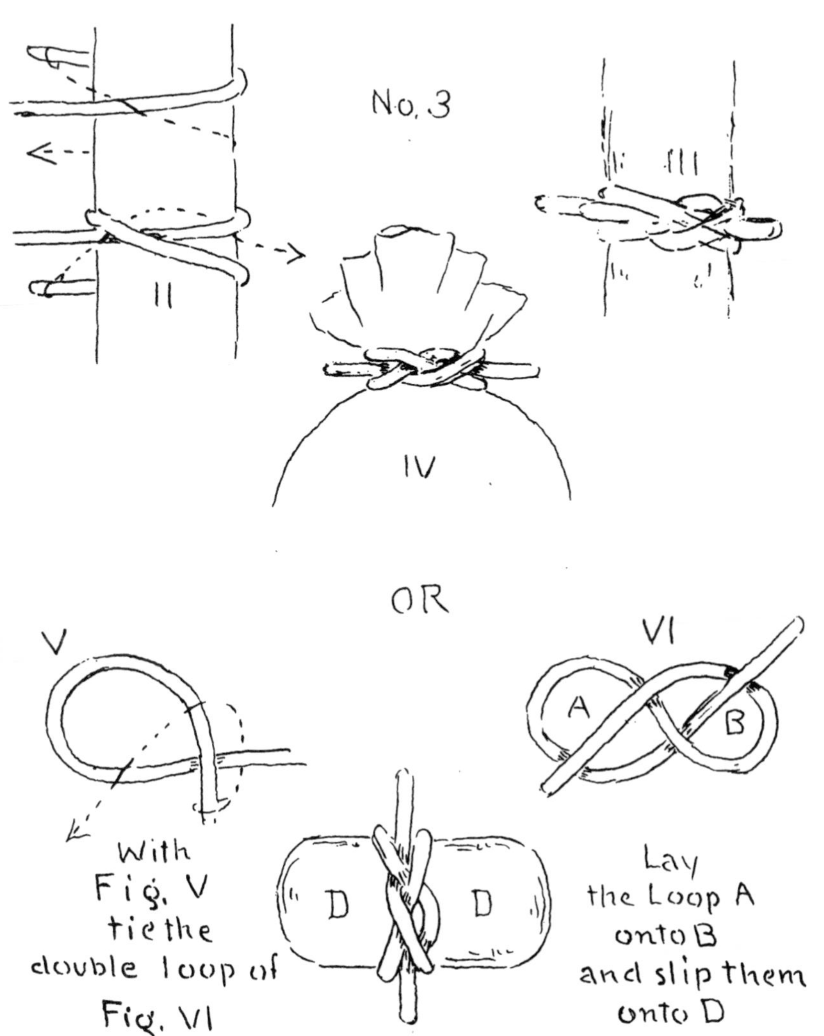
No. 3
II
III
IV
OR
V
VI
A
B
D
D
With Fig. V tie the double loop of Fig. VI
Lay the Loop A onto B and slip them onto D

SACK KNOTS

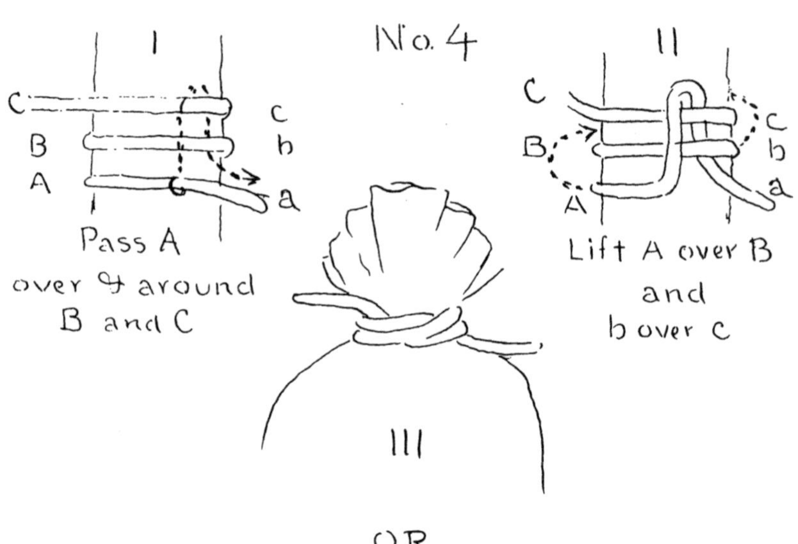
No. 4
I
C
B
A
c
b
a
Pass A
over & around
B and C
II
C
B
A
c
b
a
Lift A over B
and
b over c
III

OR

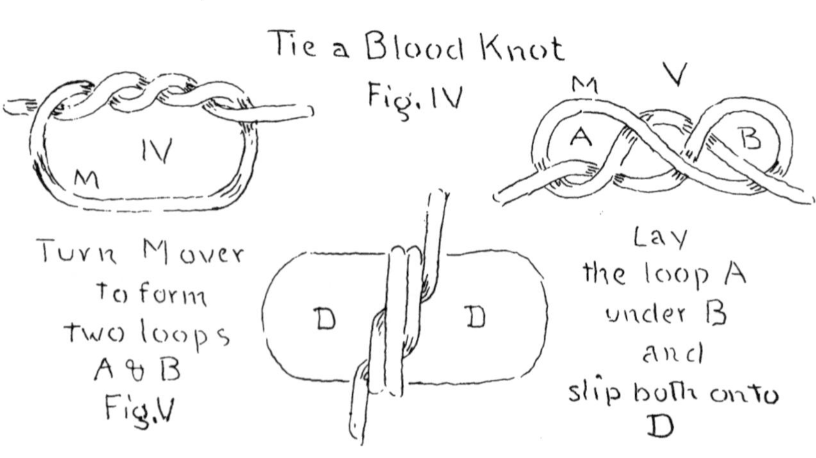
Tie a Blood Knot
Fig. IV
IV
M
V
M
A
B
D
D
Turn M over
to form
two loops
A & B
Fig. V
Lay
the loop A
under B
and
slip both onto
D

DIAMOND HITCH

A compensating device for securing the pack on a horse

A
C
B
D

The rope is adjusted to form a quadrangle on the top of the pack.

The strain that tends to pull A & B apart is held in check by a counter-strain at the points C & D

JAR SLING

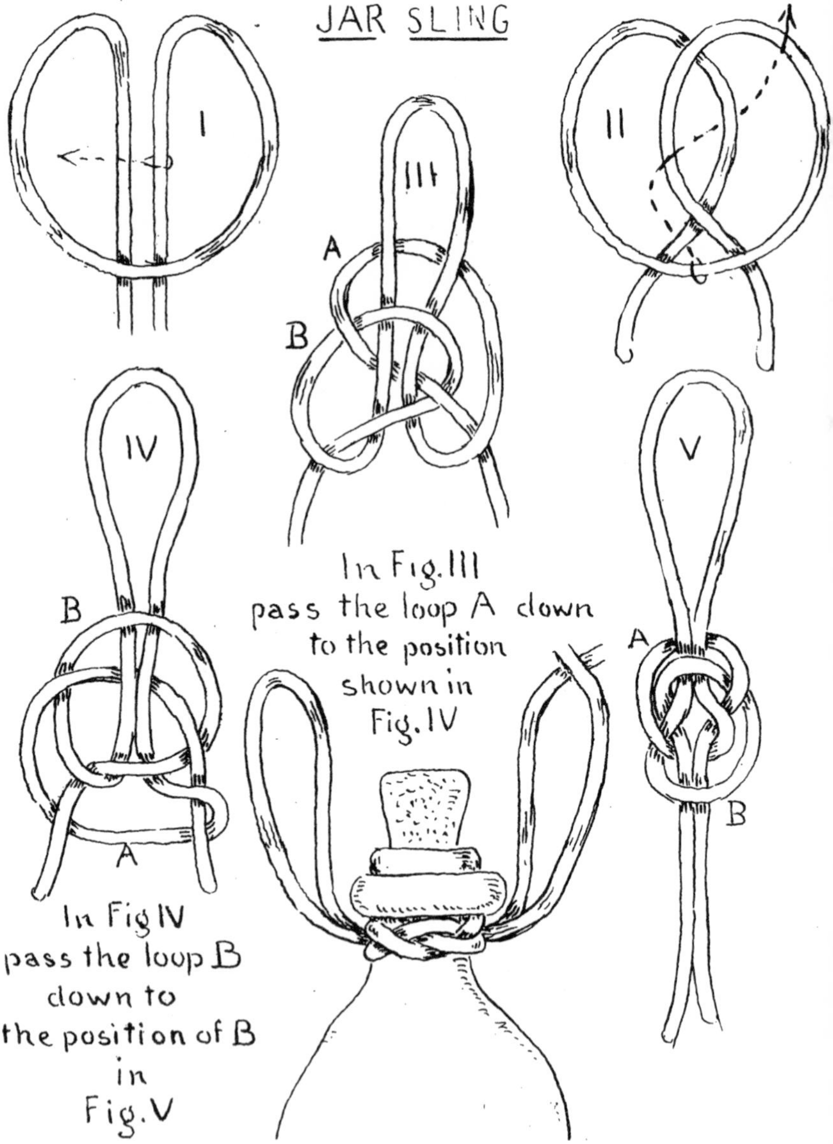

I
II
III
A
B
IV
B
A
V
A
B

In Fig. III
pass the loop A down
to the position
shown in
Fig. IV

In Fig IV
pass the loop B
down to
the position of B
in
Fig. V

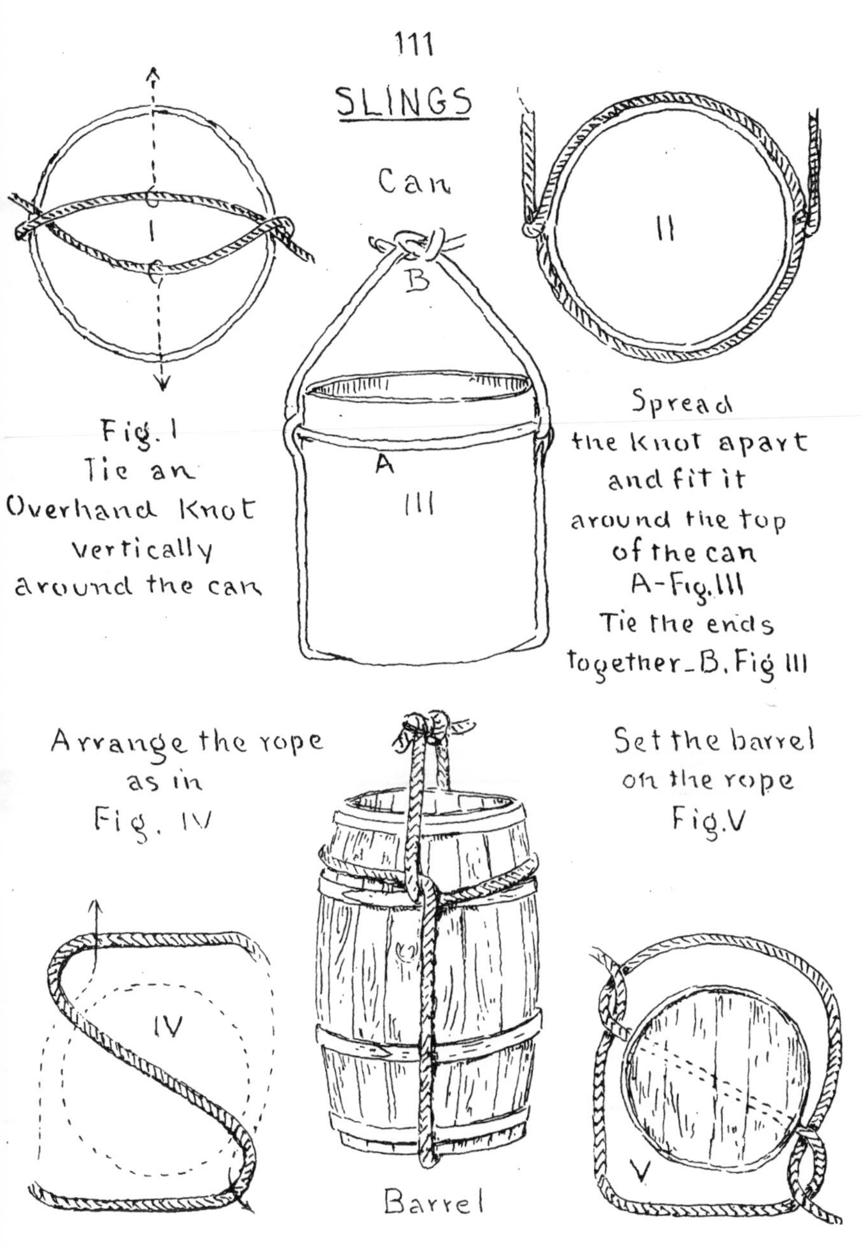
SLINGS
Can
I
II
B
A
III
Fig. I
Tie an
Overhand Knot
vertically
around the can
Spread
the knot apart
and fit it
around the top
of the can
A-Fig. III
Tie the ends
together_B. Fig III
Arrange the rope
as in
Fig. IV
Set the barrel
on the rope
Fig. V
IV
V
Barrel

LADDERS

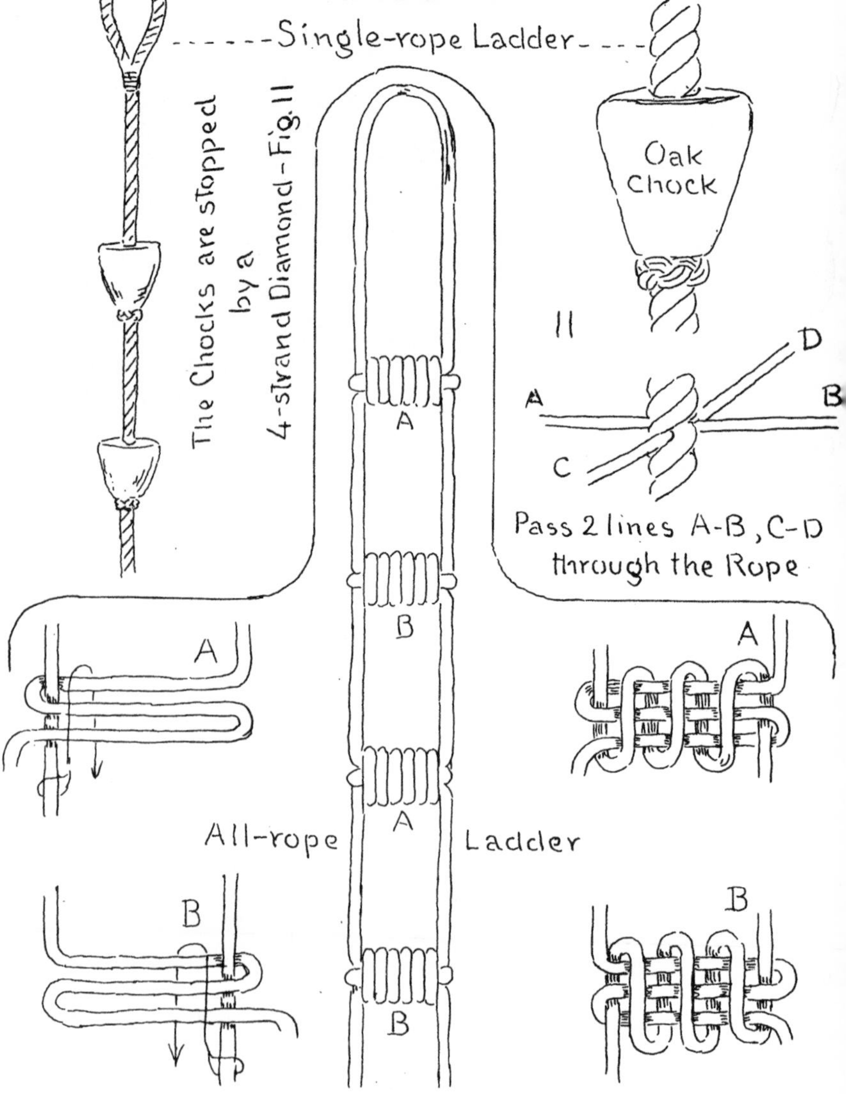

Single-rope Ladder

The Chocks are stopped by a 4-strand Diamond-Fig. 11

Oak Chock

11

A

B

C

D

Pass 2 lines A-B, C-D through the Rope

A

B

A

B

A

A

B

All-rope Ladder

B

B

113

ANGLER'S KNOTS

Line and Leader

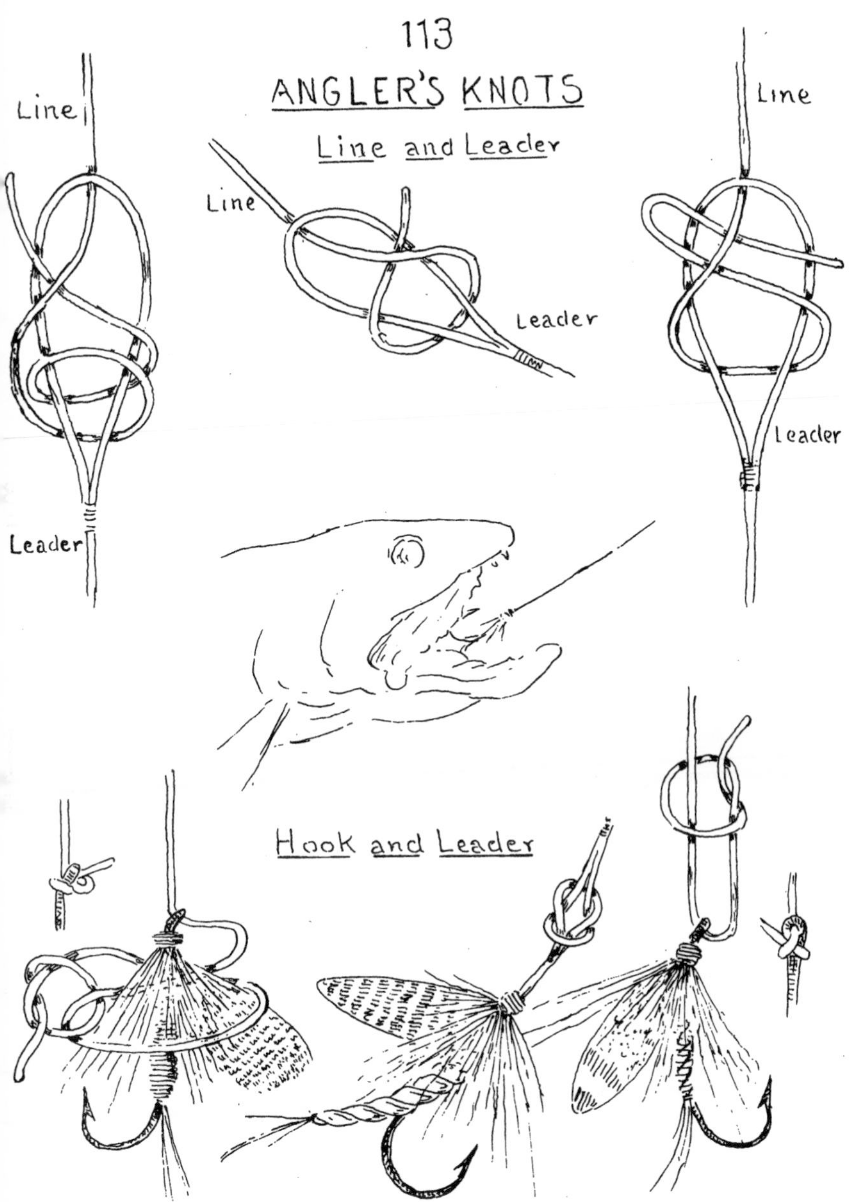

Line
Leader
Line
Leader
Line
Leader
Hook and Leader

TYING LEADERS

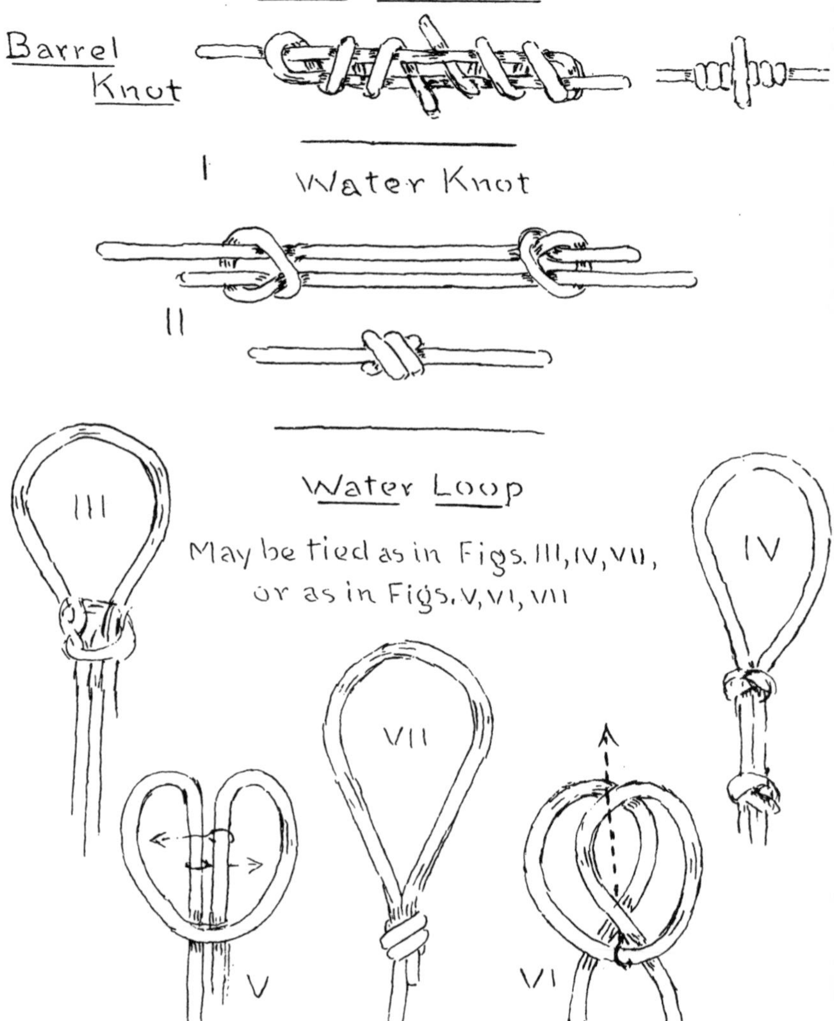
Barrel Knot
I
Water Knot
II
Water Loop
May be tied as in Figs. III, IV, VII,
or as in Figs. V, VI, VII
III
IV
VII
V
VI

For Angler's Loop see page 43

TYING FLIES

A simple and effective artificial fly may be tied with a fish hook, a length of colored silk, and a hackle from the neck of a cock.

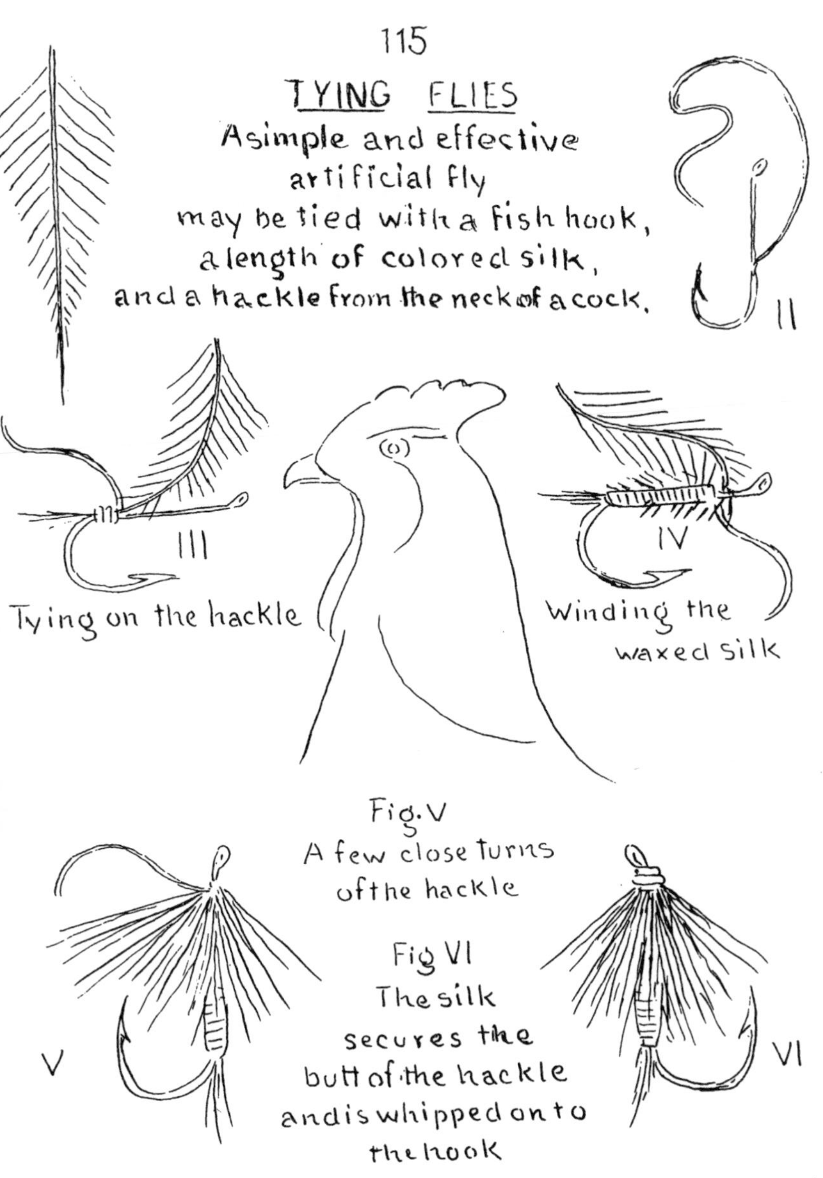
II
III
IV
V
VI

Tying on the hackle

Winding the waxed silk

Fig. V
A few close turns of the hackle

Fig VI
The silk secures the butt of the hackle and is whipped on to the hook to form the head of the fly – A drop of varnish on the head

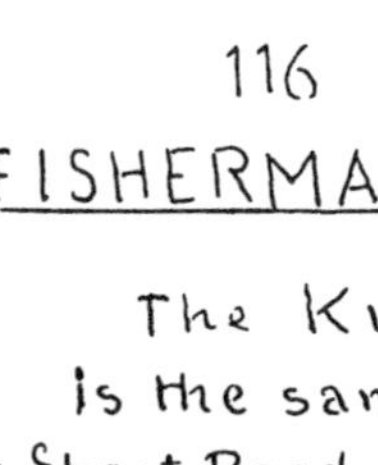

FISHERMAN'S NET

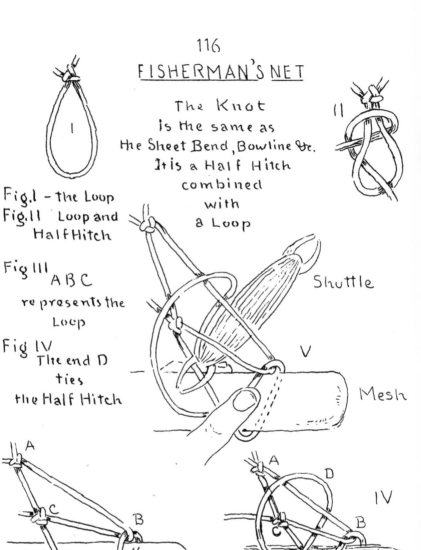

The Knot
is the same as
the Sheet Bend, Bowline &c.
It is a Half Hitch
combined
with
a Loop

Fig.I – the Loop
Fig.II Loop and Half Hitch

Fig III ABC represents the Loop

Fig IV The end D ties the Half Hitch

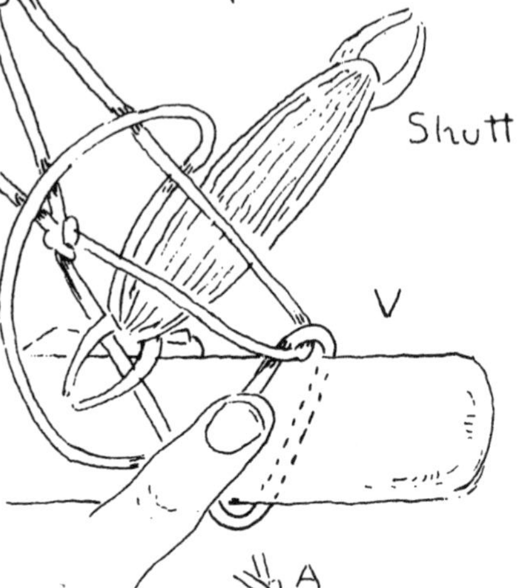
Shuttle
V
Mesh

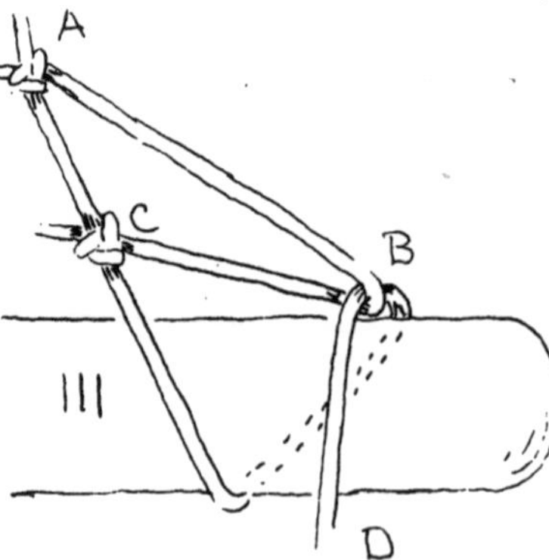
A
C
B
III
D

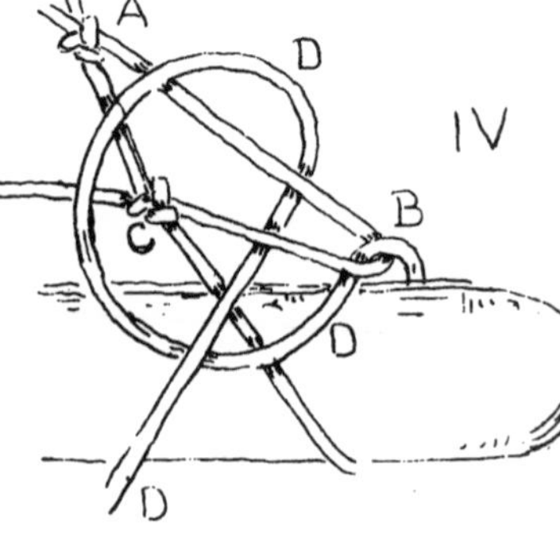
A
D
IV
B
C
D
D

CIRCULAR NET

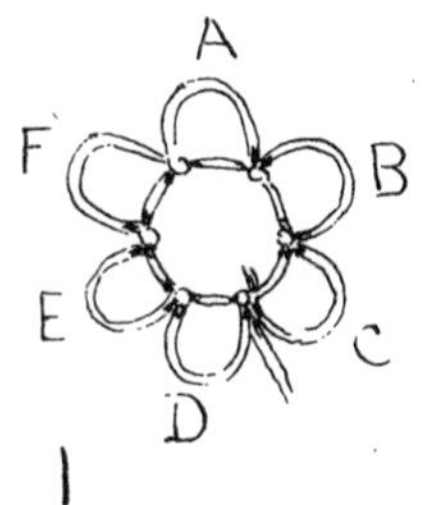
A
B
C
D
E
F
I

Fig. I
Tie 6 loops
on a centre loop

Fig II
Tie 2 Knots on each loop

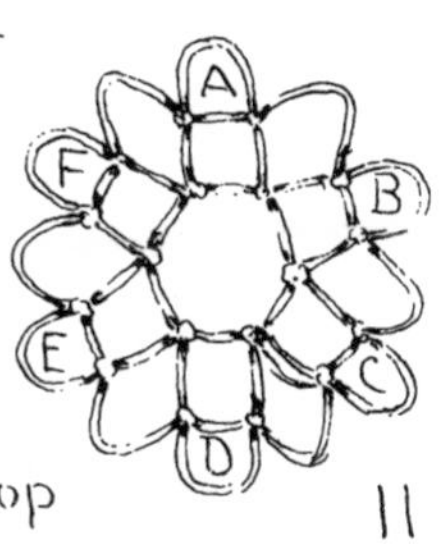
A
B
C
D
E
F
II

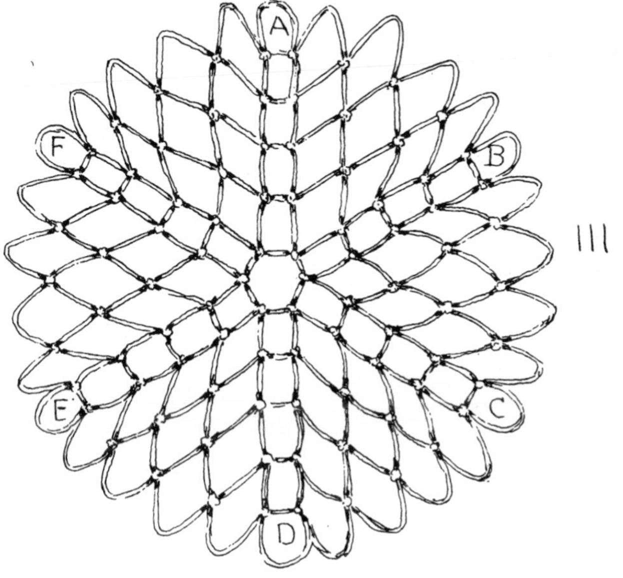
A
B
C
D
E
F
III

Fig III
The diameter of the net increases by tying 2 Knots on each of the loops that lie on the three lines AD-BE-CF

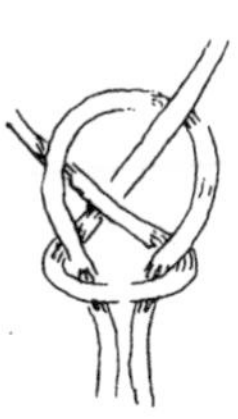

This net can be tied

118
TENNIS NET

without mesh or shuttle

Tied with short lines – A, A

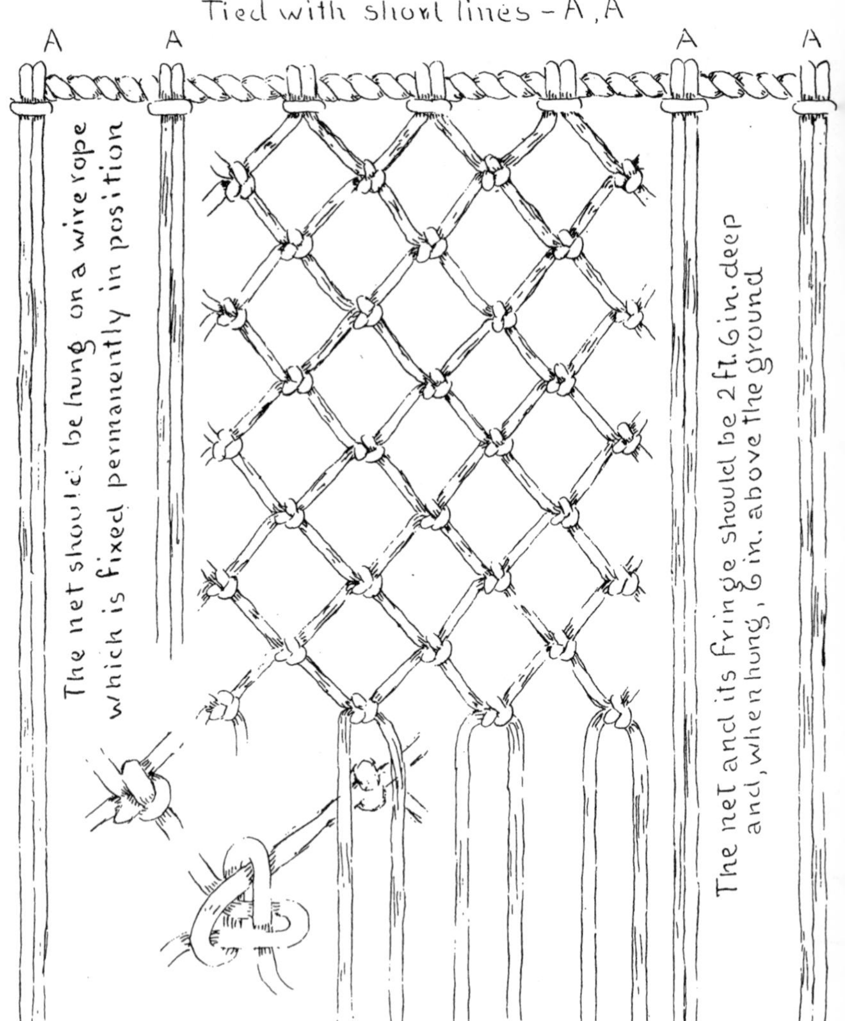
A
A
A
A
The net should be hung on a wire rope which is fixed permanently in position
The net and its fringe should be 2 ft. 6 in. deep and, when hung, 6 in. above the ground

NETTING

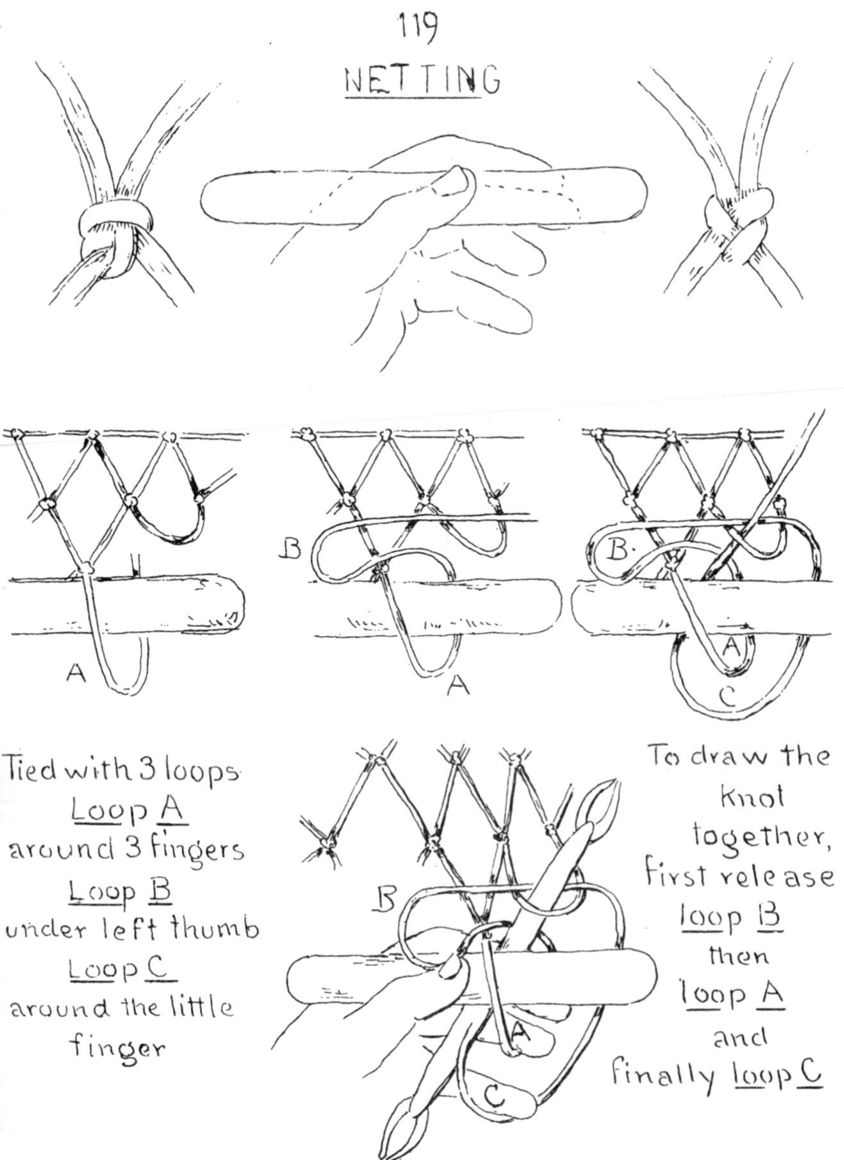
B
A
B
A
B.
A
C
Tied with 3 loops
Loop A
around 3 fingers
Loop B
under left thumb
Loop C
around the little
finger
B
A
C
To draw the
knot
together,
first release
loop B
then
loop A
and
finally loop C

TYING PACKAGES

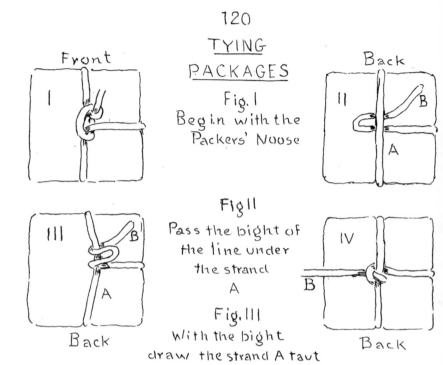

Front

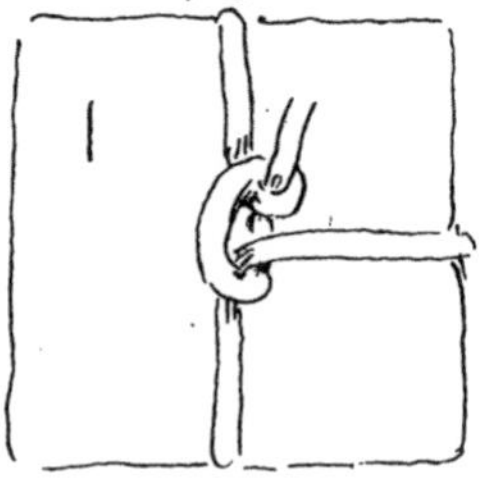

Back

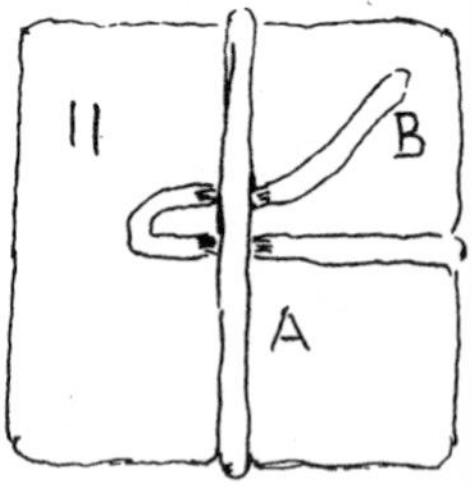

Fig. I
Begin with the Packers' Noose

Fig II
Pass the bight of the line under the strand A

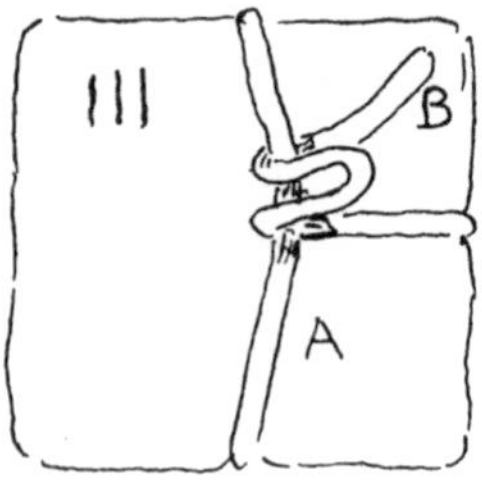

Back

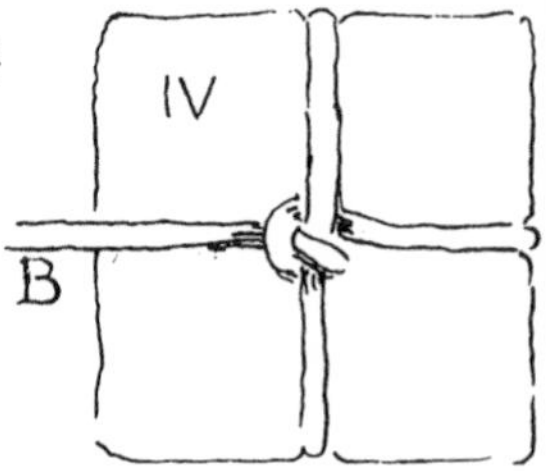

Back

Fig. III
With the bight draw the strand A taut

Fig. IV
Pass the end B through the bight and draw the knot taut

Figs. V and VI
Finish with two or three Half Hitches

Front

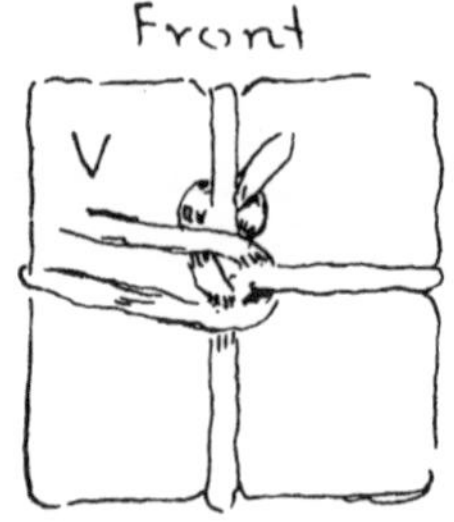
V

Front

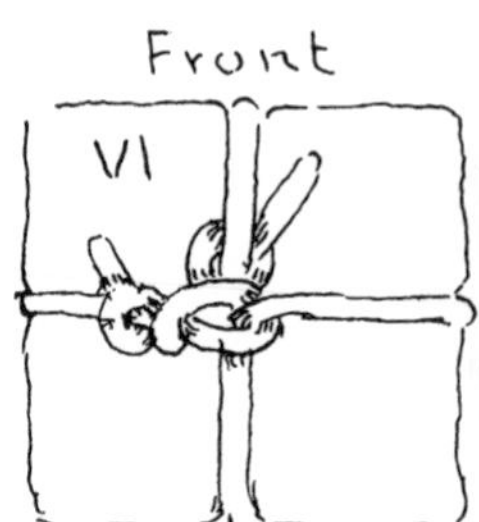
VI

TYING PACKAGES

Fig 1

Introduced here as a not-too-difficult puzzle

{To tie a 4-strand package with a single line, the beginning and the end not shown}

Diamond Tie

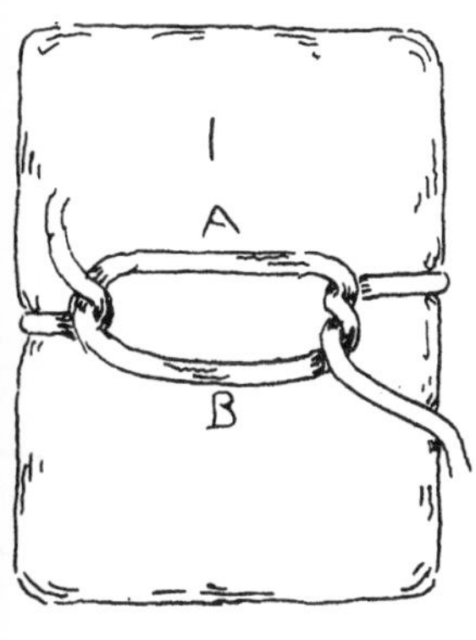
I
A
B

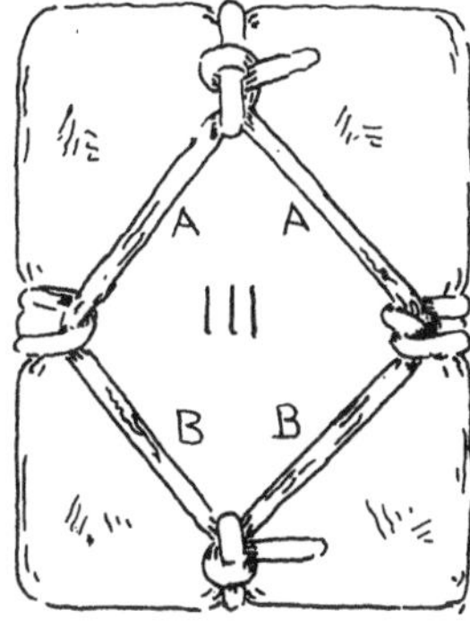
A A
III
B B

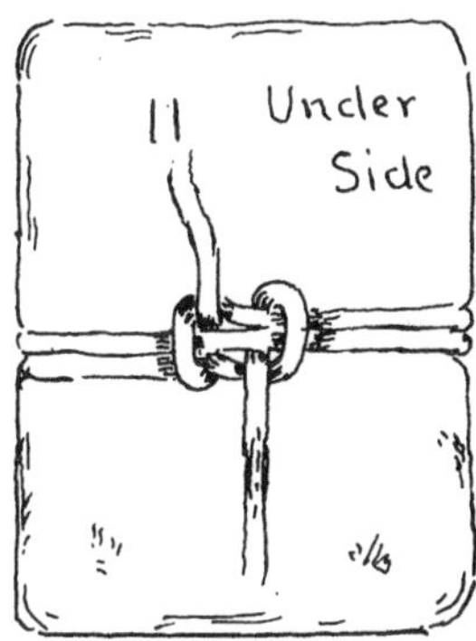
II
Under Side

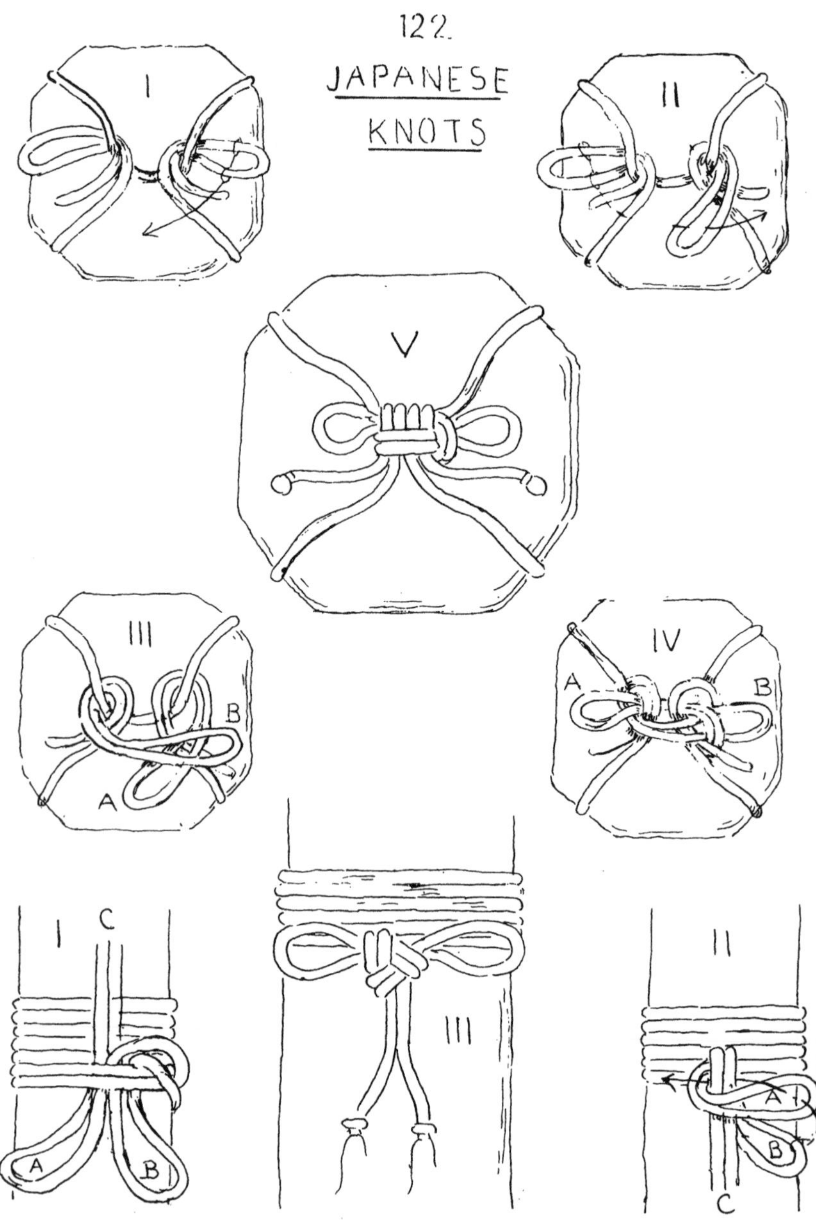
122.
JAPANESE KNOTS
I
II
V
III
B
A
IV
A
B
I
C
A
B
III
II
A
B
C

123

KNIFE – LANYARD

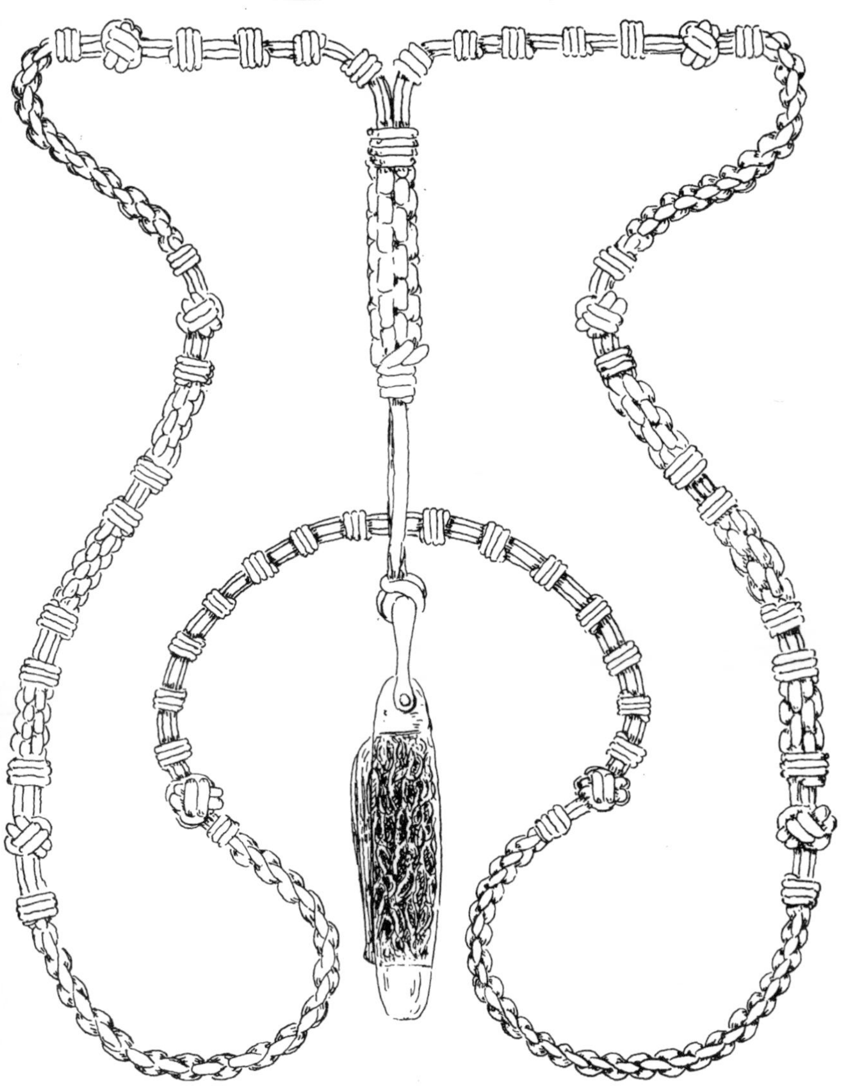

WATCH FOB

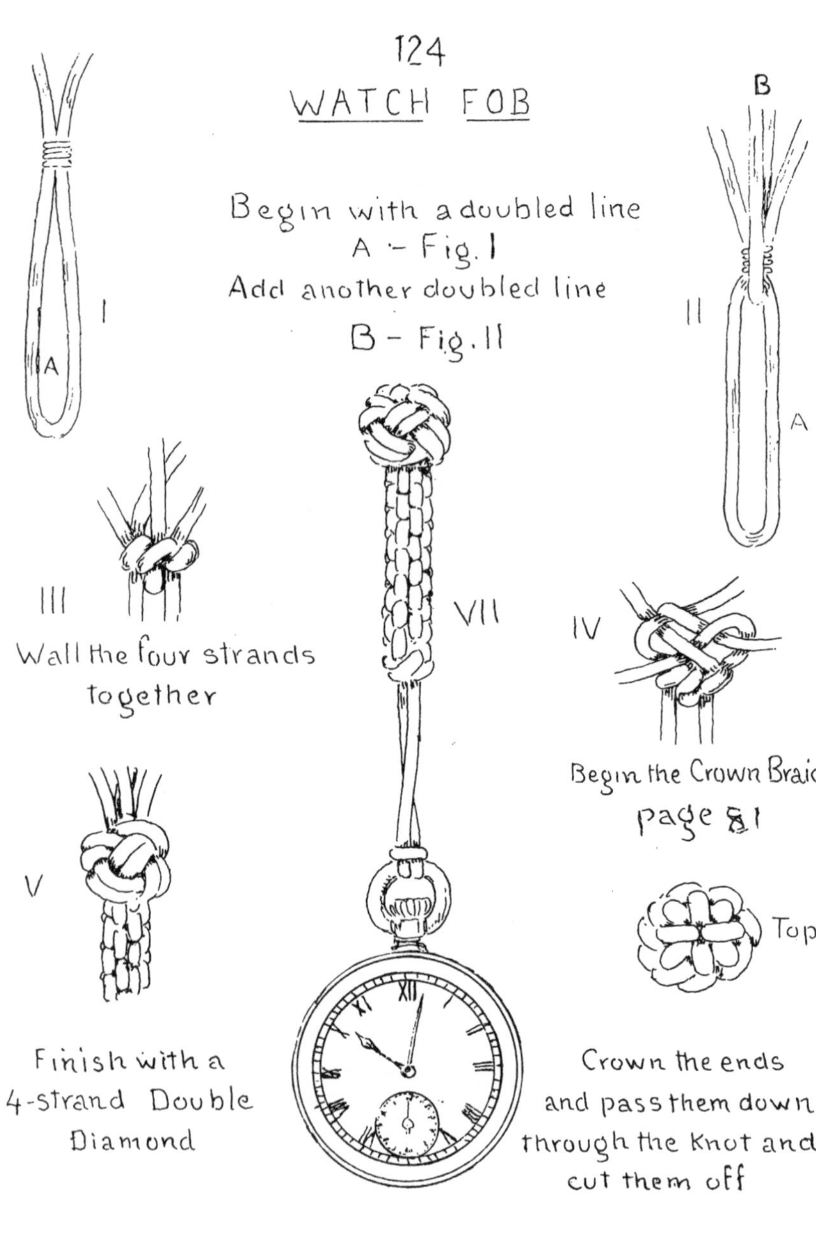
Begin with a doubled line
A – Fig. I
Add another doubled line
B – Fig. II
I
A
B
II
A
III
Wall the four strands together
VII
IV
Begin the Crown Braid
page 81
V
Top
Finish with a 4-strand Double Diamond
Crown the ends and pass them down through the knot and cut them off

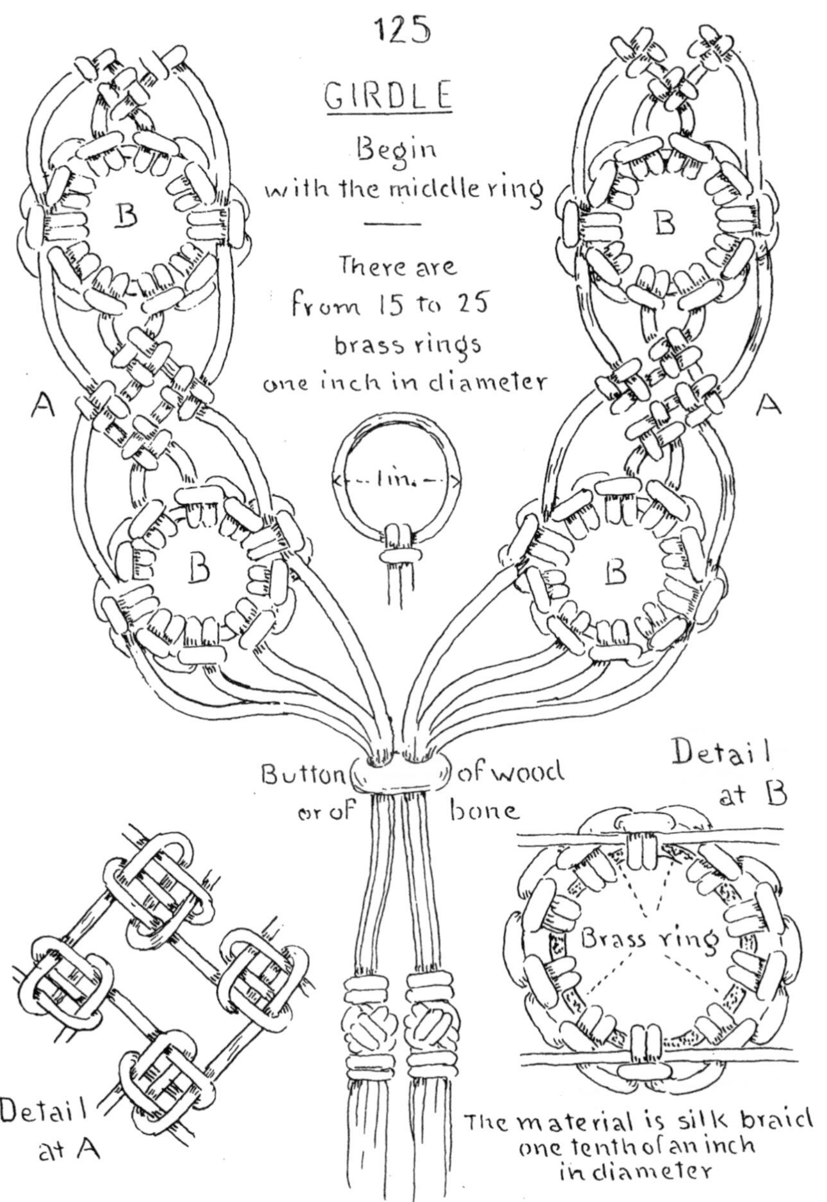
GIRDLE
Begin
with the middle ring
There are
from 15 to 25
brass rings
one inch in diameter
1 in.
A
A
B
B
B
B
Button of wood
or of bone
Detail
at B
Brass ring
Detail
at A
The material is silk braid
one tenth of an inch
in diameter

LEATHER FASTENING FOR A Girdle

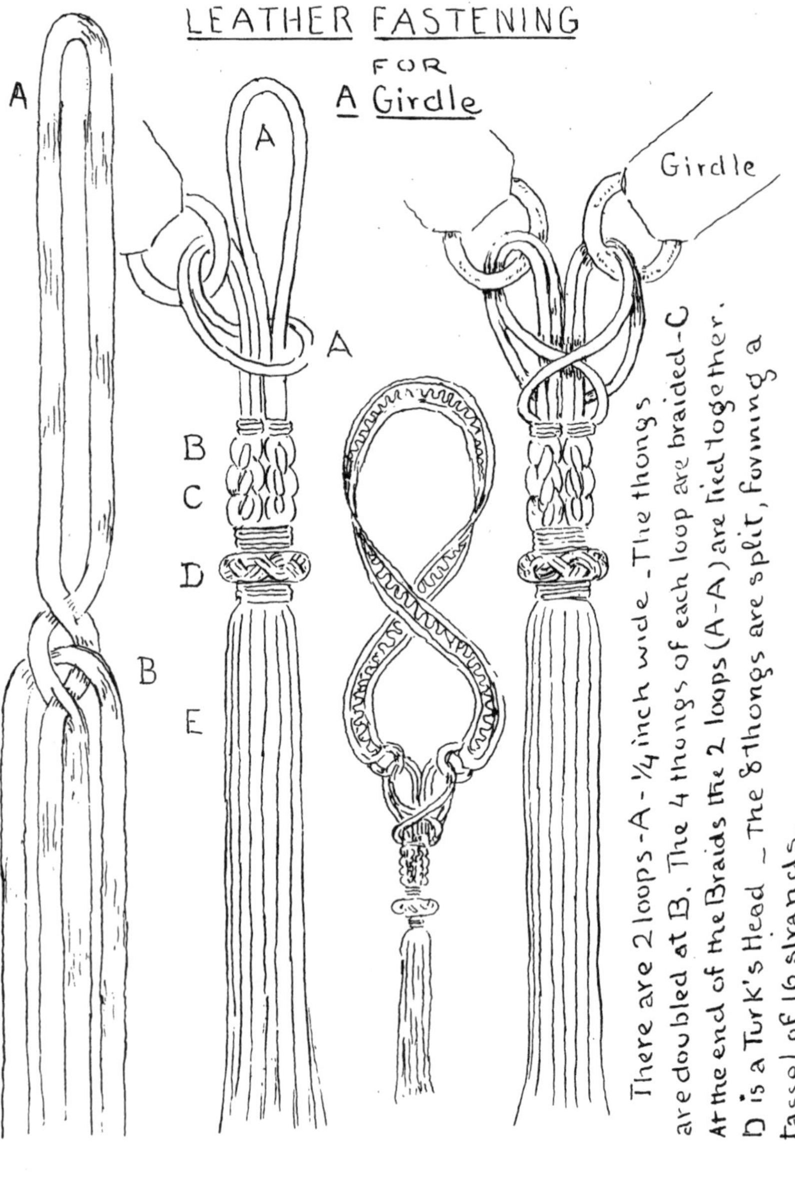
A
A
A
B
C
D
E
B
Girdle

There are 2 loops - A - ¼ inch wide _ The thongs are doubled at B. The 4 thongs of each loop are braided - C At the end of the Braids the 2 loops (A-A) are tied together. D is a Turk's Head _ The 8 thongs are split, forming a tassel of 16 strands.

LEATHER BELT and BUCKLE

Fig. I
A - Part of Belt slit into three Strands - See page 86

Fig. I
B - Two iron or brass rings

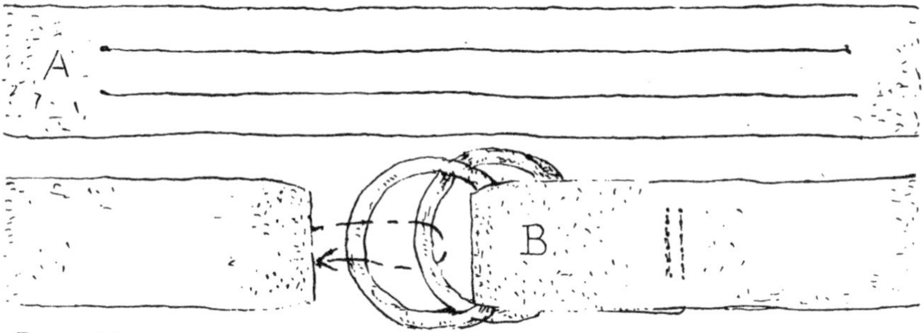

A
B

Fig II - A - The strands braided - B - The buckle fastened

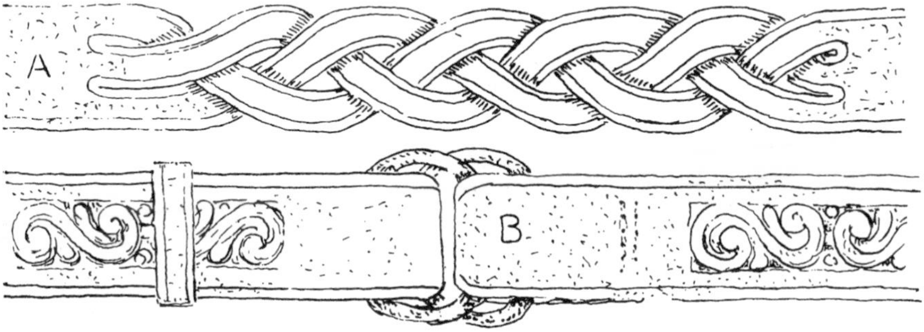

A
B

Fig. III - The inside of Buckle - The rings enlarged to show method more clearly

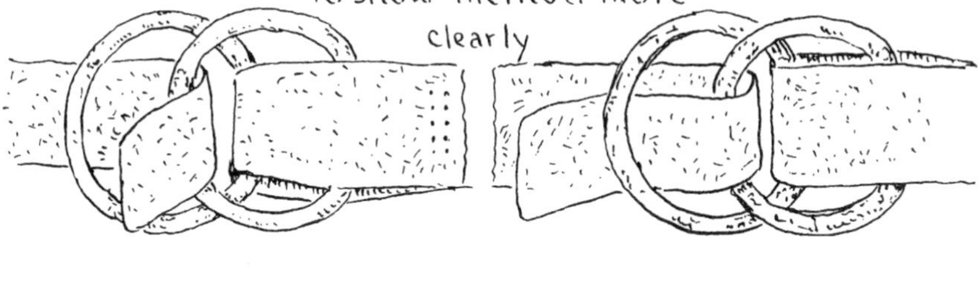

MACRAMÉ KNOTS

These are
The Square Knot, the Half Hitch and the Granny
tied around
one or more idle lines
drawn taut

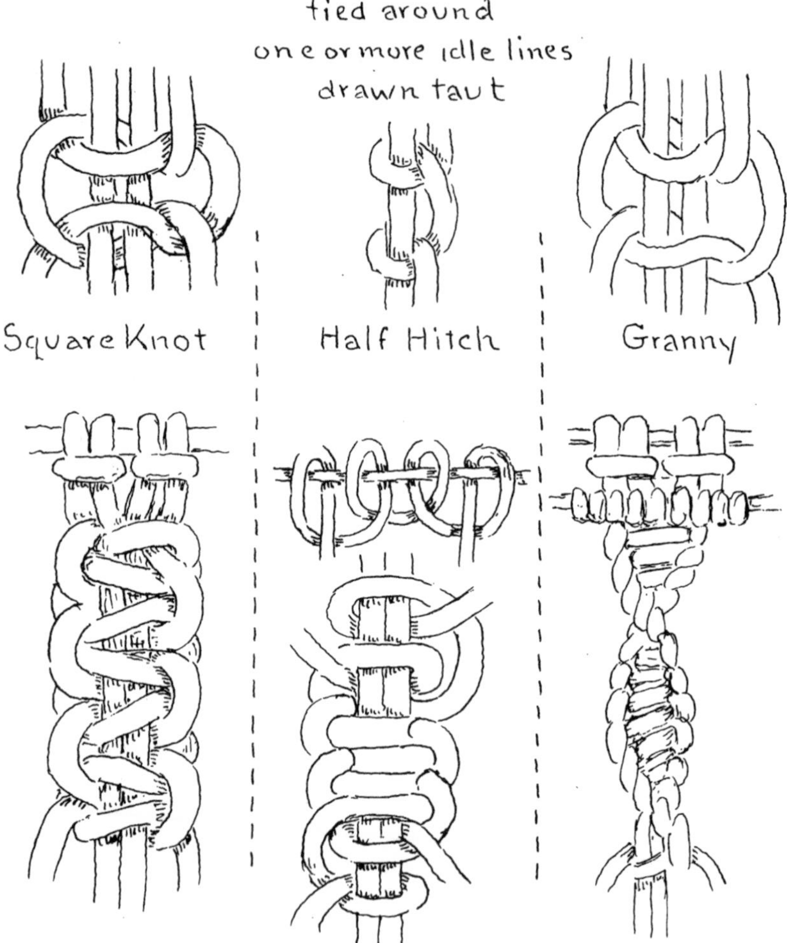
Square Knot
Half Hitch
Granny

129
MACRAME KNOTS

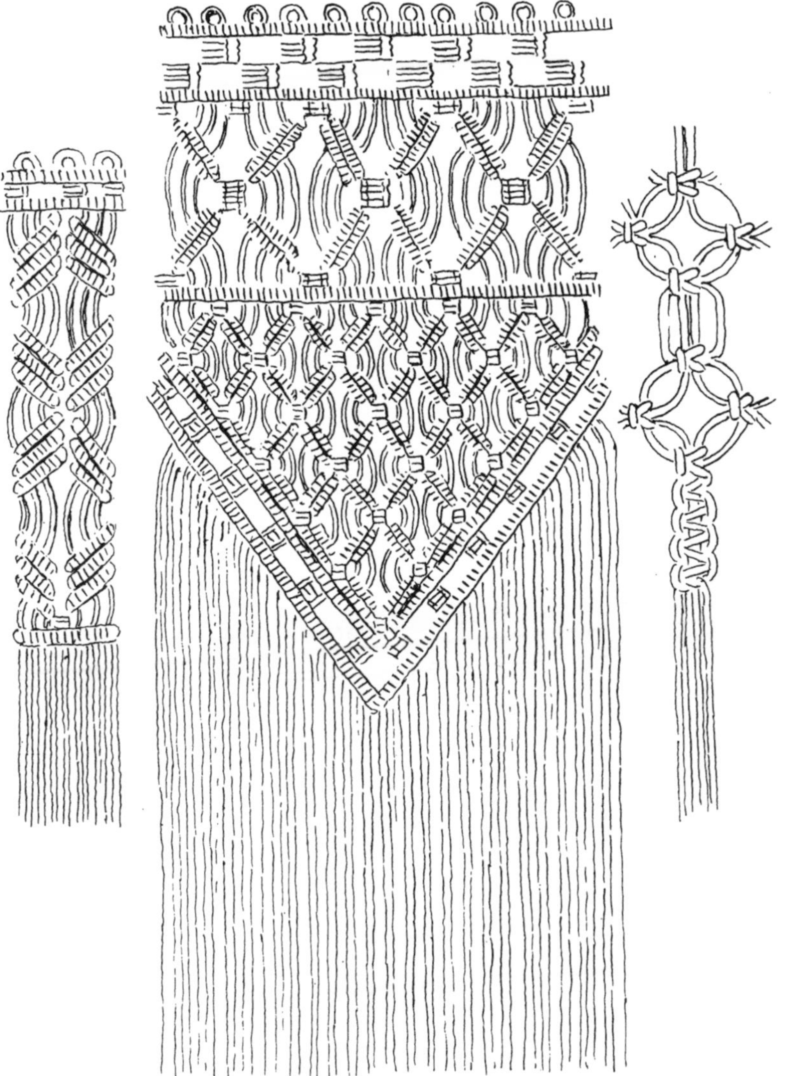

TATTING LOOP

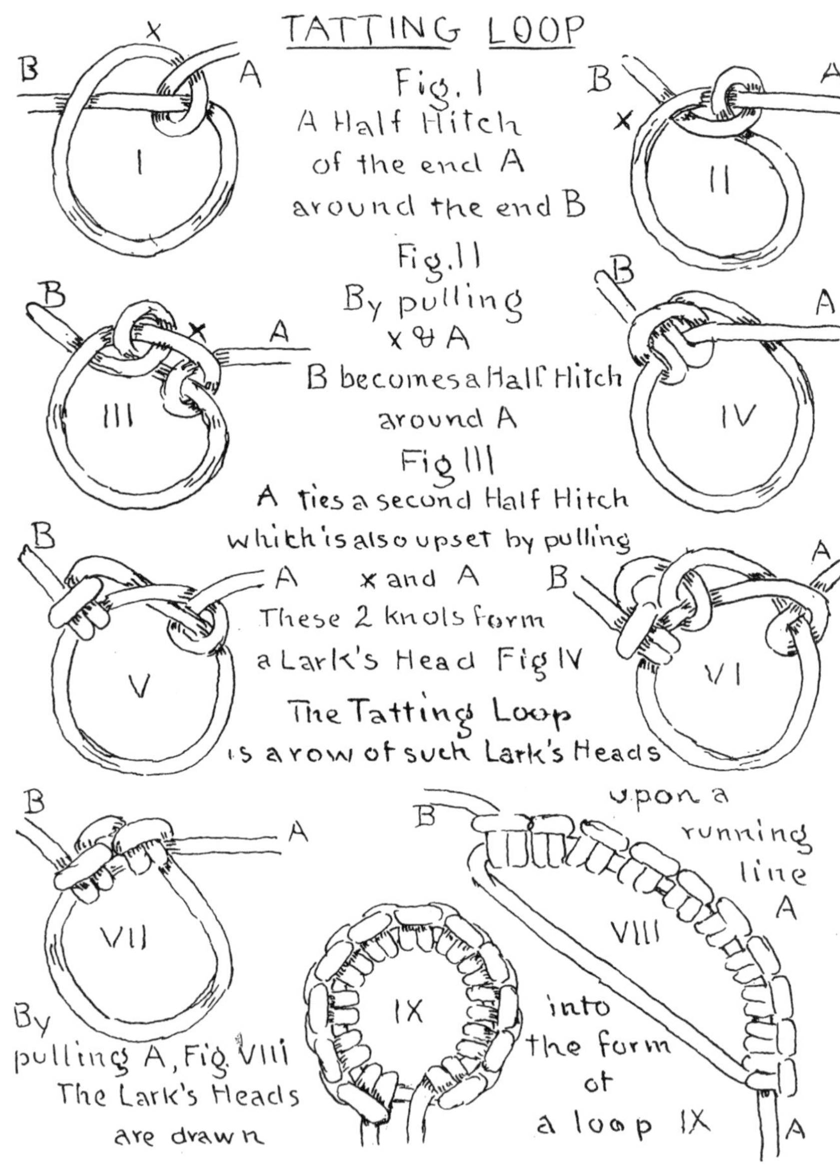
B
x
A
I
Fig. I
A Half Hitch
of the end A
around the end B
B
A
x
II
Fig. II
By pulling
x & A
B becomes a Half Hitch
around A
B
x
A
III
B
A
IV
Fig III
A ties a second Half Hitch
which is also upset by pulling
x and A
These 2 knots form
a Lark's Head Fig IV
B
A
V
B
A
VI
The Tatting Loop
is a row of such Lark's Heads
upon a
running
line
B
A
VII
B
A
VIII
A
IX
By
pulling A, Fig. VIII
The Lark's Heads
are drawn
into
the form
of
a loop IX

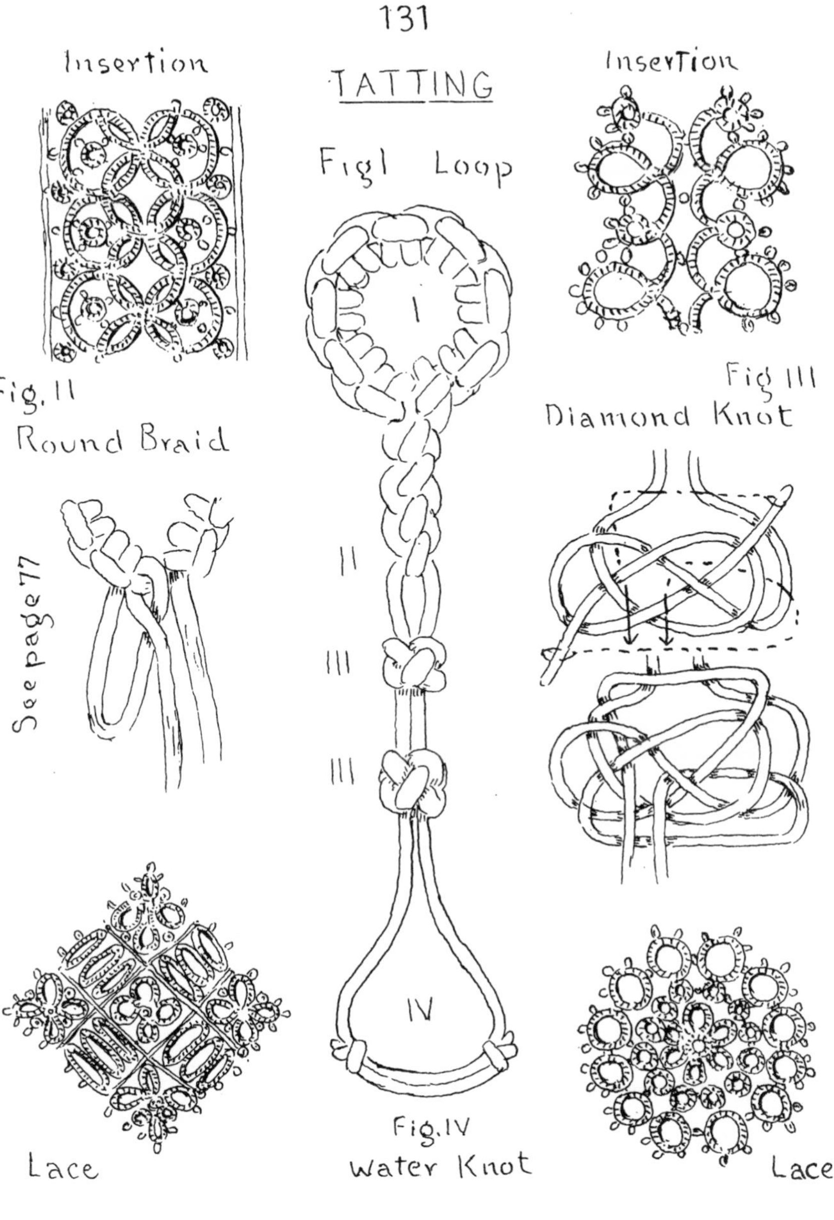
Insertion
TATTING
Insertion
Fig I Loop
I
II
III
III
IV
Fig. II
Round Braid
See page 77
Fig III
Diamond Knot
Fig. IV
Water Knot
Lace
Lace

BOOK COVER

BOOK COVER

ORIENTAL RUGS

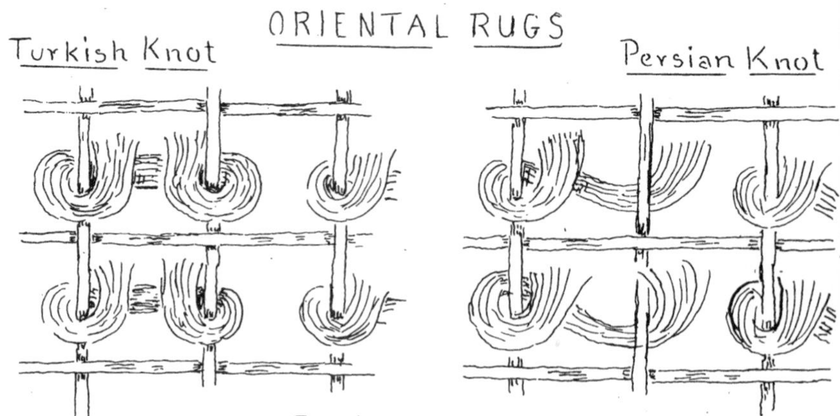
Turkish Knot
Persian Knot

Five hundred Knots
to the square inch are not unusual

KNOTS
IN
HERALDRY

CHINESE KNOT

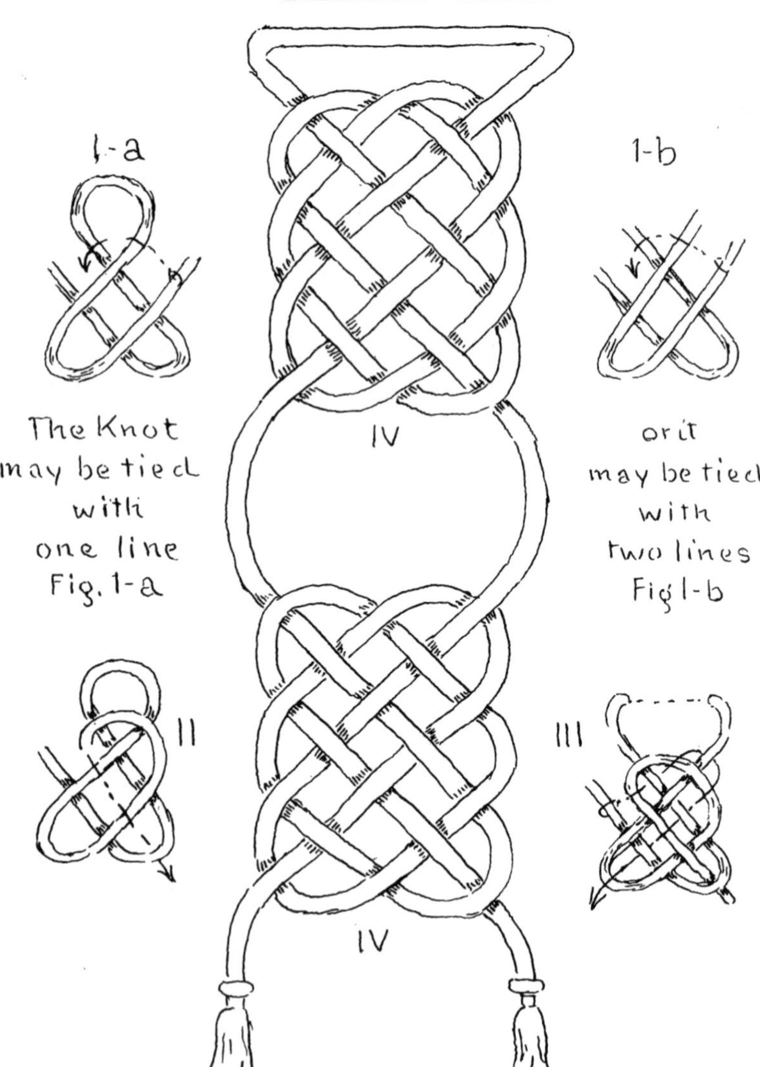
1-a
1-b
The Knot may be tied with one line Fig. 1-a
or it may be tied with two lines Fig 1-b
IV
II
III
IV

ADDING STRANDS to the CHINESE KNOT

I
II
V
V
III
IV

DEVELOPMENT

of Interlacings of any number of strands

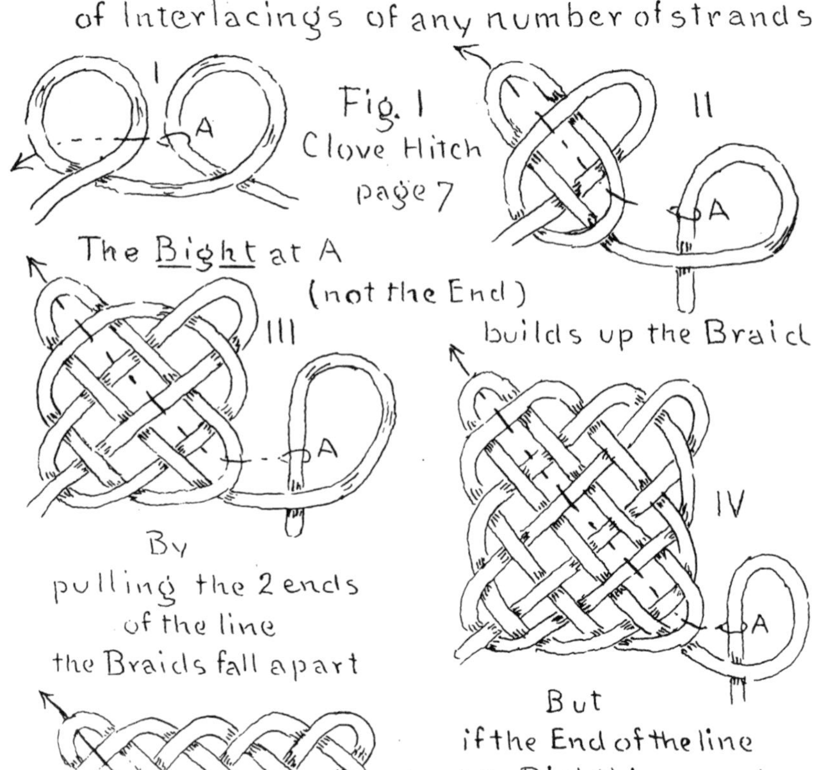
I
A
II
A
III
A
IV
A
V

Fig. I Clove Hitch page 7

The Bight at A (not the End) builds up the Braid

By pulling the 2 ends of the line the Braids fall apart

But if the End of the line (not the Bight) is passed through the Braid as in Fig. V the Interlacing cannot fall apart and the work can be so ended at any one of its stages.

139

TEMPLE ORNAMENTS

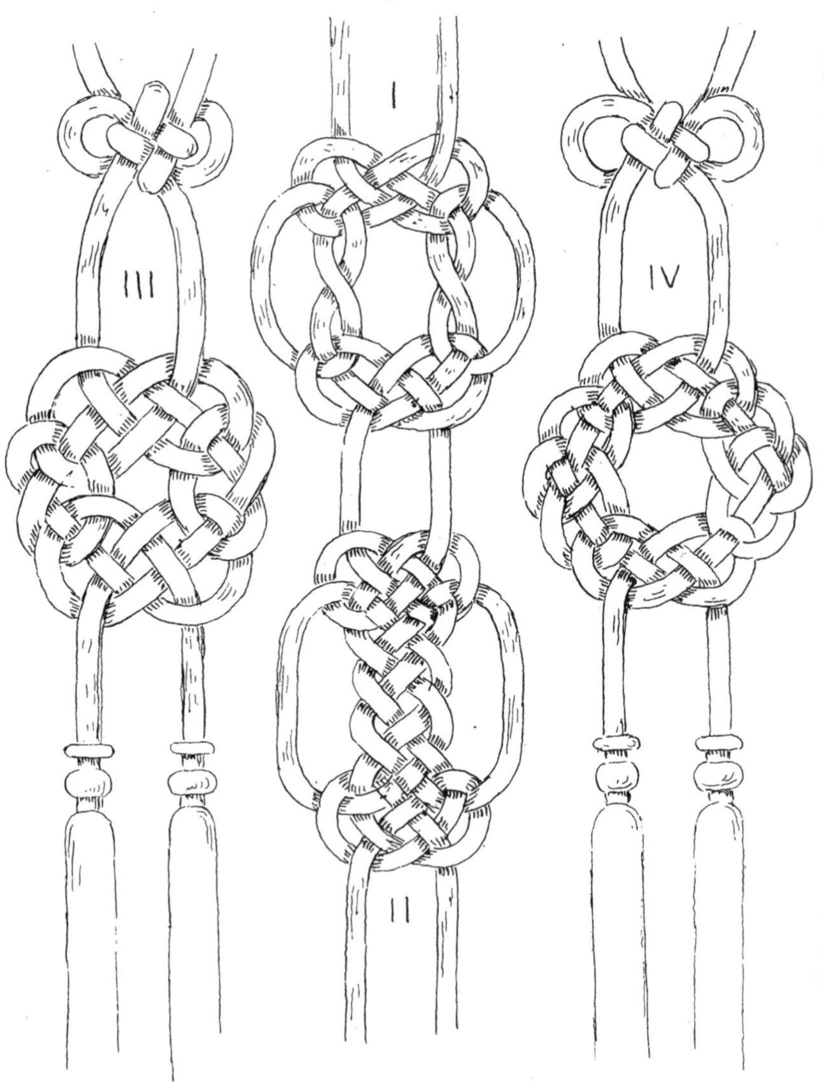
I
III
IV
II

141

Details of Temple Ornaments

A - begins all four Knots

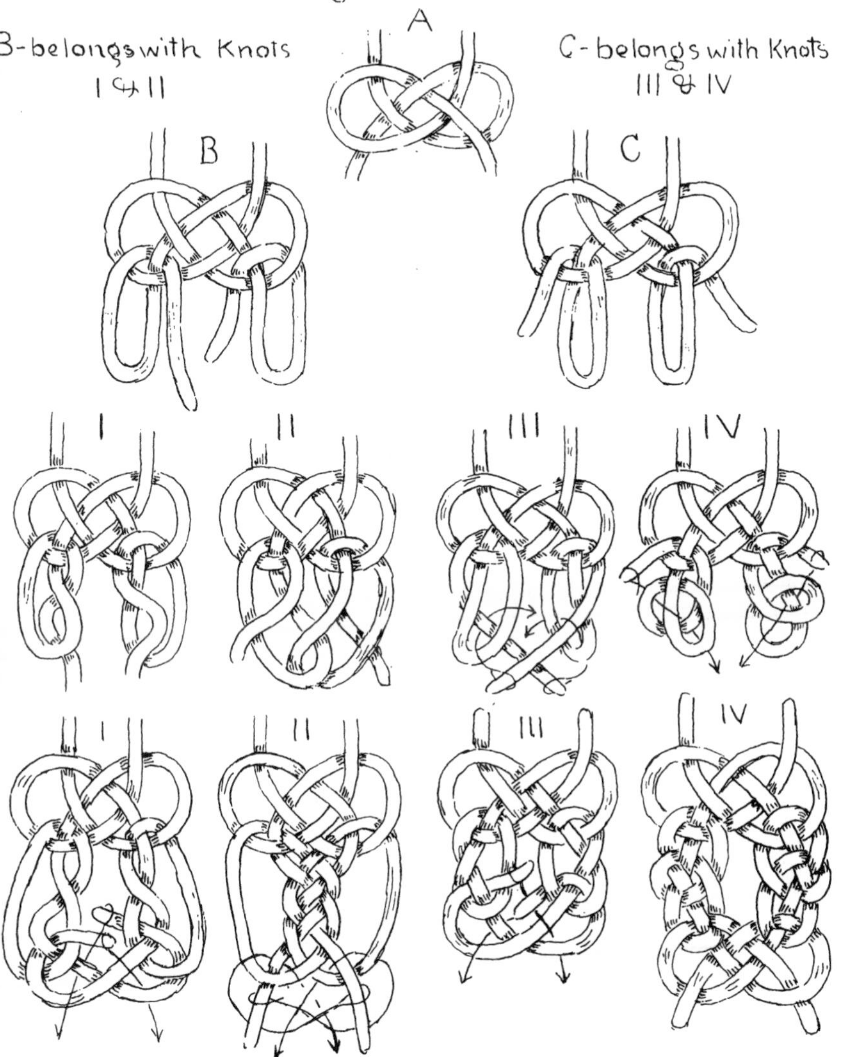

A
B - belongs with Knots
I & II
C - belongs with Knots
III & IV
B
C
I
II
III
IV
I
II
III
IV

142

ORNAMENTAL FORMS

based on the

Overhand Knot

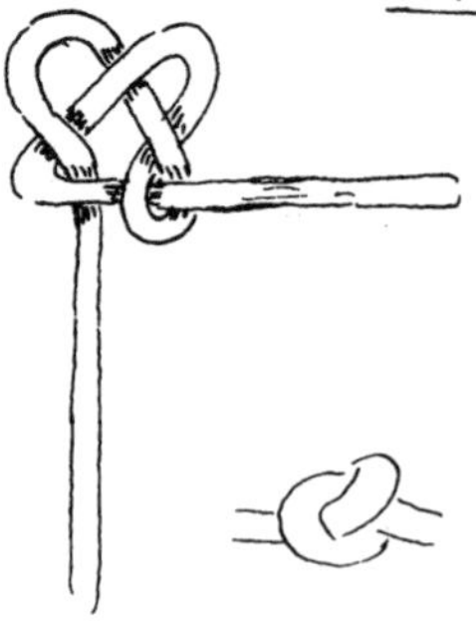

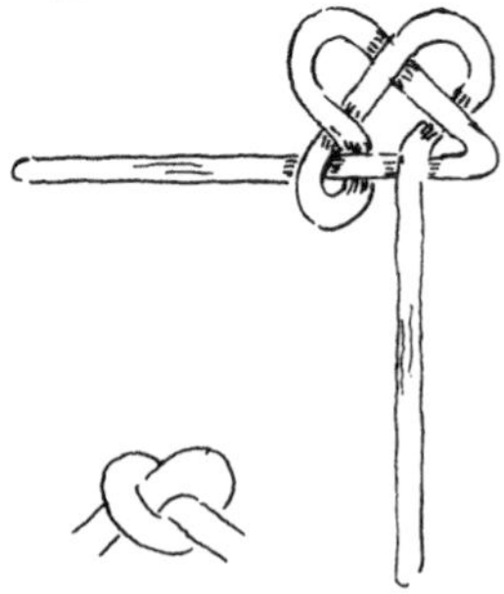

143

DOUBLE CARRICK

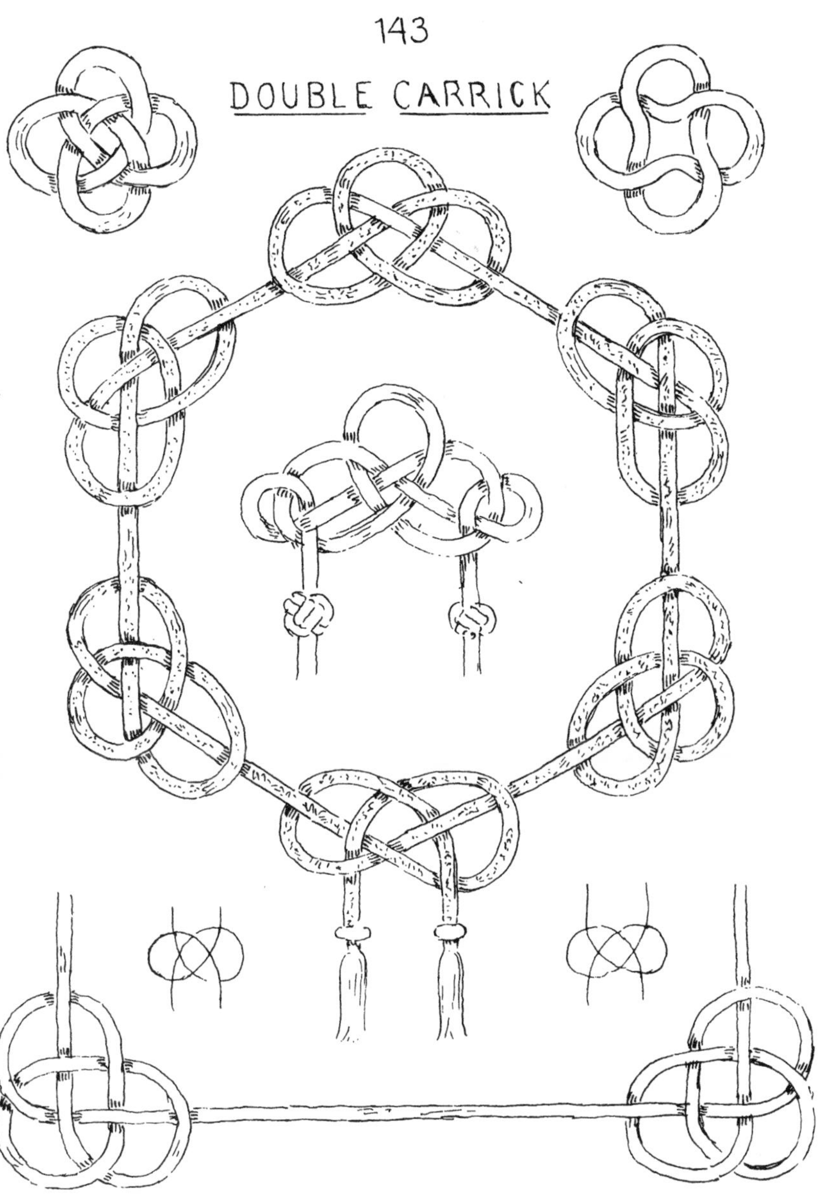

144

ORNAMENTAL KNOTS

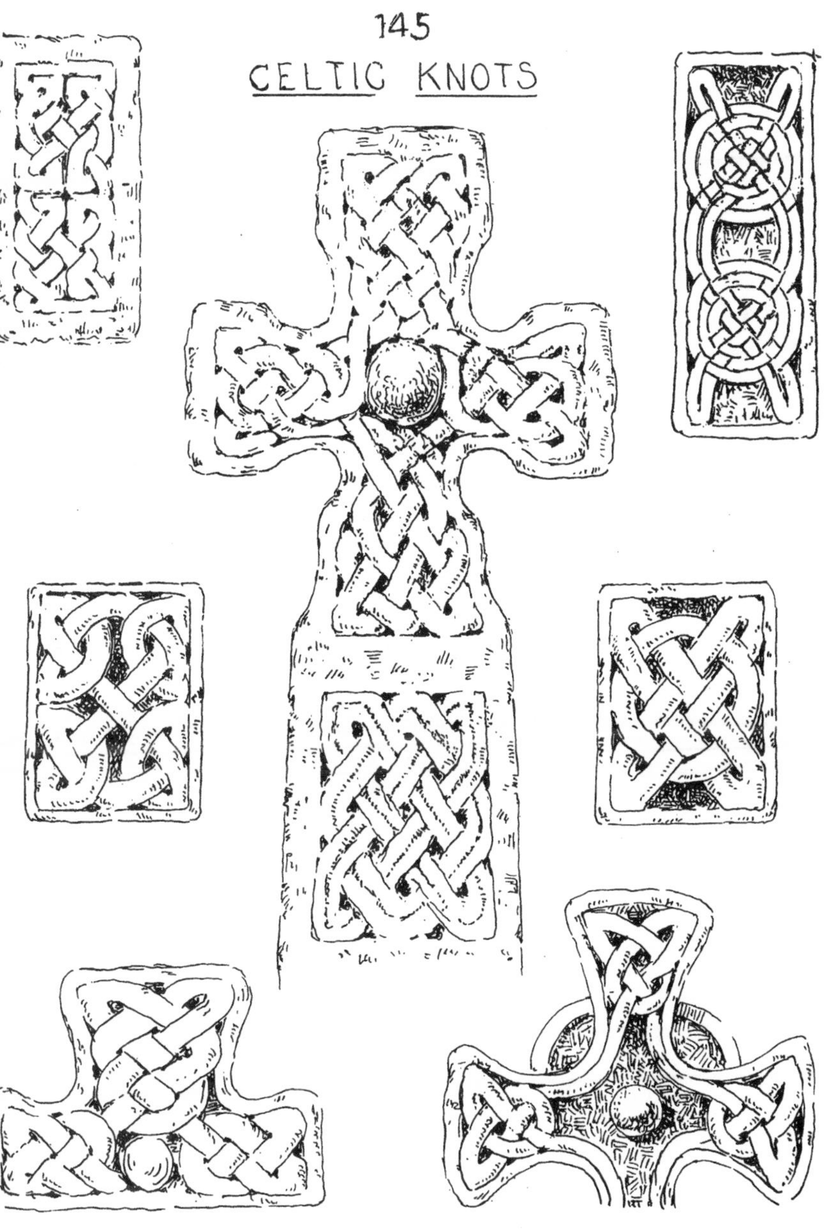
145
CELTIC KNOTS

CELTIC INTERLACINGS

Panels
II, III, IV & V
are modifications
of panel I
II
III
I
A
B
C
D
Fig. A
may be changed to B
or to
IV
V
Fig. C
can be changed to D

CELTIC KNOTS

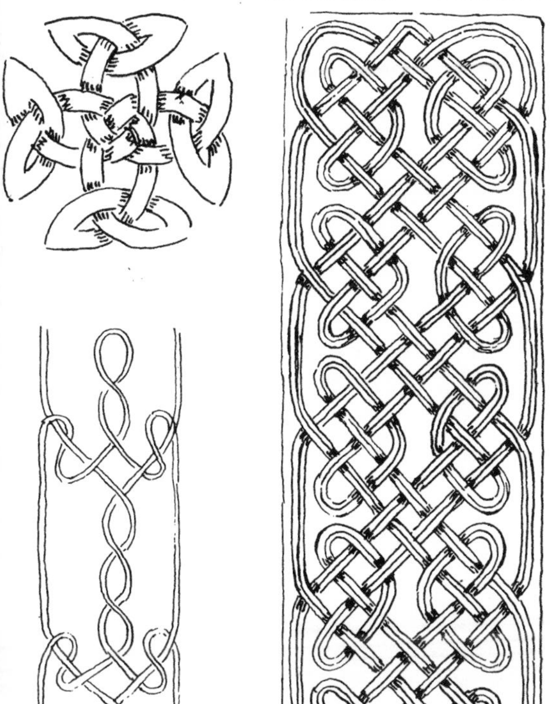

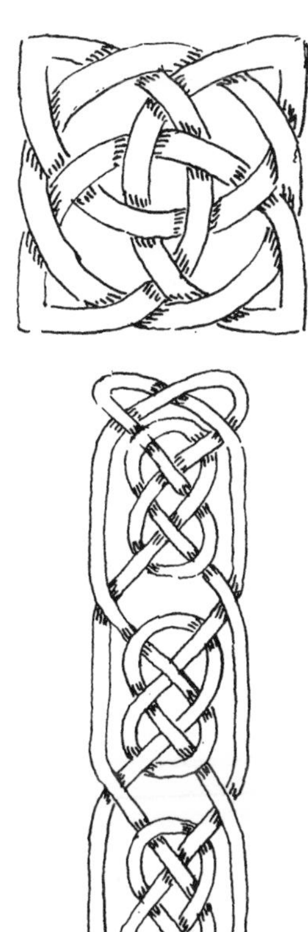

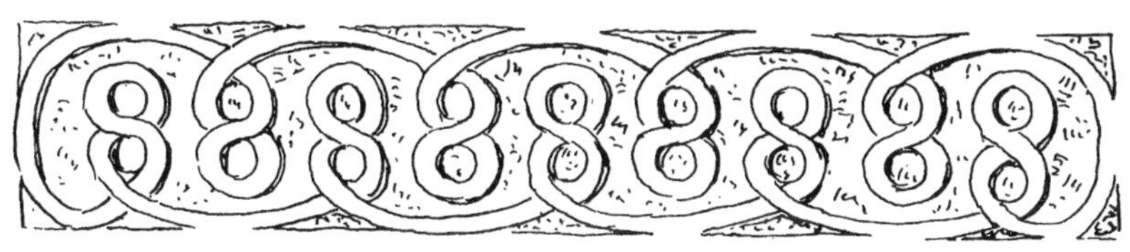

JAPANESE KNOTS

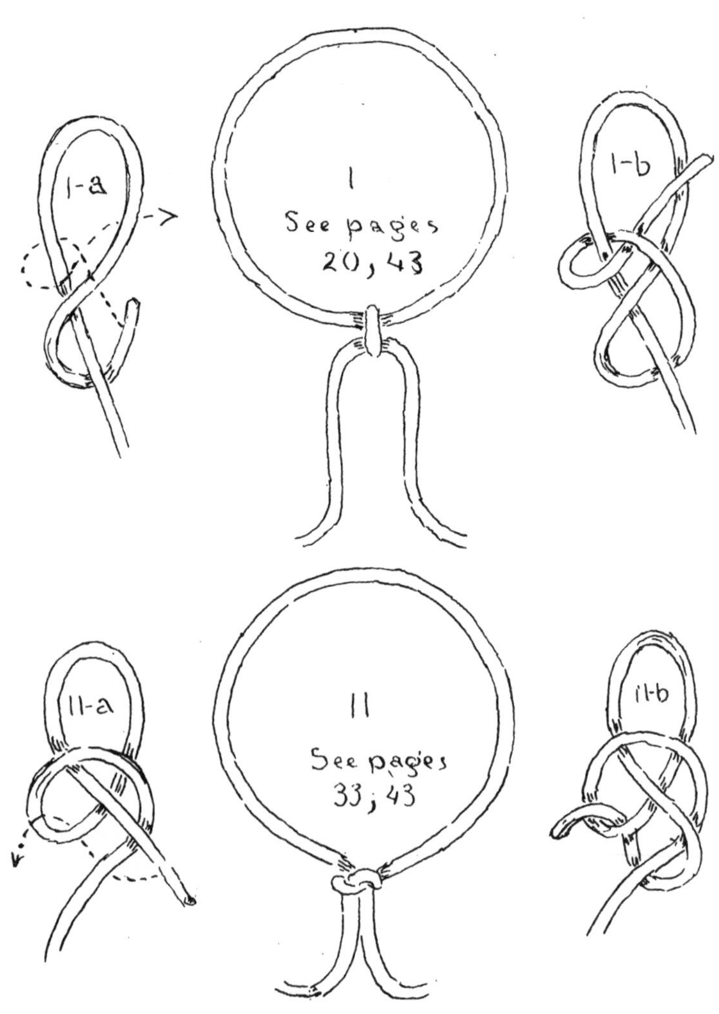

1-a
I
See pages
20, 43
1-b
II-a
II
See pages
33; 43
II-b

149 JAPANESE CROWN KNOT

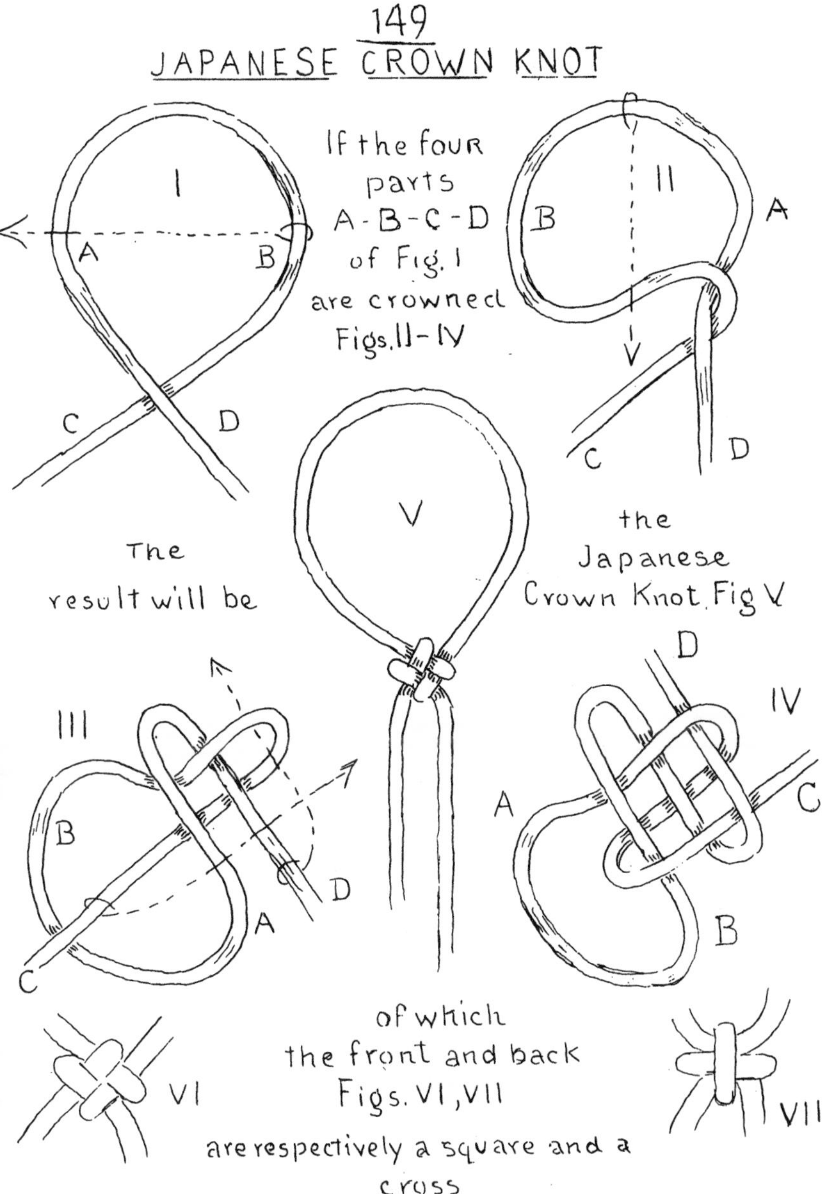

If the four parts A-B-C-D of Fig. I are crowned Figs. II-IV
I
A
B
C
D
II
B
A
C
D
The result will be
V
the Japanese Crown Knot. Fig V
III
B
A
C
D
D
IV
A
C
B
of which the front and back Figs. VI, VII
VI
VII
are respectively a square and a cross

150

ANOTHER METHOD

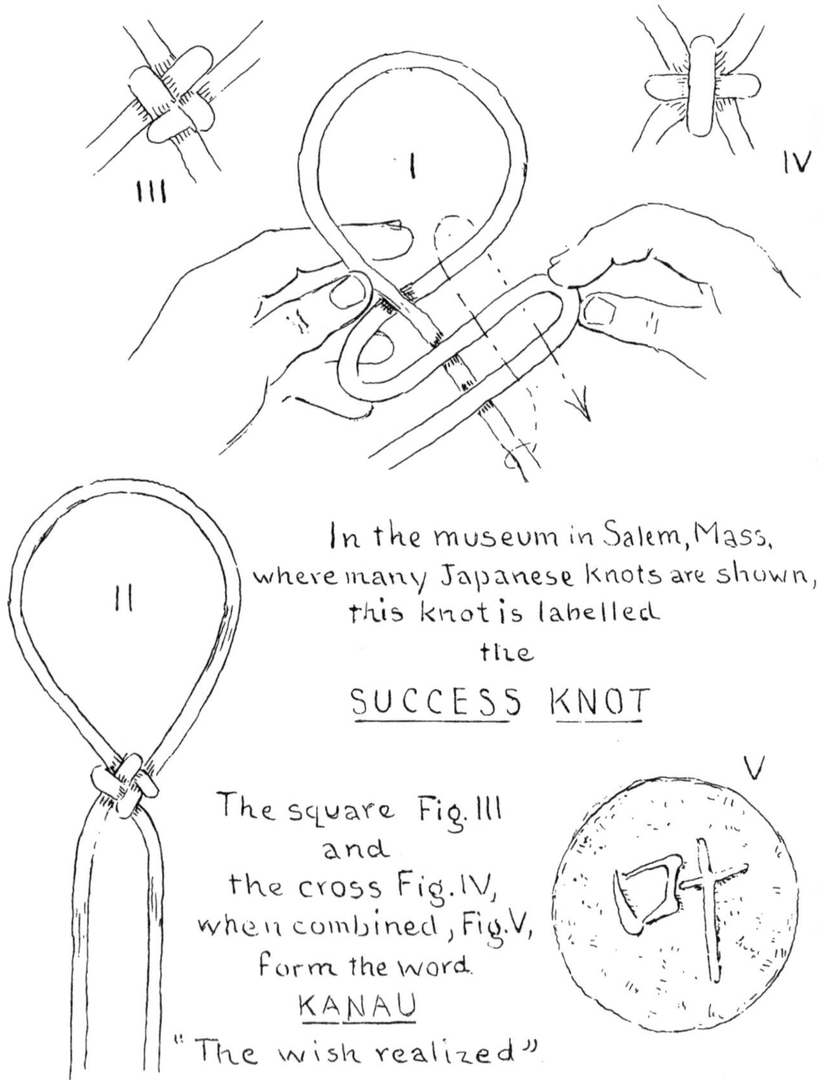
III
I
IV
II
In the museum in Salem, Mass.
where many Japanese knots are shown,
this knot is labelled
the
SUCCESS KNOT
V
The square Fig. III
and
the cross Fig. IV,
when combined, Fig. V,
form the word
KANAU
"The wish realized"

ANOTHER METHOD

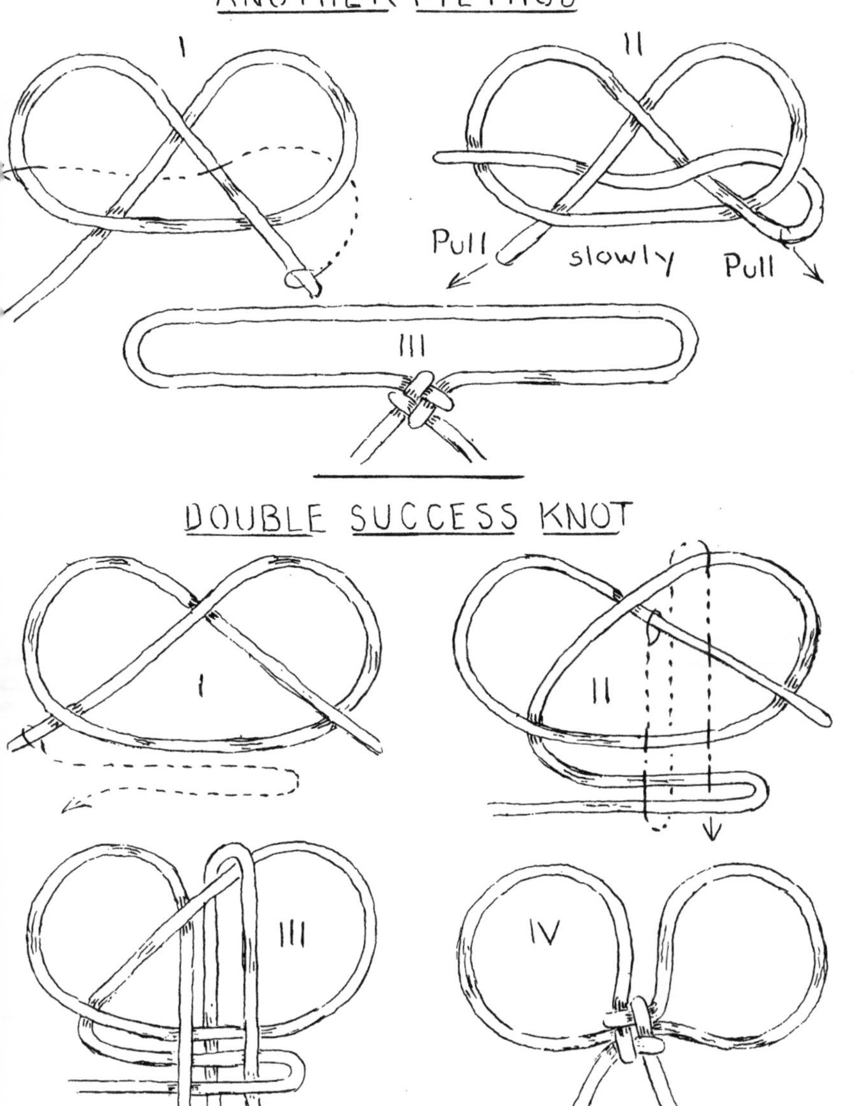
I
II
Pull
slowly
Pull
III
I
II
III
IV

DOUBLE SUCCESS KNOT

JAPANESE KNOTS

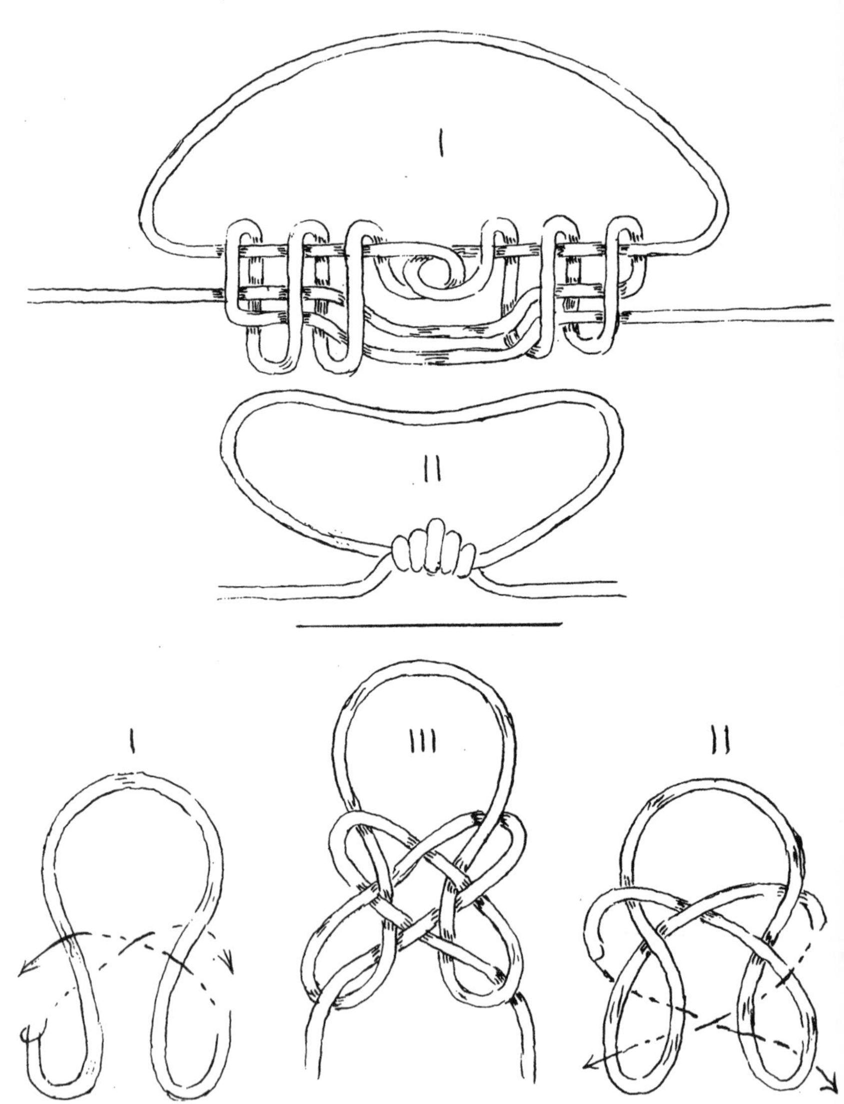
I
II
I
III
II

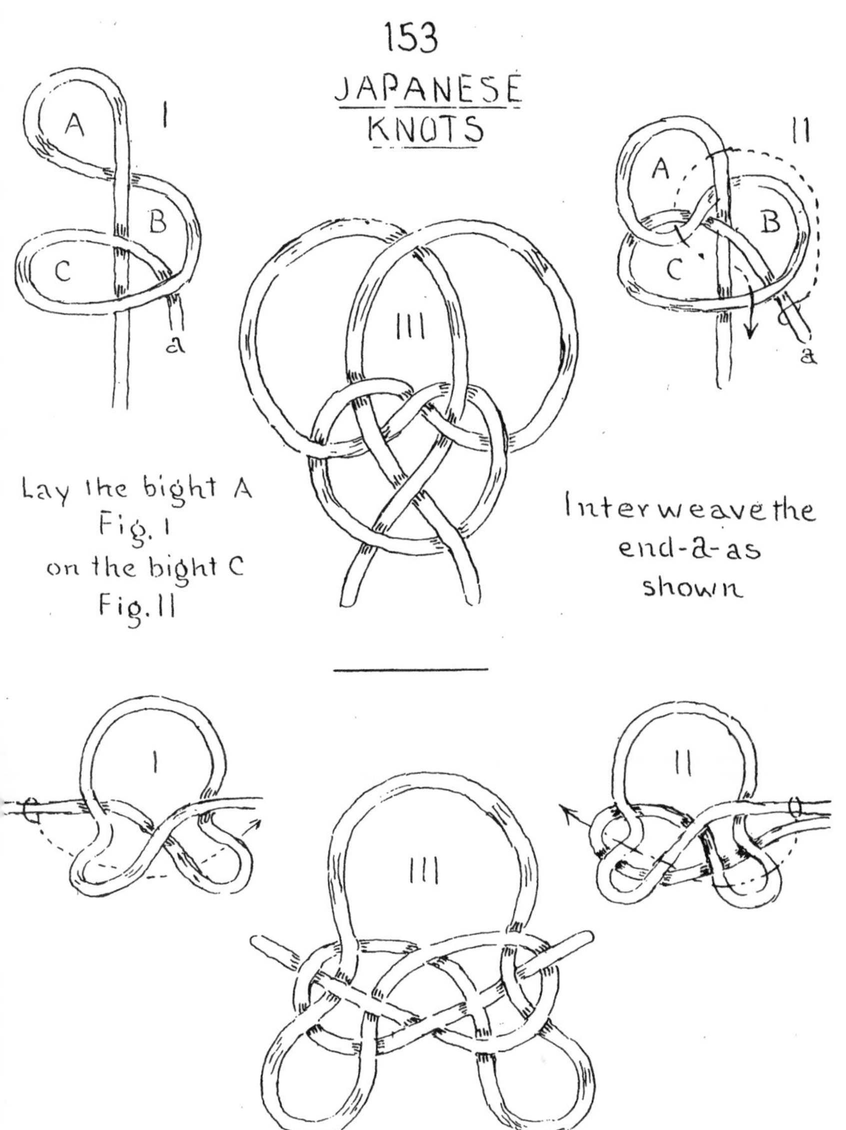
153
JAPANESE
KNOTS
I
A
B
C
a
II
A
B
C
a
III
Lay the bight A
Fig. I
on the bight C
Fig. II
Interweave the
end-a-as
shown
I
II
III

154
JAPANESE KNOTS

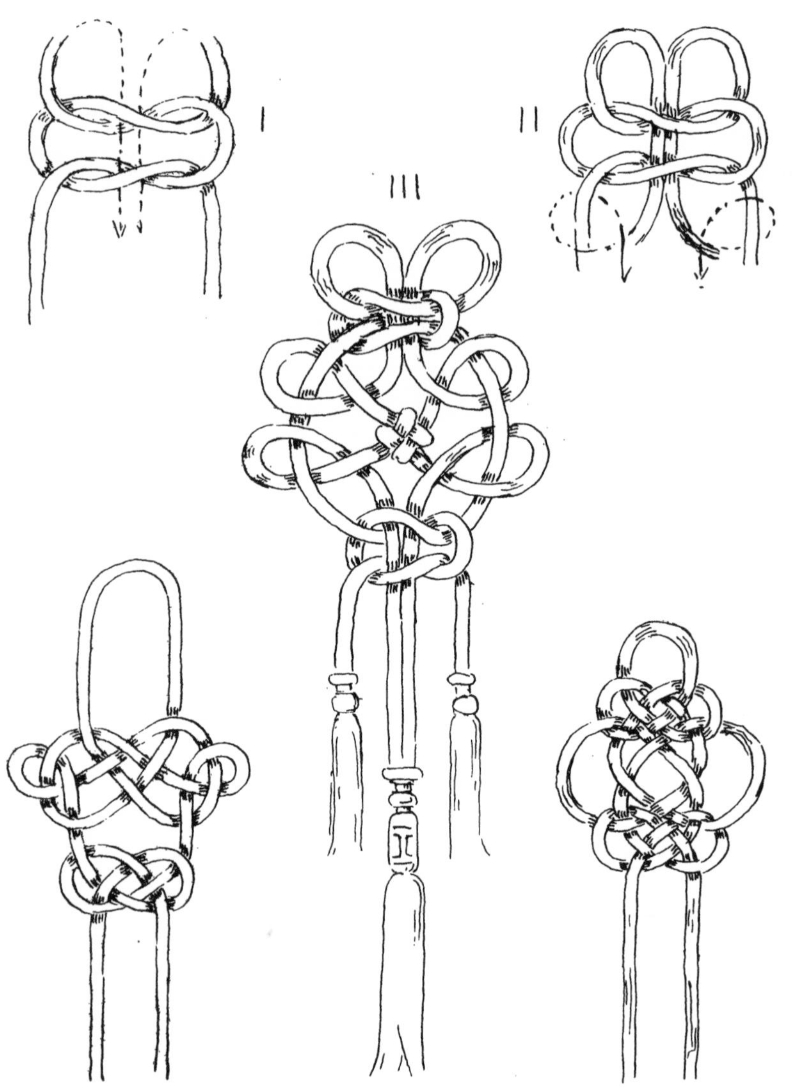

I
II
III

ORIENTAL KNOTS

Suggesting the outline of Flowers and of Insects &c

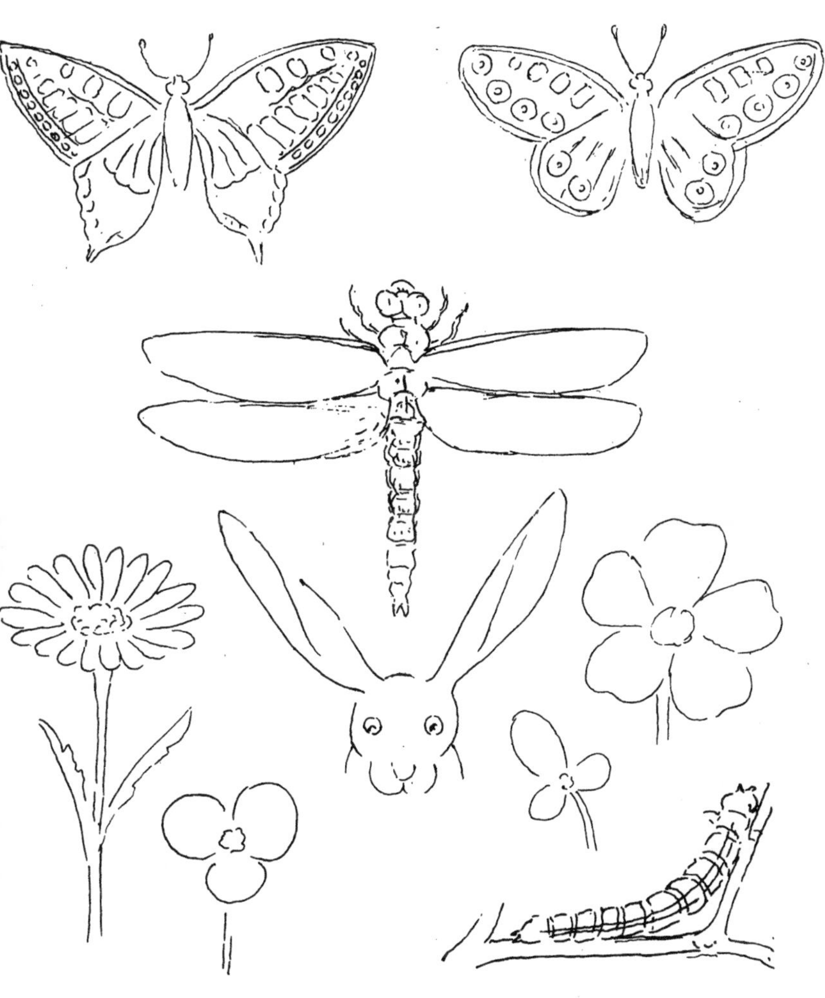

156 BUTTERFLY

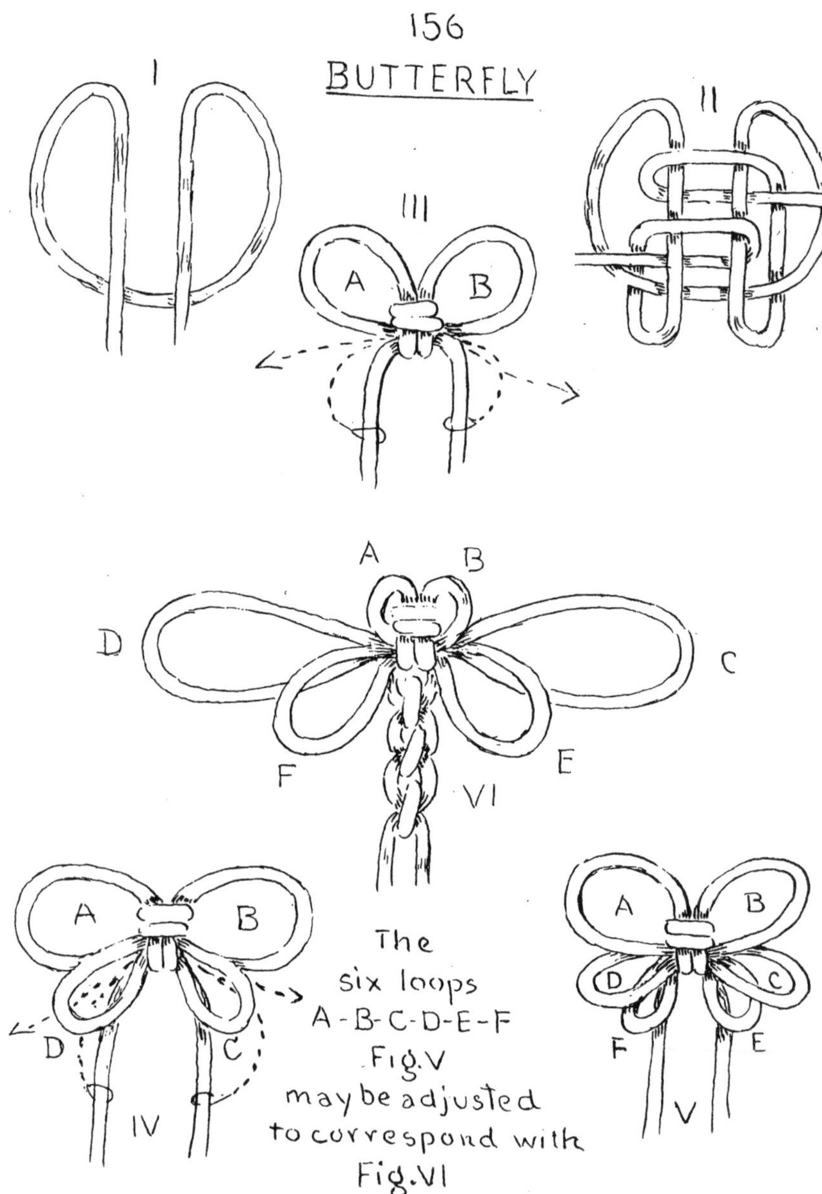
I
II
III
A
B
A
B
D
C
F
E
VI
A
B
D
C
IV
The six loops A-B-C-D-E-F Fig.V may be adjusted to correspond with Fig.VI
A
B
D
C
F
E
V

BUTTERFLY

Fig I-a
The Double-triangular Knot, page 171.
Its parts may be adjusted
to form Fig I-b

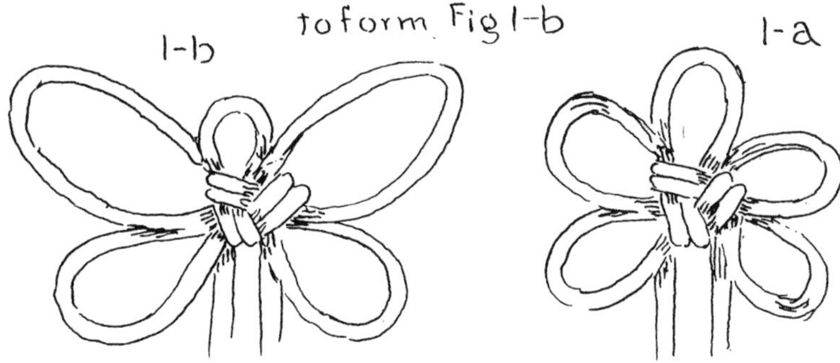
I-b
I-a

Fig. II-a
The Hexagonal Knot, page 176.
Its. parts may also be adjusted
to form
a Butterfly Knot

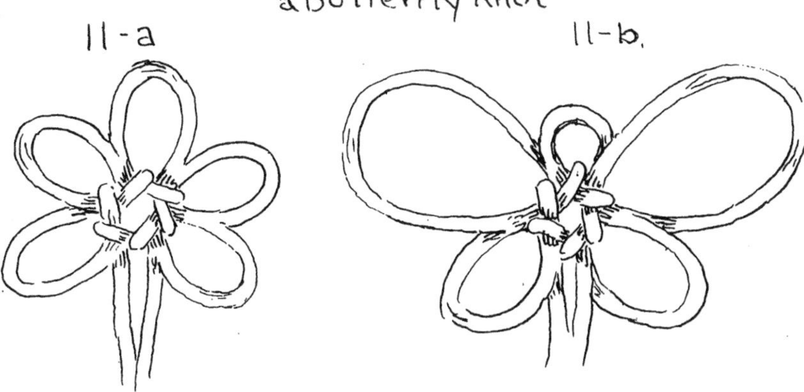
II-a
II-b.

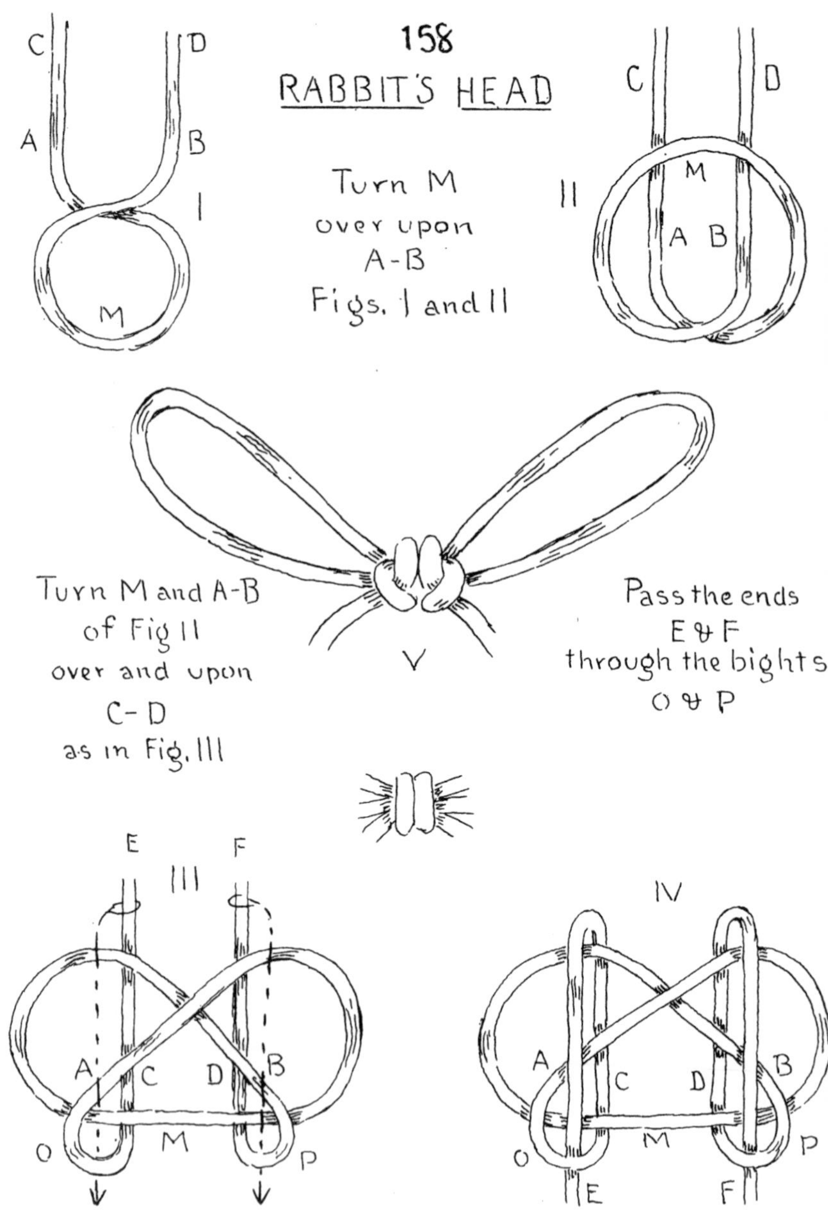
158
RABBIT'S HEAD
Turn M over upon A-B Figs. I and II
Turn M and A-B of Fig II over and upon C-D as in Fig. III
Pass the ends E & F through the bights O & P
C
D
A
B
I
M
II
C
D
M
A B
V
III
E
F
A
C
D
B
O
M
P
IV
A
C
D
B
O
M
P
E
F

THE DRAGON FLY

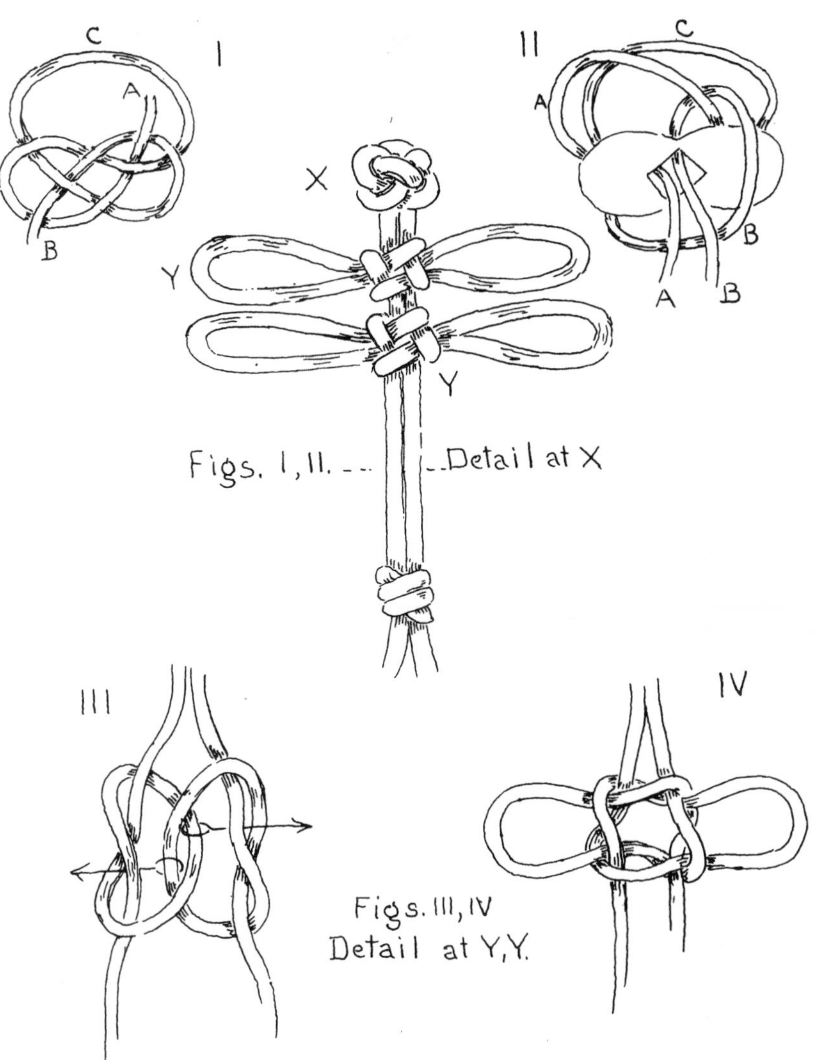
C
I
A
B
II
C
A
B
A
B
X
Y
Y
III
IV

Figs. I, II. ---Detail at X

Figs. III, IV
Detail at Y, Y.

INSECT

In the Museum in Salem Mass. are two Japanese Knots with the label "Insect"

I

One of them, Fig I, is a three-strand Sennit, page 72 and probably represents an

EARTHWORM

III

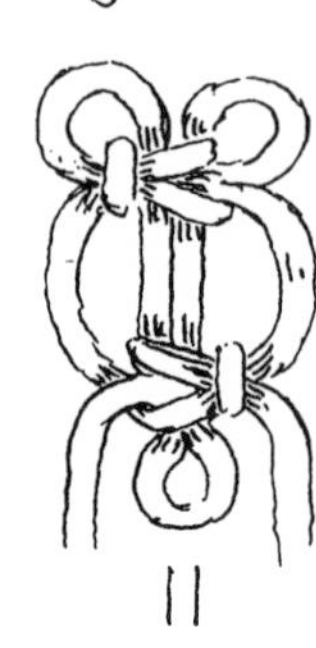

II

The other, Fig. II, is a combination of two Macrame' Square Knots, see page 128, and may possibly represent a

BEETLE

IV

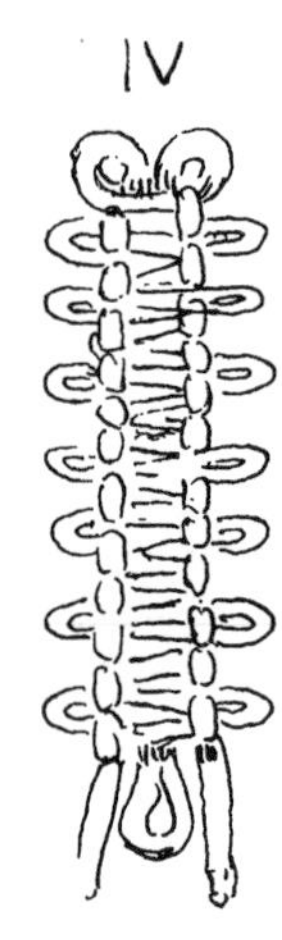

Fig. II suggests a method for tying a

CATERPILLAR

Fig. III is a series of Square Knots & spaces around two idle lines on which the knots are free to run. By sliding the Knots together, Fig. IV is the result

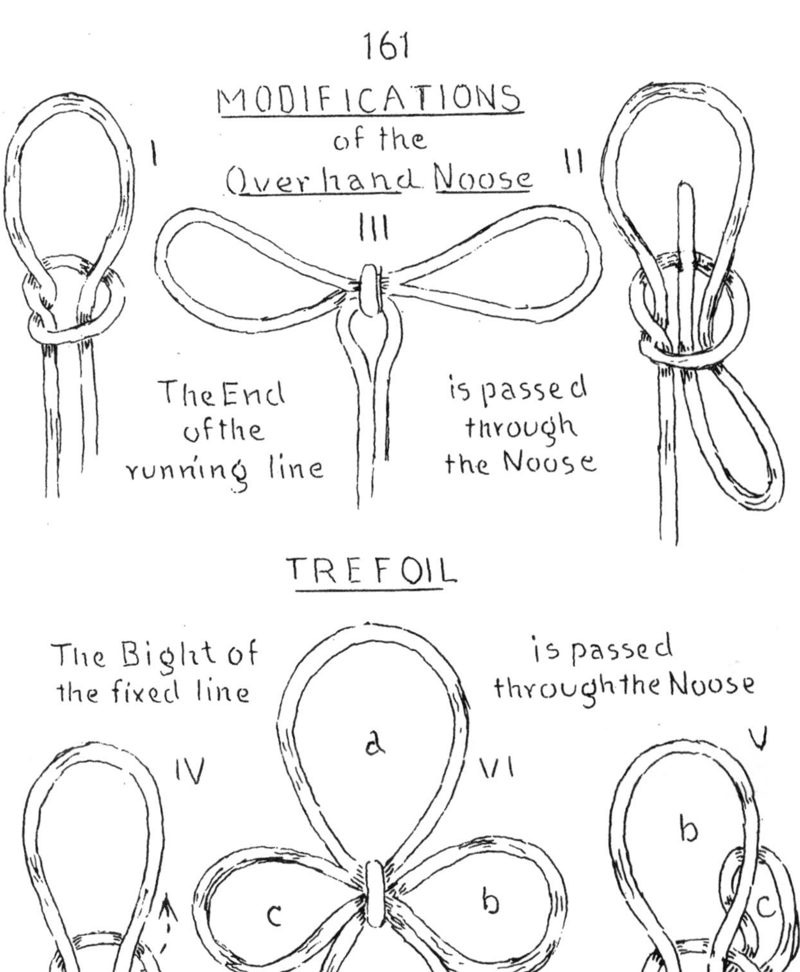
MODIFICATIONS
of the
Overhand Noose
I
II
III
The End
of the
running line
is passed
through
the Noose
TREFOIL
The Bight of
the fixed line
is passed
through the Noose
IV
VI
V
a
b
c
b
c
a

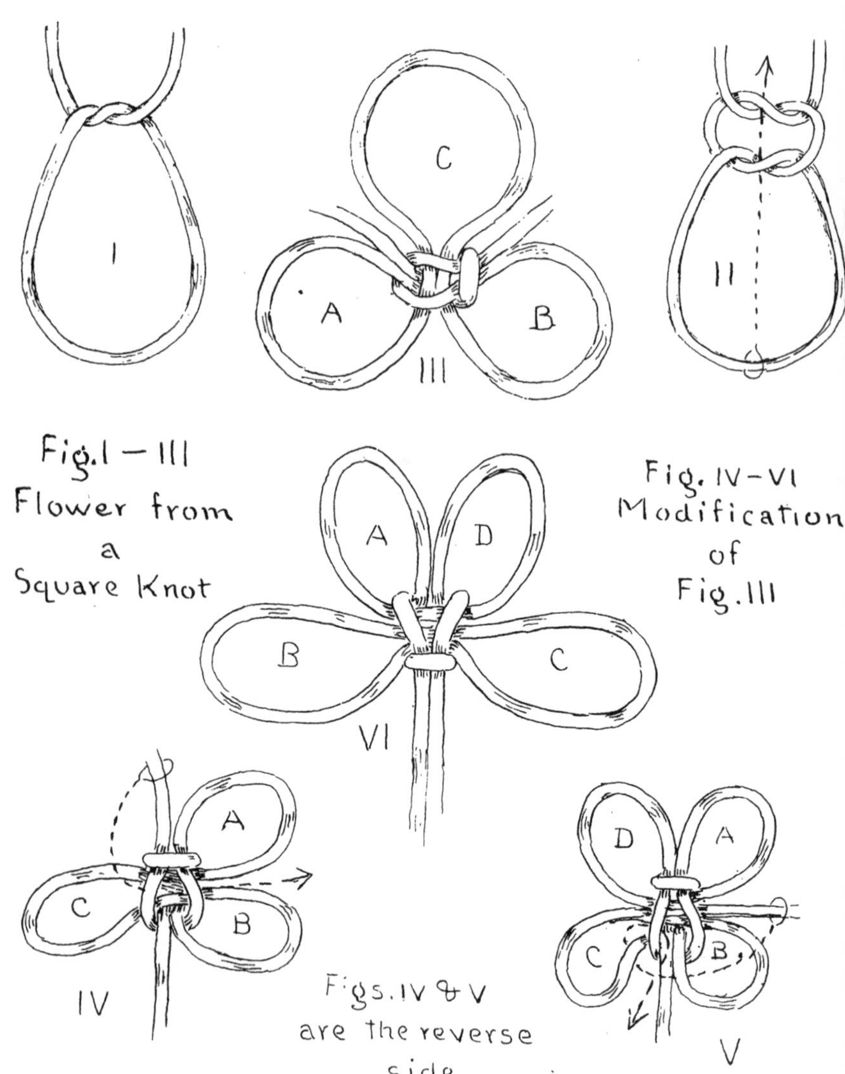
C
I
A
B
III
II
A
D
B
C
VI
A
C
B
IV
D
A
C
B
V

Fig. I – III
Flower from
a
Square Knot

Fig. IV – VI
Modification
of
Fig. III

Figs. IV & V
are the reverse
side

FLOWER KNOT

A
D
B
C

Fig. I
Position
of
the strands

C
II
D
B
A

Fig. II
Crowning
the
four parts

Another Method
V

Fig. III
Flower
of
three petals

Fig. IV
Reverse side
of
Fig. II

III

For Flowers
of
seven & Eleven
petals
see
next two pages

A
D
IV
B
C

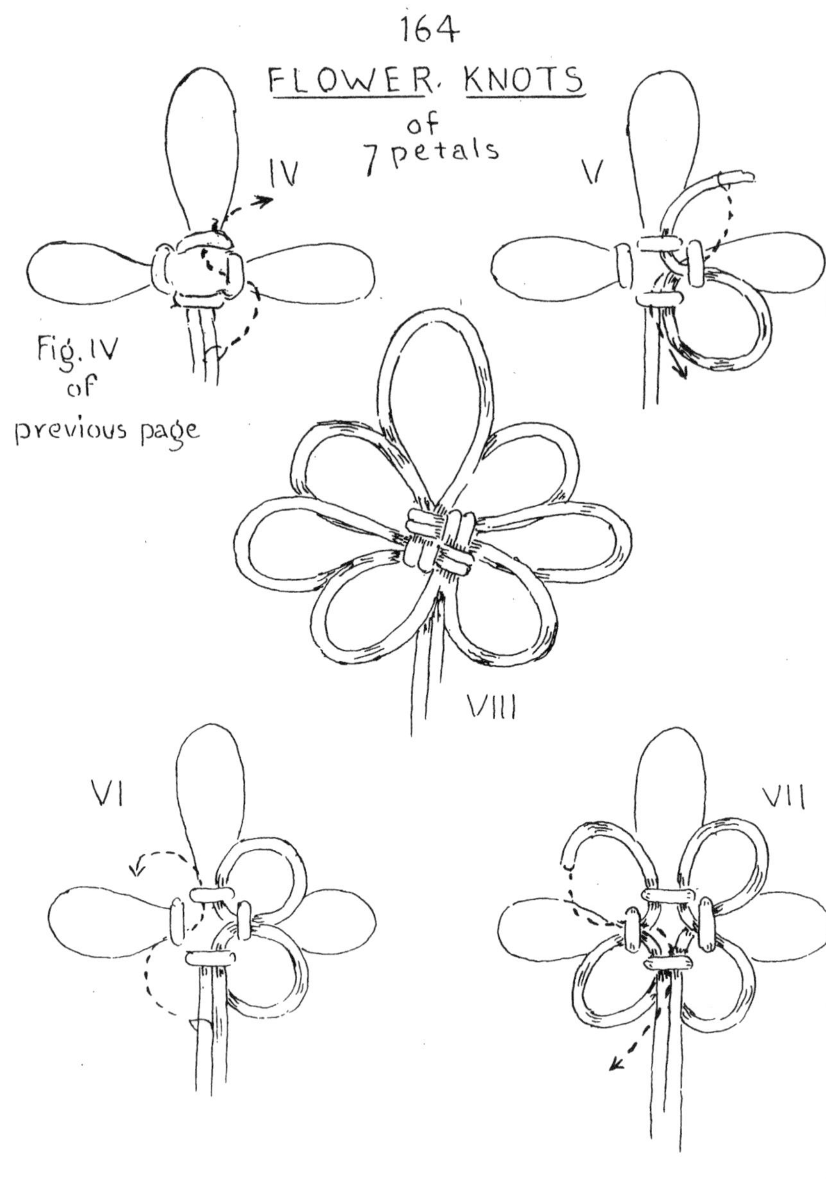
164
FLOWER KNOTS
of
7 petals
IV
V
Fig. IV
of
previous page
VIII
VI
VII

165

CHRYSANTHEMUM

of
eleven petals

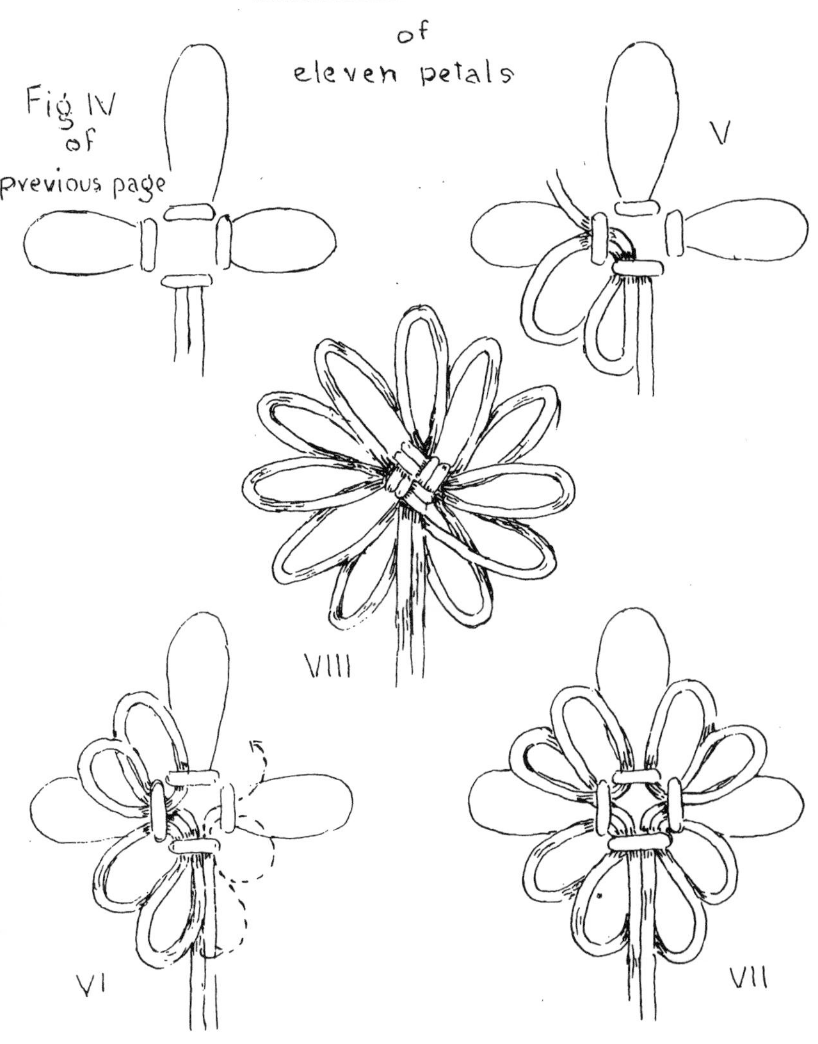

Fig IV
of
previous page
V
VIII
VI
VII

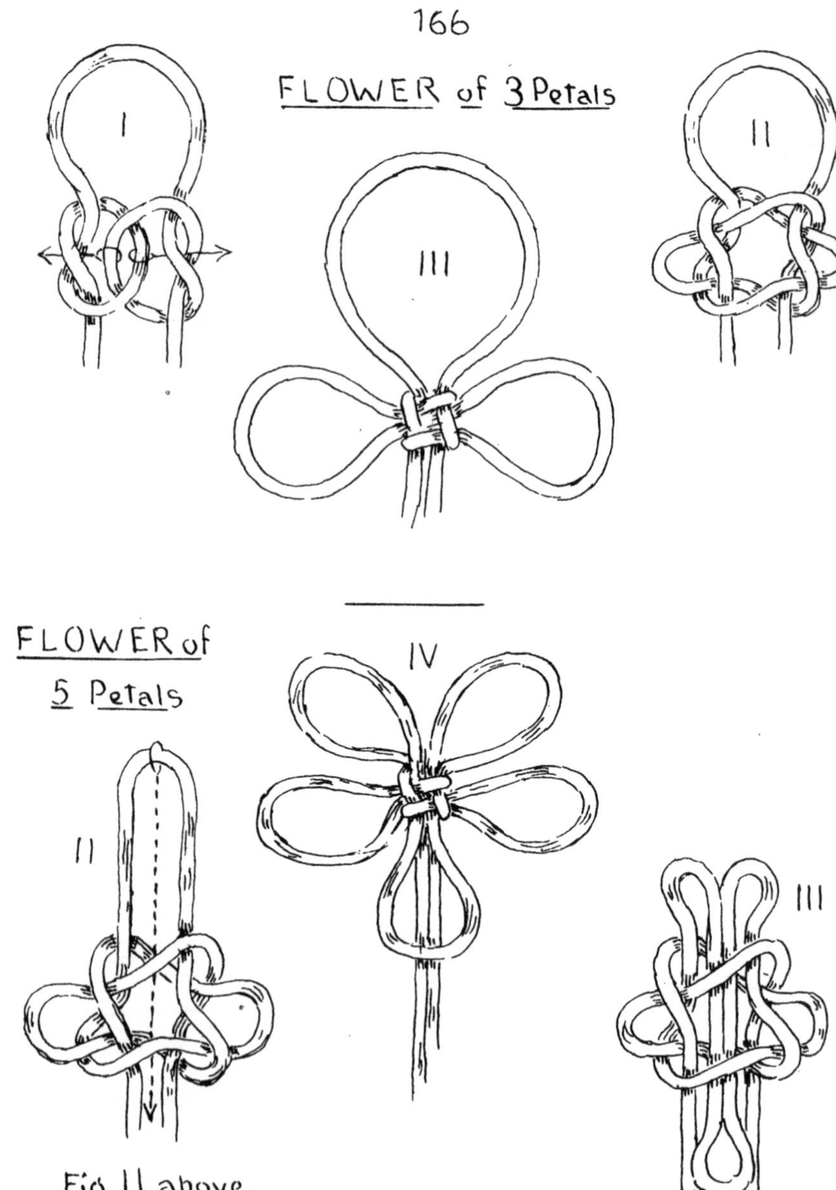
FLOWER of 3 Petals
I
II
III
FLOWER of 5 Petals
IV
II
III
Fig II above

167

FLOWER OF THE PLUM

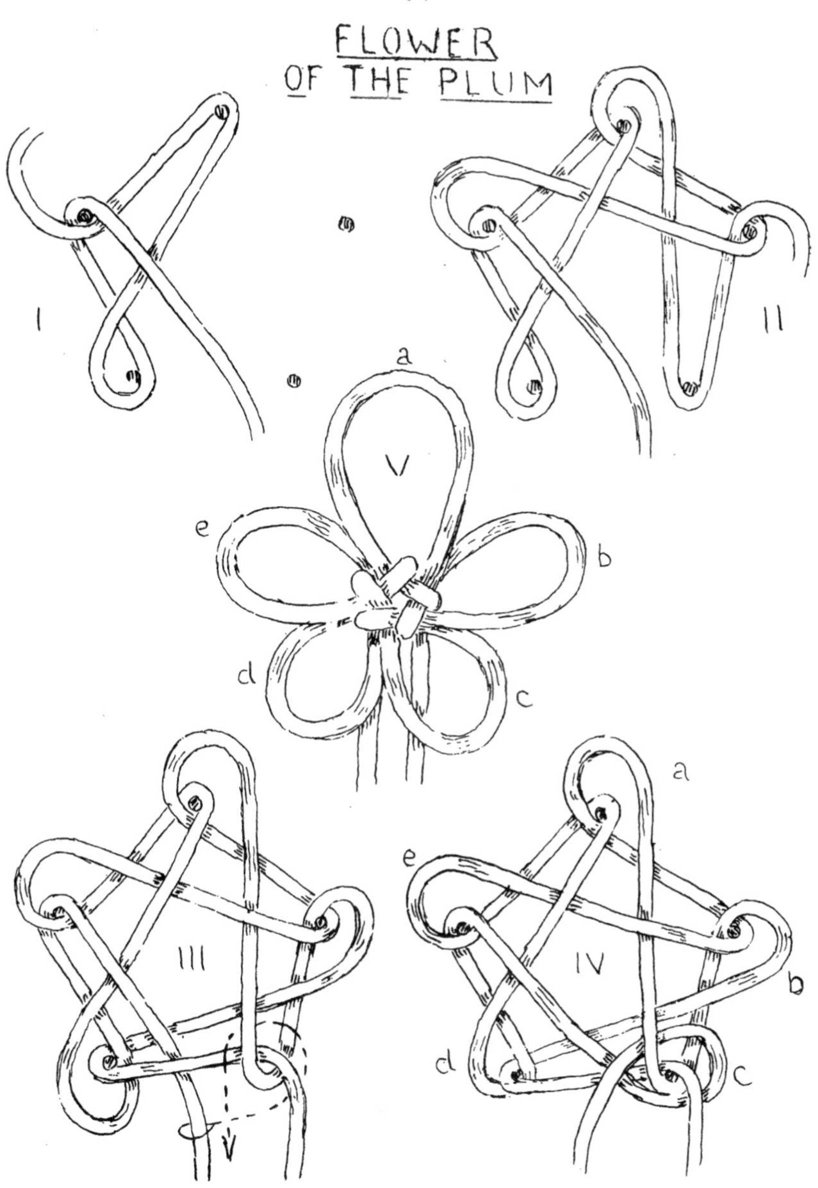

I
II
V
a
b
c
d
e
III
IV
a
b
c
d
e

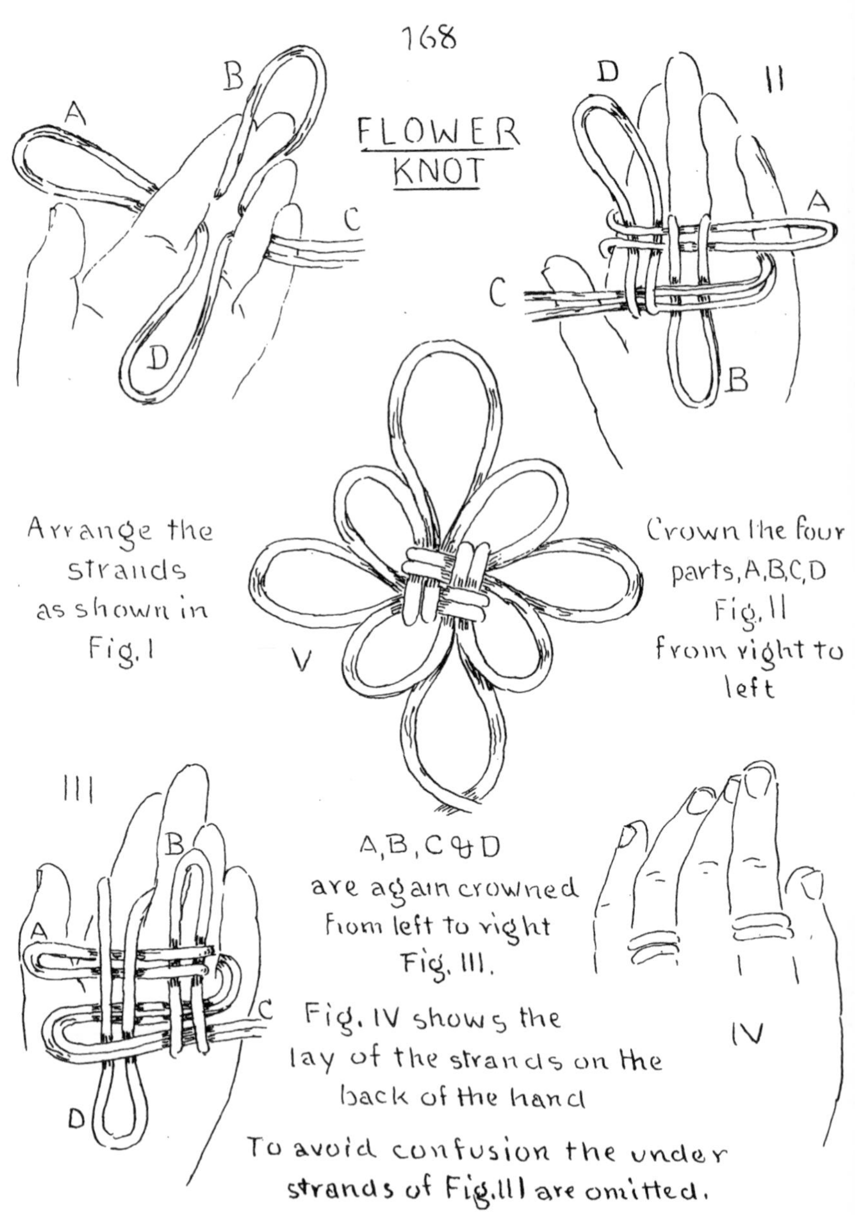
FLOWER KNOT
A
B
C
D
II
D
A
C
B
Arrange the strands as shown in Fig. I
V
Crown the four parts, A,B,C,D Fig. II from right to left
III
B
A
C
D
A,B,C & D are again crowned from left to right Fig. III.
IV
Fig. IV shows the lay of the strands on the back of the hand
To avoid confusion the under strands of Fig. III are omitted.

169

POLYGONAL KNOTS

These Knots are probably of Chinese origin
They may be tied with the aid of pins placed at the angles of a triangle, square, pentagon or other regular polygon

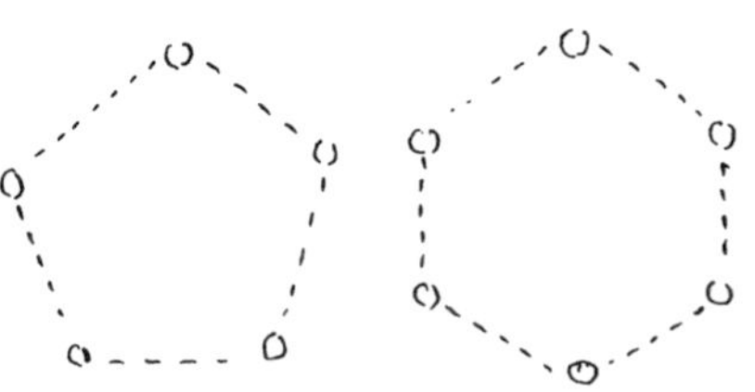

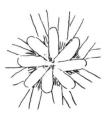

The radiating strands at the center of the knot are double.
There is a top and bottom layer which are alike

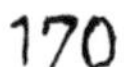
170

TRIANGULAR KNOT

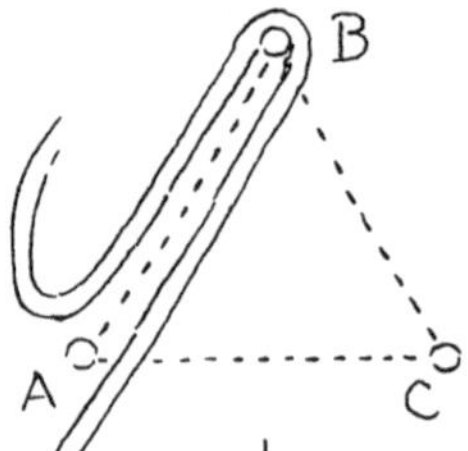

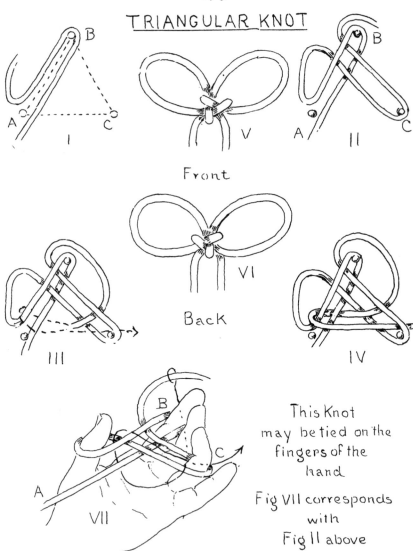

A B C

I

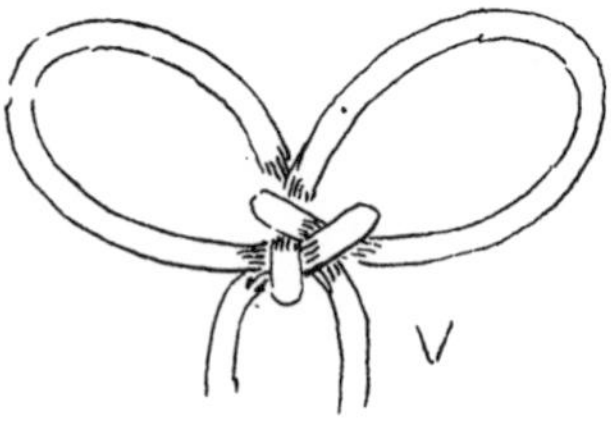

V

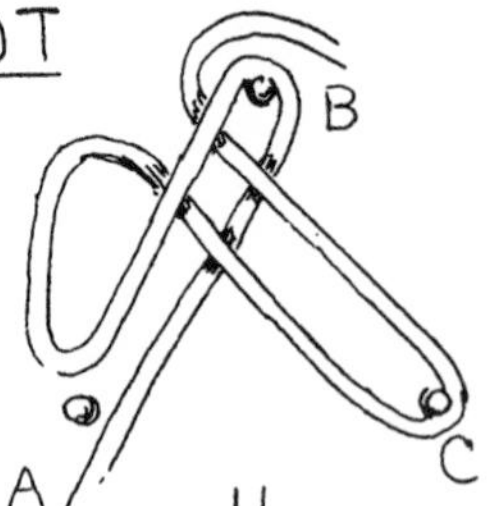

A B C

II

Front

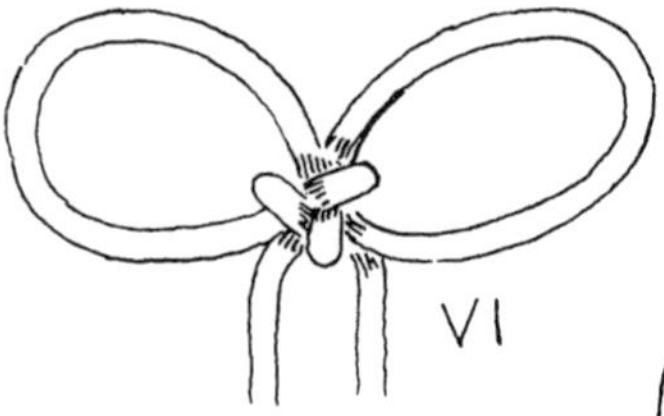

VI

Back

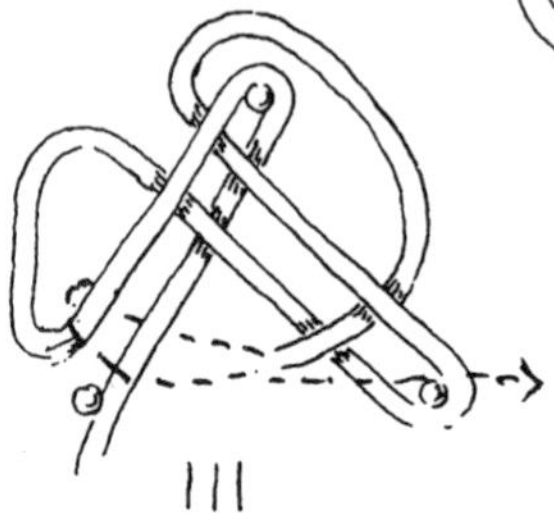

III

IV

B

A C

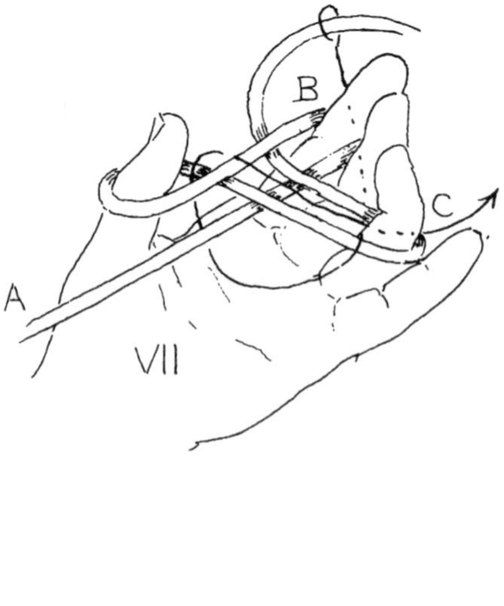

VII

This Knot may be tied on the fingers of the hand

Fig VII corresponds with Fig II above

171

DOUBLE TRIANGULAR KNOT

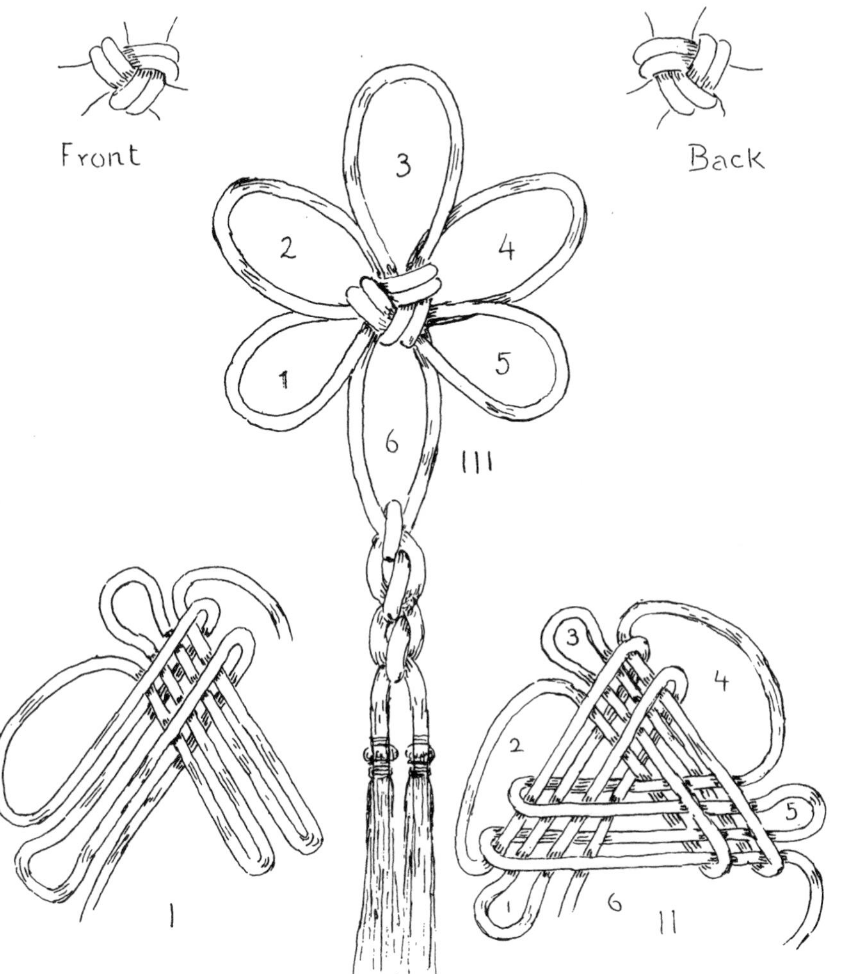
Front
Back
3
2
4
1
5
6
III
3
4
2
5
1
6
I
II

SINGLE QUADRANGULAR-KNOT

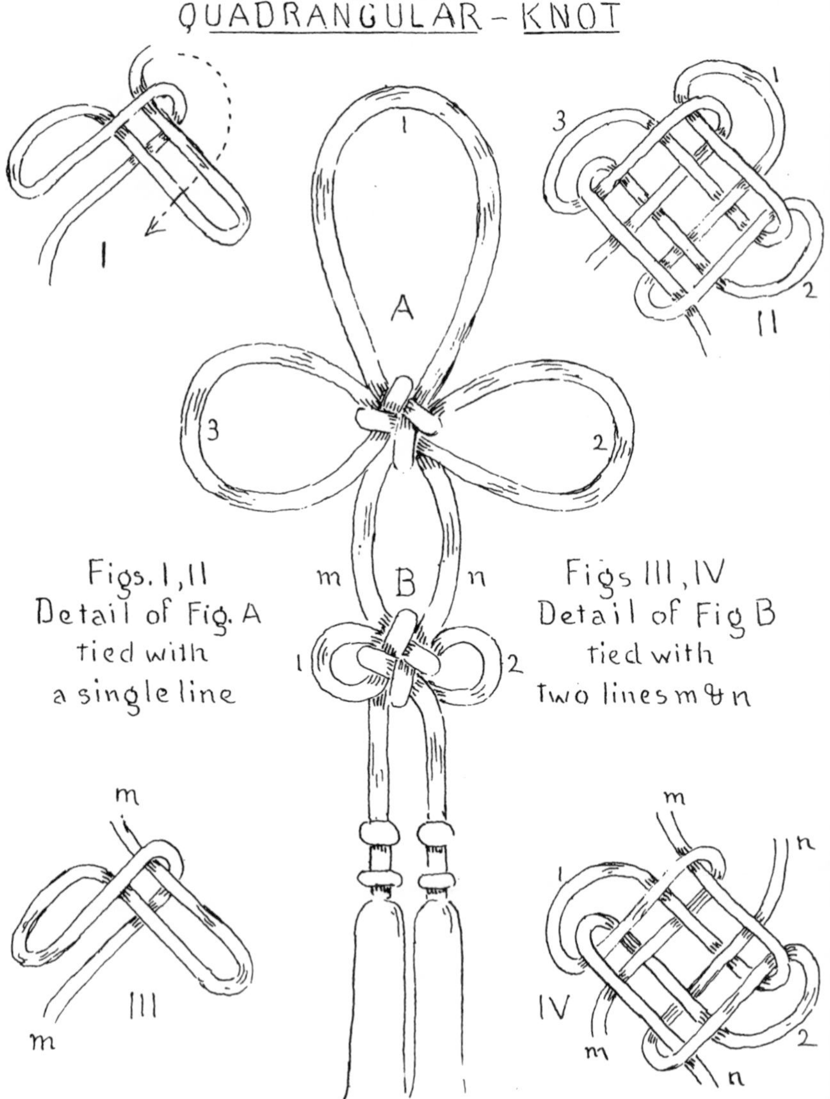
I
II
A
B
1
2
3
m
n
III
IV
Figs. I, II
Detail of Fig. A
tied with
a single line
Figs III, IV
Detail of Fig B
tied with
two lines m & n

173
DOUBLE QUADRANGULAR-KNOT

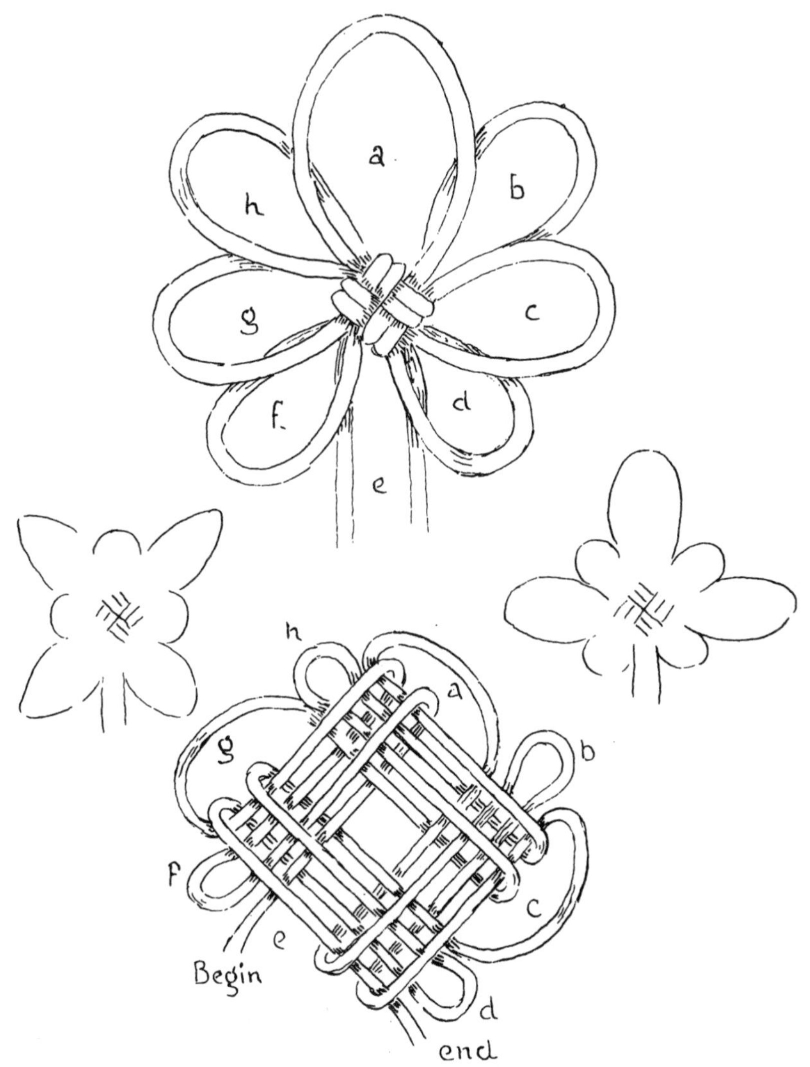

a
b
c
d
e
f
g
h
h
a
b
g
f
c
e
Begin
d
end

174

TRIPLE QUADRANGULAR-KNOT

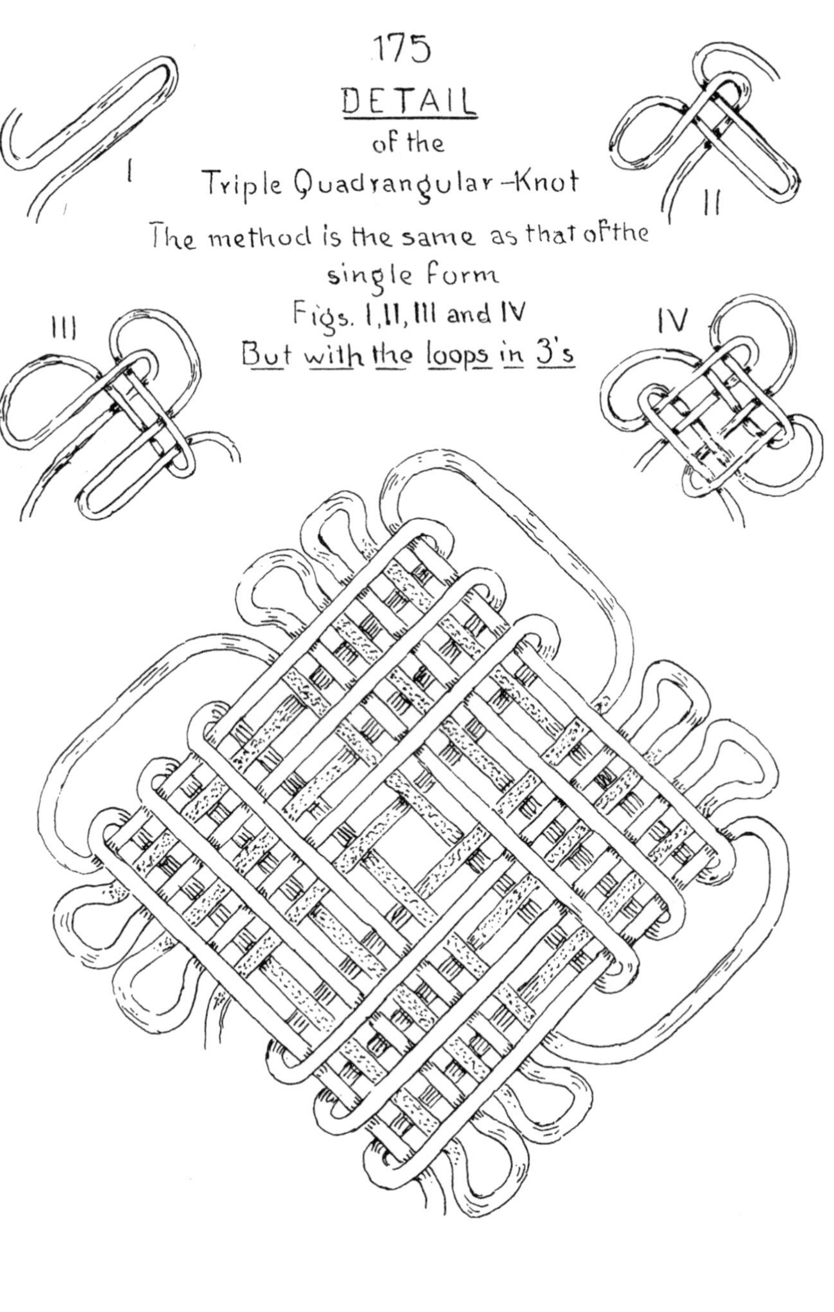
175
DETAIL
of the
Triple Quadrangular-Knot
The method is the same as that of the
single form
Figs. I, II, III and IV
But with the loops in 3's
I
II
III
IV

176

HEXAGONAL KNOT

Each Bight passes through 2 Loops

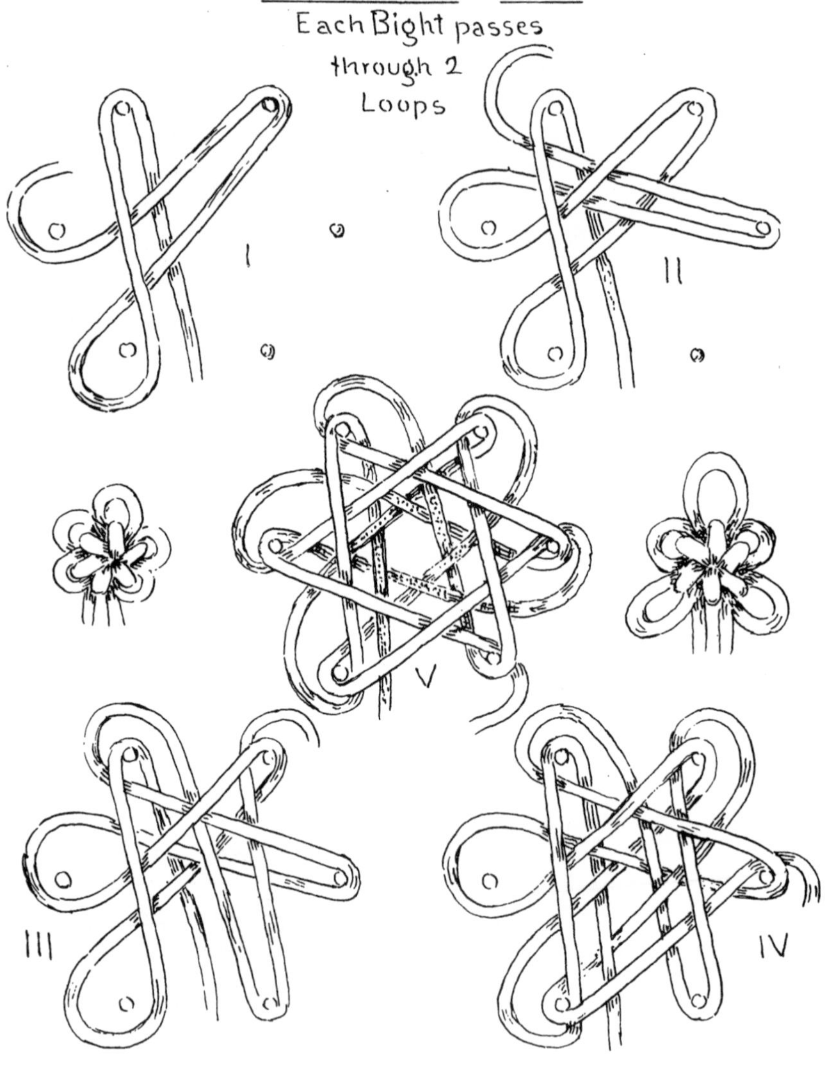
I
II
V
III
IV

177

OCTAGONAL KNOT

where
each Bight passes
through 2
Loops

I
II
III
IV

DECAGONAL KNOT

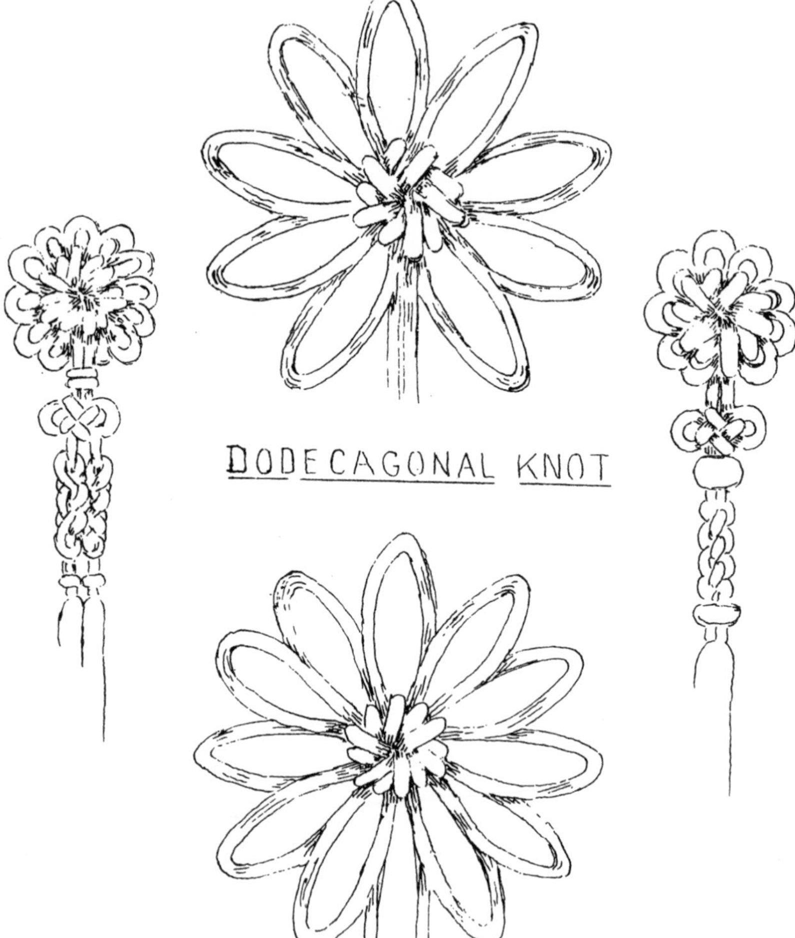
DODECAGONAL KNOT

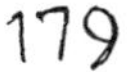
179

DECAGONAL KNOT

Detail

Each Bight passes through 3 Loops

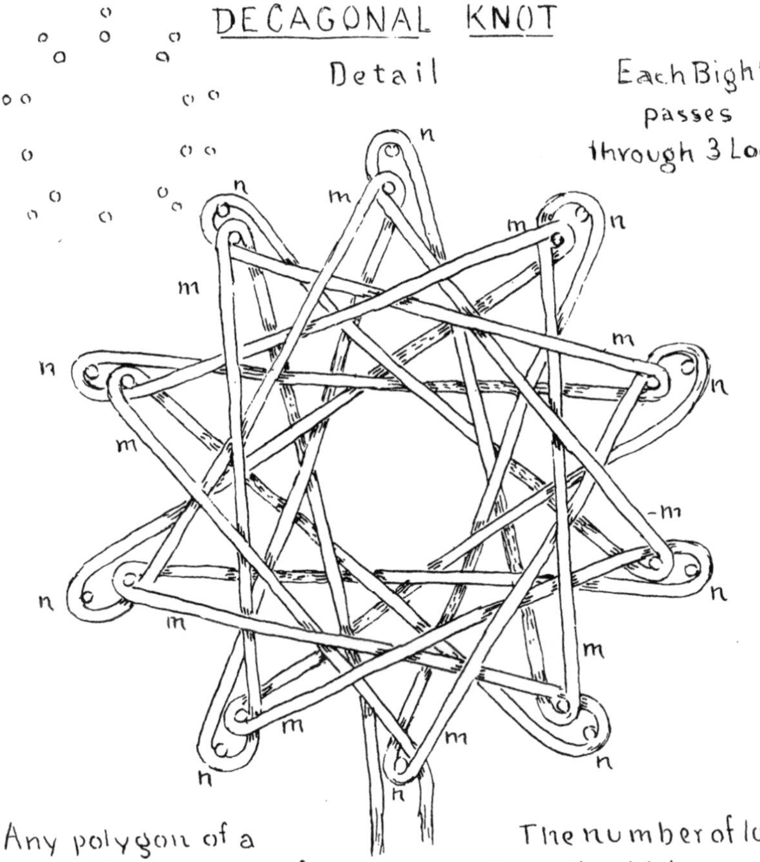

Any polygon of a convenient number of angles may serve as a foundation for this Knot

The number of loops through which each bight passes must be less than one half the number of angles

In adjusting the knot release all the bights m, m, m, - - -

pull gradually and equally all the bights n, n, n, - - -

180

CHINESE TASSEL

DOUBLE INTERLACING

These Knots (probably Chinese) are based on the Quadrangular Knot page 172

I

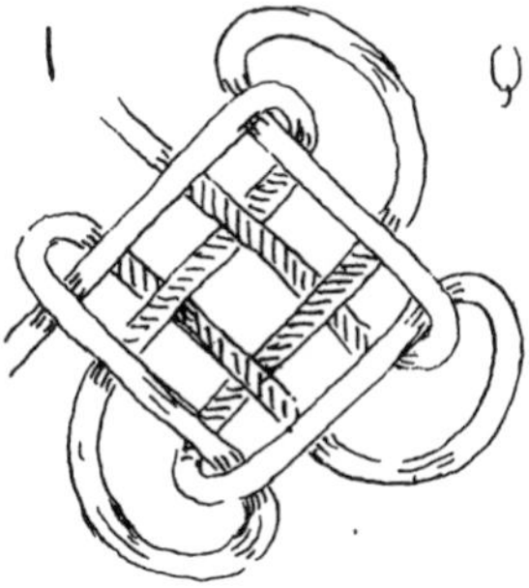

II

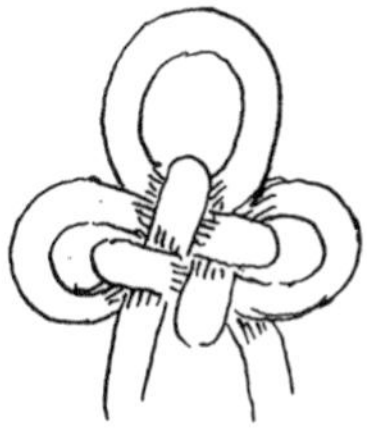

Fig. I shows the upper and lower strands, the lower strands shaded

The number of strands in each layer may vary from two to four, six or any convenient even number

In the process of tying the knot, elaborations may be introduced in which the Carrick Bend appears, pages 185, 186, 188

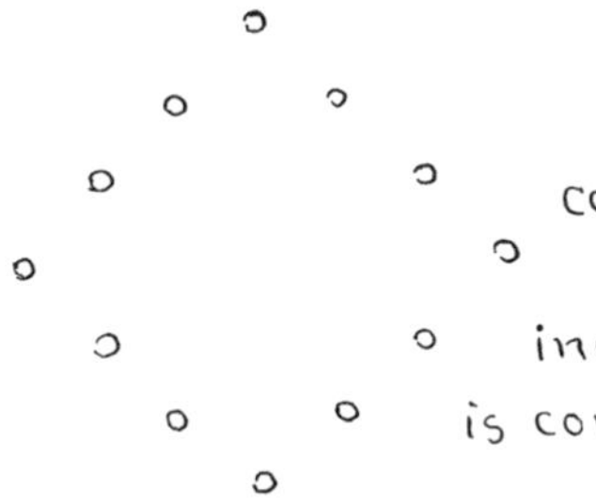

A diagram with pins, that correspond with the number of strands, is necessary, also pins to hold the strands in place as the work progresses

A cork board 6 or 8 inches square is convenient for this and other intricate Knots

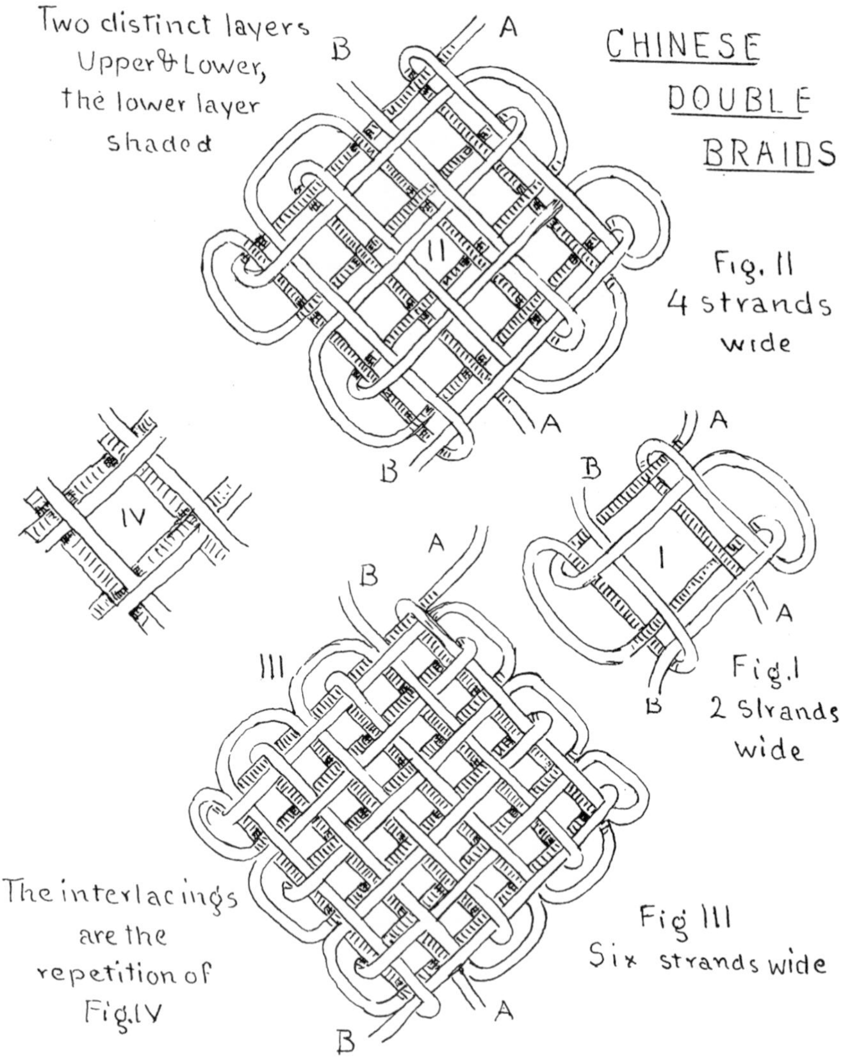
Two distinct layers
Upper & Lower,
the lower layer
shaded
CHINESE
DOUBLE
BRAIDS
A
B
II
A
B
Fig. II
4 strands
wide
IV
A
B
I
A
B
Fig. I
2 Strands
wide
A
B
III
The interlacings
are the
repetition of
Fig. IV
Fig III
Six strands wide
A
B

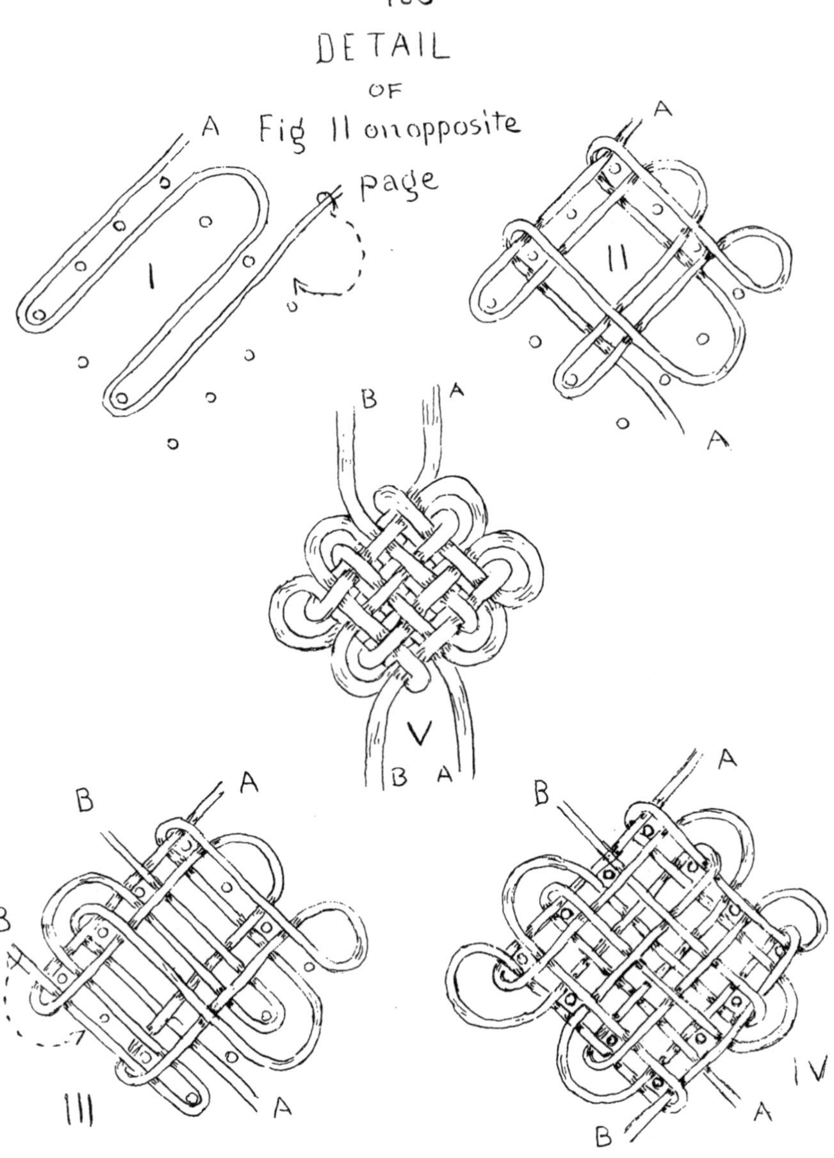

DETAIL
OF
Fig II on opposite
page
A
I
A
II
A
B
A
V
B
A
B
A
B
III
A
B
A
B
IV
A
B

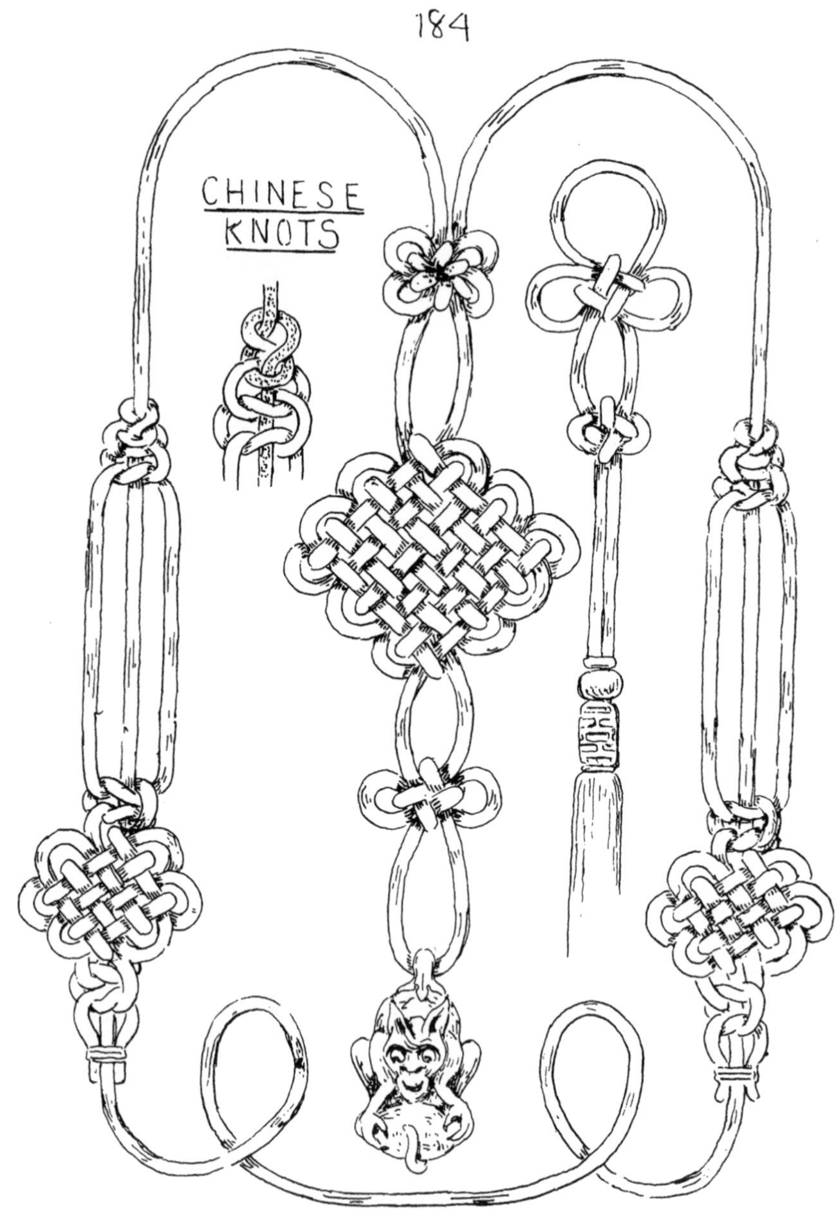
CHINESE
KNOTS

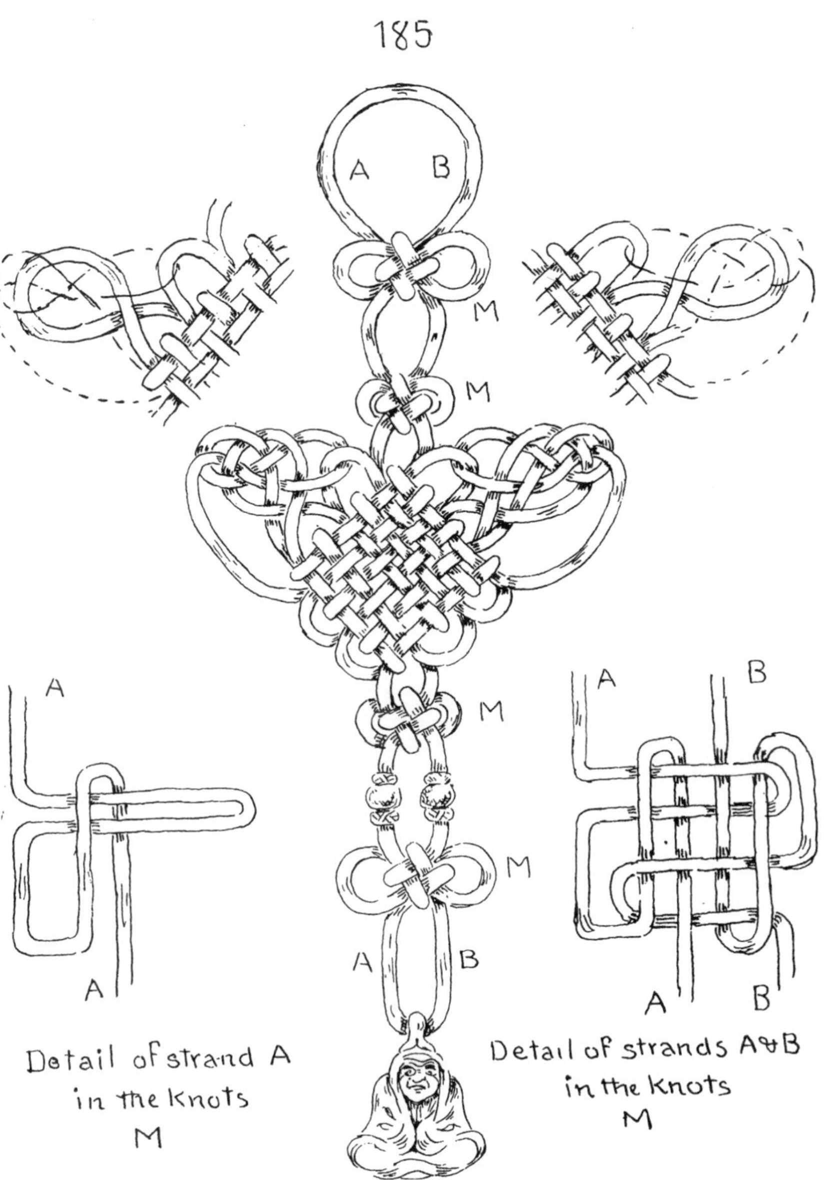
185
A
B
M
M
M
M
A
B
A
A
A
B
A
B
Detail of strand A
in the knots
M
Detail of strands A&B
in the knots
M

186

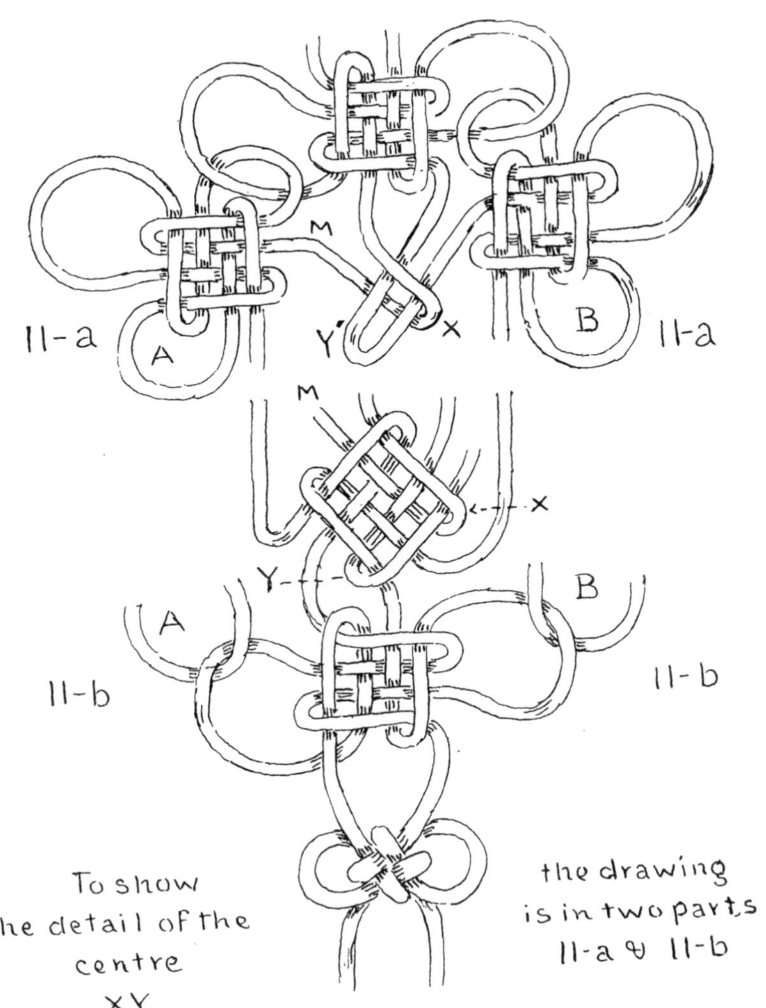
M
11-a
A
Y
X
B
11-a
M
X
Y
A
B
11-b
11-b
To show
the detail of the
centre
XY
the drawing
is in two parts
11-a & 11-b

188

CARRICK BEND and CHINESE DOUBLE BRAID in combination

Fig. I

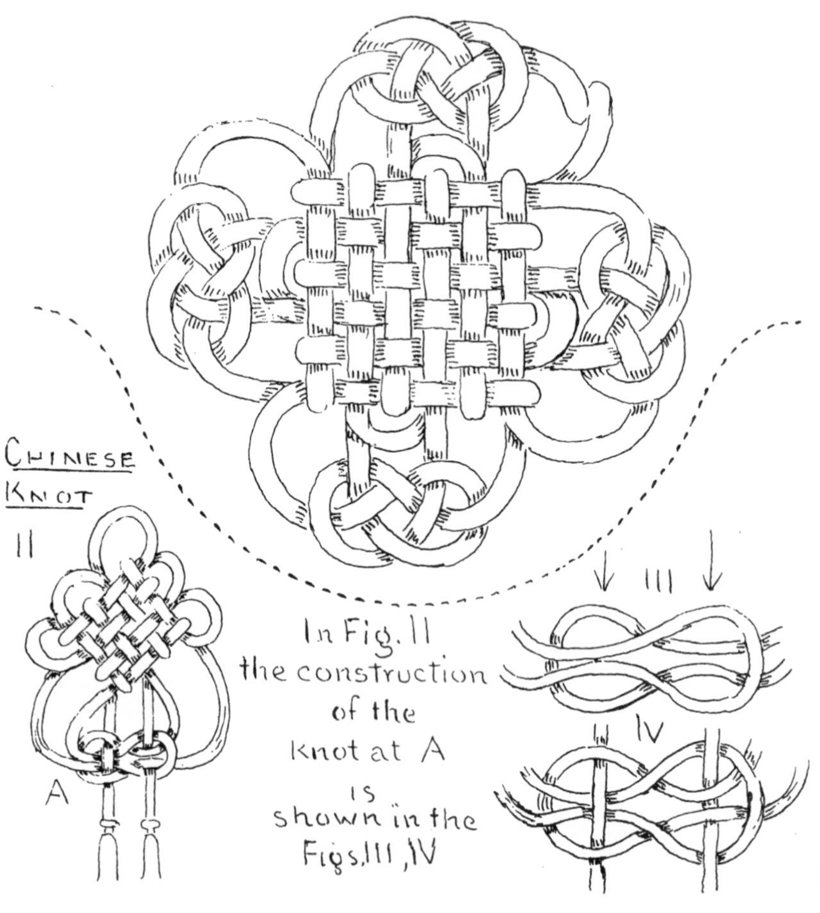
CHINESE KNOT
II
A
In Fig. II the construction of the Knot at A is shown in the Figs. III, IV
III
IV

TRICK KNOTS

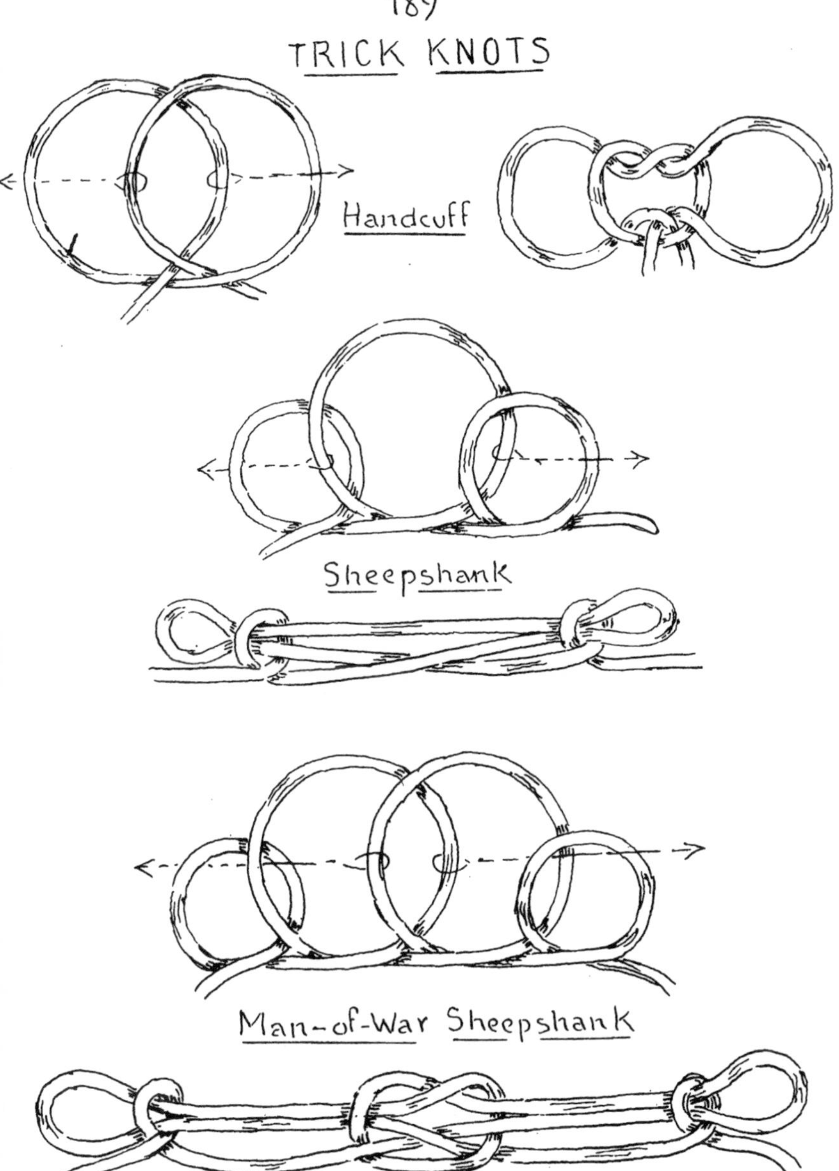
Handcuff
Sheepshank
Man-of-War Sheepshank

A KNOT TIED WITH ONE HAND

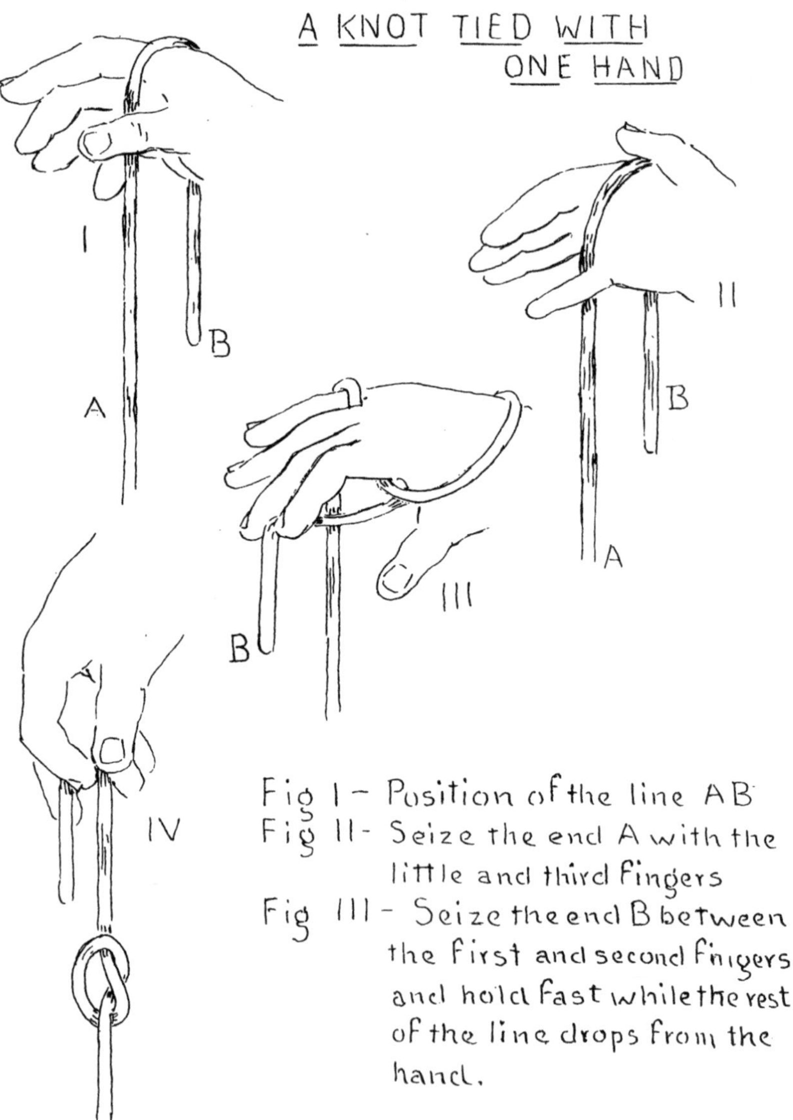
I
B
A
II
B
A
III
B
IV

Fig I – Position of the line AB

Fig II – Seize the end A with the little and third fingers

Fig III – Seize the end B between the first and second fingers and hold fast while the rest of the line drops from the hand.

TRICK KNOTS

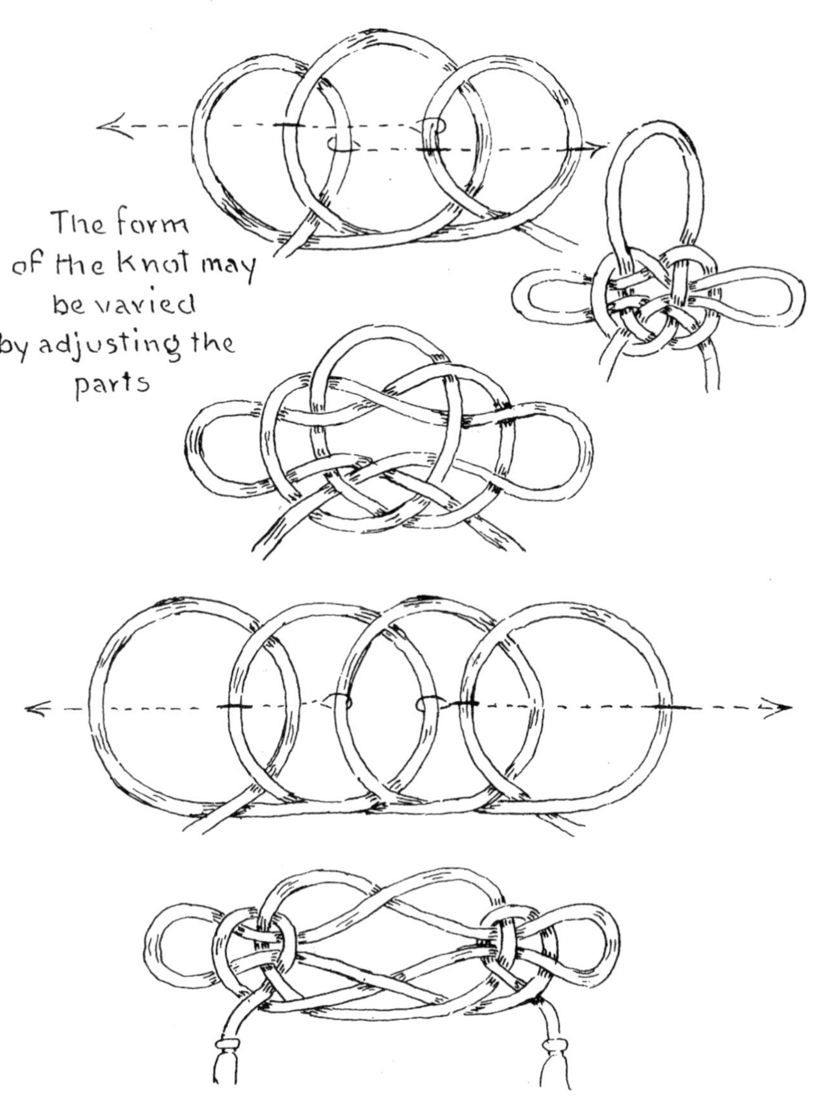
The form
of the knot may
be varied
by adjusting the
parts

192 JURY KNOT

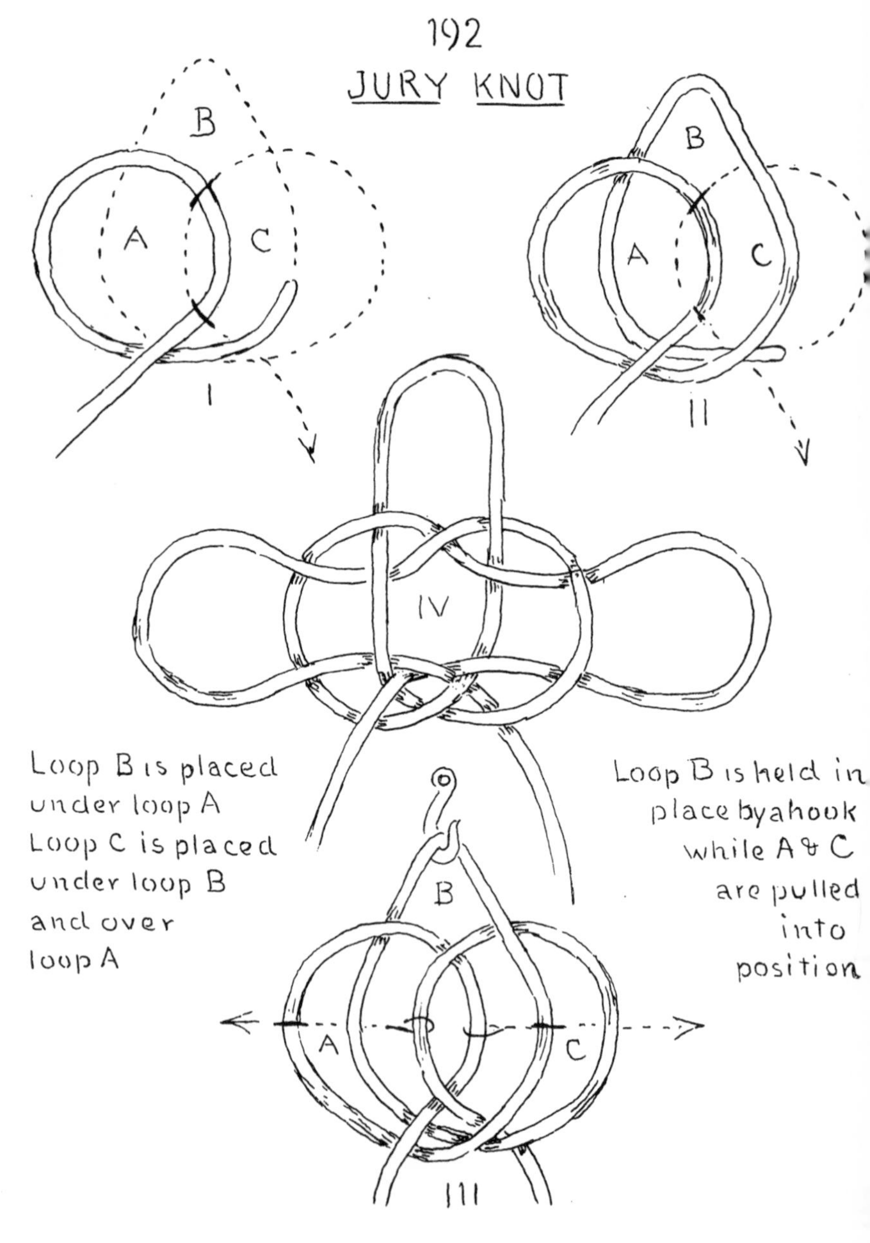
B
A
C
I
B
A
C
II
IV
Loop B is placed under loop A Loop C is placed under loop B and over loop A
Loop B is held in place by a hook while A & C are pulled into position
B
A
C
III

TRICK KNOTS

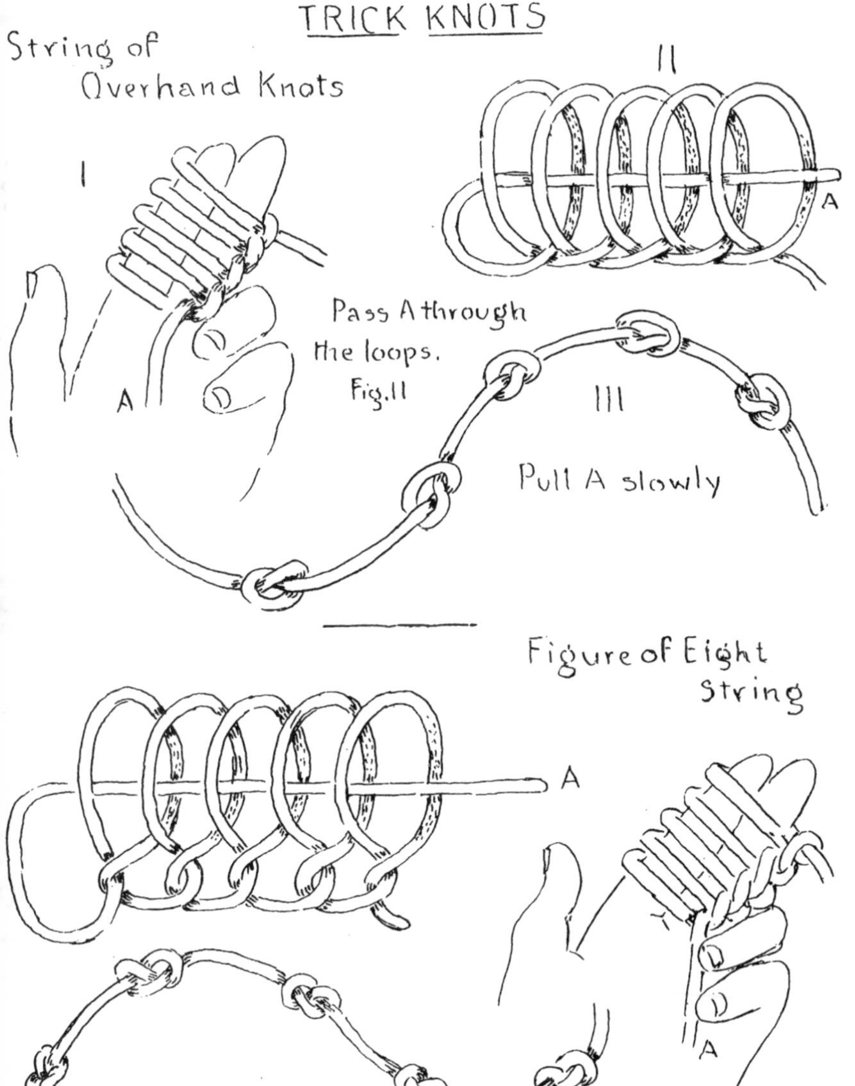
String of
Overhand Knots
I
II
A
A
Pass A through
the loops.
Fig. II
III
Pull A slowly
Figure of Eight
String
A
A

A CATALOG OF SELECTED DOVER BOOKS IN ALL FIELDS OF INTEREST

CONCERNING THE SPIRITUAL IN ART, Wassily Kandinsky. Pioneering work by father of abstract art. Thoughts on color theory, nature of art. Analysis of earlier masters. 12 illustrations. 80pp. of text. 5⅜ x 8½. 0-486-23411-8

CELTIC ART: The Methods of Construction, George Bain. Simple geometric techniques for making Celtic interlacements, spirals, Kells-type initials, animals, humans, etc. Over 500 illustrations. 160pp. 9 x 12. (Available in U.S. only.) 0-486-22923-8

AN ATLAS OF ANATOMY FOR ARTISTS, Fritz Schider. Most thorough reference work on art anatomy in the world. Hundreds of illustrations, including selections from works by Vesalius, Leonardo, Goya, Ingres, Michelangelo, others. 593 illustrations. 192pp. 7⅛ x 10¼. 0-486-20241-0

CELTIC HAND STROKE-BY-STROKE (Irish Half-Uncial from "The Book of Kells"): An Arthur Baker Calligraphy Manual, Arthur Baker. Complete guide to creating each letter of the alphabet in distinctive Celtic manner. Covers hand position, strokes, pens, inks, paper, more. Illustrated. 48pp. 8¼ x 11. 0-486-24336-2

EASY ORIGAMI, John Montroll. Charming collection of 32 projects (hat, cup, pelican, piano, swan, many more) specially designed for the novice origami hobbyist. Clearly illustrated easy-to-follow instructions insure that even beginning papercrafters will achieve successful results. 48pp. 8¼ x 11. 0-486-27298-2

BLOOMINGDALE'S ILLUSTRATED 1886 CATALOG: Fashions, Dry Goods and Housewares, Bloomingdale Brothers. Famed merchants' extremely rare catalog depicting about 1,700 products: clothing, housewares, firearms, dry goods, jewelry, more. Invaluable for dating, identifying vintage items. Also, copyright-free graphics for artists, designers. Co-published with Henry Ford Museum & Greenfield Village. 160pp. 8¼ x 11. 0-486-25780-0

THE ART OF WORLDLY WISDOM, Baltasar Gracian. "Think with the few and speak with the many," "Friends are a second existence," and "Be able to forget" are among this 1637 volume's 300 pithy maxims. A perfect source of mental and spiritual refreshment, it can be opened at random and appreciated either in brief or at length. 128pp. 5⅜ x 8½. 0-486-44034-6

JOHNSON'S DICTIONARY: A Modern Selection, Samuel Johnson (E. L. McAdam and George Milne, eds.). This modern version reduces the original 1755 edition's 2,300 pages of definitions and literary examples to a more manageable length, retaining the verbal pleasure and historical curiosity of the original. 480pp. 5³⁄₁₆ x 8¼. 0-486-44089-3

ADVENTURES OF HUCKLEBERRY FINN, Mark Twain, Illustrated by E. W. Kemble. A work of eternal richness and complexity, a source of ongoing critical debate, and a literary landmark, Twain's 1885 masterpiece about a barefoot boy's journey of self-discovery has enthralled readers around the world. This handsome clothbound reproduction of the first edition features all 174 of the original black-and-white illustrations. 368pp. 5⅜ x 8½. 0-486-44322-1

THE MALLEUS MALEFICARUM OF KRAMER AND SPRENGER, translated by Montague Summers. Full text of most important witchhunter's "bible," used by both Catholics and Protestants. 278pp. 6⅝ x 10. 0-486-22802-9

SPANISH STORIES/CUENTOS ESPAÑOLES: A Dual-Language Book, Angel Flores (ed.). Unique format offers 13 great stories in Spanish by Cervantes, Borges, others. Faithful English translations on facing pages. 352pp. 5⅜ x 8½. 0-486-25399-6

GARDEN CITY, LONG ISLAND, IN EARLY PHOTOGRAPHS, 1869–1919, Mildred H. Smith. Handsome treasury of 118 vintage pictures, accompanied by carefully researched captions, document the Garden City Hotel fire (1899), the Vanderbilt Cup Race (1908), the first airmail flight departing from the Nassau Boulevard Aerodrome (1911), and much more. 96pp. 8⅞ x 11¾. 0-486-40669-5

OLD QUEENS, N.Y., IN EARLY PHOTOGRAPHS, Vincent F. Seyfried and William Asadorian. Over 160 rare photographs of Maspeth, Jamaica, Jackson Heights, and other areas. Vintage views of DeWitt Clinton mansion, 1939 World's Fair and more. Captions. 192pp. 8⅞ x 11. 0-486-26358-4

CAPTURED BY THE INDIANS: 15 Firsthand Accounts, 1750-1870, Frederick Drimmer. Astounding true historical accounts of grisly torture, bloody conflicts, relentless pursuits, miraculous escapes and more, by people who lived to tell the tale. 384pp. 5⅜ x 8½. 0-486-24901-8

THE WORLD'S GREAT SPEECHES (Fourth Enlarged Edition), Lewis Copeland, Lawrence W. Lamm, and Stephen J. McKenna. Nearly 300 speeches provide public speakers with a wealth of updated quotes and inspiration–from Pericles' funeral oration and William Jennings Bryan's "Cross of Gold Speech" to Malcolm X's powerful words on the Black Revolution and Earl of Spenser's tribute to his sister, Diana, Princess of Wales. 944pp. 5⅜ x 8⅜. 0-486-40903-1

THE BOOK OF THE SWORD, Sir Richard F. Burton. Great Victorian scholar/adventurer's eloquent, erudite history of the "queen of weapons"–from prehistory to early Roman Empire. Evolution and development of early swords, variations (sabre, broadsword, cutlass, scimitar, etc.), much more. 336pp. 6⅛ x 9¼. 0-486-25434-8

AUTOBIOGRAPHY: The Story of My Experiments with Truth, Mohandas K. Gandhi. Boyhood, legal studies, purification, the growth of the Satyagraha (nonviolent protest) movement. Critical, inspiring work of the man responsible for the freedom of India. 480pp. 5⅜ x 8½. (Available in U.S. only.) 0-486-24593-4

CELTIC MYTHS AND LEGENDS, T. W. Rolleston. Masterful retelling of Irish and Welsh stories and tales. Cuchulain, King Arthur, Deirdre, the Grail, many more. First paperback edition. 58 full-page illustrations. 512pp. 5⅜ x 8½. 0-486-26507-2

THE PRINCIPLES OF PSYCHOLOGY, William James. Famous long course complete, unabridged. Stream of thought, time perception, memory, experimental methods; great work decades ahead of its time. 94 figures. 1,391pp. 5⅜ x 8½. 2-vol. set. Vol. I: 0-486-20381-6 Vol. II: 0-486-20382-4

THE WORLD AS WILL AND REPRESENTATION, Arthur Schopenhauer. Definitive English translation of Schopenhauer's life work, correcting more than 1,000 errors, omissions in earlier translations. Translated by E. F. J. Payne. Total of 1,269pp. 5⅜ x 8½. 2-vol. set. Vol. 1: 0-486-21761-2 Vol. 2: 0-486-21762-0

CATALOG OF DOVER BOOKS

LIGHT AND SHADE: A Classic Approach to Three-Dimensional Drawing, Mrs. Mary P. Merrifield. Handy reference clearly demonstrates principles of light and shade by revealing effects of common daylight, sunshine, and candle or artificial light on geometrical solids. 13 plates. 64pp. 5⅜ x 8½. 0-486-44143-1

ASTROLOGY AND ASTRONOMY: A Pictorial Archive of Signs and Symbols, Ernst and Johanna Lehner. Treasure trove of stories, lore, and myth, accompanied by more than 300 rare illustrations of planets, the Milky Way, signs of the zodiac, comets, meteors, and other astronomical phenomena. 192pp. 8⅜ x 11. 0-486-43981-X

JEWELRY MAKING: Techniques for Metal, Tim McCreight. Easy-to-follow instructions and carefully executed illustrations describe tools and techniques, use of gems and enamels, wire inlay, casting, and other topics. 72 line illustrations and diagrams. 176pp. 8¼ x 10⅞. 0-486-44043-5

MAKING BIRDHOUSES: Easy and Advanced Projects, Gladstone Califf. Easy-to-follow instructions include diagrams for everything from a one-room house for bluebirds to a forty-two-room structure for purple martins. 56 plates; 4 figures. 80pp. 8¾ x 6⅜. 0-486-44183-0

LITTLE BOOK OF LOG CABINS: How to Build and Furnish Them, William S. Wicks. Handy how-to manual, with instructions and illustrations for building cabins in the Adirondack style, fireplaces, stairways, furniture, beamed ceilings, and more. 102 line drawings. 96pp. 8¾ x 6⅜. 0-486-44259-4

THE SEASONS OF AMERICA PAST, Eric Sloane. From "sugaring time" and strawberry picking to Indian summer and fall harvest, a whole year's activities described in charming prose and enhanced with 79 of the author's own illustrations. 160pp. 8¼ x 11. 0-486-44220-9

THE METROPOLIS OF TOMORROW, Hugh Ferriss. Generous, prophetic vision of the metropolis of the future, as perceived in 1929. Powerful illustrations of towering structures, wide avenues, and rooftop parks–all features in many of today's modern cities. 59 illustrations. 144pp. 8¼ x 11. 0-486-43727-2

THE PATH TO ROME, Hilaire Belloc. This 1902 memoir abounds in lively vignettes from a vanished time, recounting a pilgrimage on foot across the Alps and Apennines in order to "see all Europe which the Christian Faith has saved." 77 of the author's original line drawings complement his sparkling prose. 272pp. 5⅜ x 8½. 0-486-44001-X

THE HISTORY OF RASSELAS: Prince of Abissinia, Samuel Johnson. Distinguished English writer attacks eighteenth-century optimism and man's unrealistic estimates of what life has to offer. 112pp. 5⅜ x 8½. 0-486-44094-X

A VOYAGE TO ARCTURUS, David Lindsay. A brilliant flight of pure fancy, where wild creatures crowd the fantastic landscape and demented torturers dominate victims with their bizarre mental powers. 272pp. 5⅜ x 8½. 0-486-44198-9

Paperbound unless otherwise indicated. Available at your book dealer, online at **www.doverpublications.com**, or by writing to Dept. GI, Dover Publications, Inc., 31 East 2nd Street, Mineola, NY 11501. For current price information or for free catalogs (please indicate field of interest), write to Dover Publications or log on to **www.doverpublications.com** and see every Dover book in print. Dover publishes more than 500 books each year on science, elementary and advanced mathematics, biology, music, art, literary history, social sciences, and other areas.